ALSO BY STUART STEVENS

Feeding Frenzy
Malaria Dreams
Night Train to Turkistan
Scorched Earth

THE

ENCH

*Campaign Adventures with
the Cockeyed Optimists from Texas
Who Won
the Biggest Prize in Politics*

B★I★G
ILADA

Stuart Stevens

THE FREE PRESS

NEW YORK   LONDON   TORONTO   SYDNEY   SINGAPORE

*f*P

THE FREE PRESS
A Division of Simon & Schuster, Inc.
1230 Avenue of the Americas
New York, NY 10020

Copyright © 2001 by Stuart Stevens
All rights reserved,
including the right of reproduction
in whole or in part in any form.
THE FREE PRESS and colophon are trademarks
of Simon & Schuster, Inc.
For information regarding special discounts for bulk purchases,
please contact Simon & Schuster Special Sales:
1-800-456-6798 or business@simonandschuster.com
Designed by Edith Fowler
Manufactured in the United States of America

10   9   8   7   6   5   4   3   2   1

Library of Congress Cataloging-in-Publication Data is available
ISBN 0-7432-2290-3

For Karl and Darby, Mark and Annie,
for doing so much to make us feel at home

Contents

A Note from the Author

IT IS OFTEN SAID THESE DAYS that politics has become a poison-
ous business and it seems true enough. One ingredient of this
particularly public toxin is the compulsion of those who have
been on the inside at a high level to bear witness to the horrors
they have observed. The pattern is predictable—the idealistic
aide signs on full of hope and then eventually stumbles away,
disillusioned, a touch bitter, with only his ambition intact.

This is a different story. In June 1999, I moved from New
York City to Austin, Texas, to join a group of mostly Texans
who were utterly convinced that George W. Bush was going
to be our next president. This was despite considerable evidence to the contrary—chiefly the unlikelihood of ousting an
incumbent party in an era of peace and record prosperity. In
Austin, I found myself rediscovering the peculiar pleasure of
working with people who not only respected and admired
their candidate but actually liked him. So did I.

All campaigns are strange in their own way but this one
was *really* strange in so many ways. It was exhilarating, maddening, horribly debilitating, very gratifying and, of course,
just way too damn long. This is a story by a temporary Texan
who, in what will certainly be one of my last campaigns,
found myself remembering why I was drawn to this crazy
process in the first place.

The Big
Enchilada

A Modest Landslide

1

I HAD BEEN AT THE GYM for three hours when I got the call. It was what I did on Election Day—I went to the gym and worked myself into a small frenzy waiting for the first exit polls. Each of us had his own ritual. One group, Matthew Dowd and Dan Bartlett and a bunch of guys from the press, had teed off at 7:30 A.M. and others were going to the movies. Me, I don't have the metabolic rate for golf or film on a calm day, forget about Election Day. I knew one guy who always went to strip clubs and maintained it was the only thing that could really keep him from replaying the election in his head—the things that he had done wrong, what could have been, the spots that never made it on the air. All this stuff he seemed able to forget while watching some girl feign love to a silver pole. I'm sure it beat hanging around the office poring over the last tracking numbers like a Biblical scholar given first crack at the Dead Sea Scrolls.

Tracking numbers. For years I had lived and died by tracking numbers. That's what those of us who are perverse enough to spend our lives in political combat call overnight daily polling numbers. As in, "How was the Pennsylvania track last night?" or "If our fave/unfave with married women holds up in one more track, this thing is done." In life, you have to believe in something and it was pretty much essential

1

in politics to believe your own tracking. It was like what they said about religion in combat—in a crazed and chaotic world that didn't seem to make much sense from one moment (or news cycle) to the next, you needed something to cling to, something to bring order and a semblance of rationality to your world when more often than not, it felt like the sun was busy rising over that western horizon.

Tracking. Somewhere in little cubicles in some call center in Omaha (good midwestern accents, flat, and close to two time zones) or Phoenix or Chicago, perfectly innocent strangers were calling other innocent strangers to interrupt their dinner or television joy with, "We're conducting a nationwide survey of voters and would like to ask you a few questions . . ." Maybe the person who answered was having an argument with their spouse, maybe their favorite team was winning big or their kid just got into college or just wrecked the car or those test results from the doctor didn't look so good—none of that was supposed to matter. That person was expected to spend ten or fifteen minutes revealing their innermost political secrets and passions. We call that a completed interview or simply a "complete." You get two hundred completes a night, subject them to this mysterious polling mumbo jumbo called "weighting," and, presto, out come the voting intentions of a state the size of, well, Florida.

Of course, every pollster tells you not to put too much faith in one night's track but instead look at what they call "the roll." That's when you average together, say, three nights of tracking. It's never really made sense to me that one night was untrustworthy but if you put together three nights of these untrustworthy numbers, you came up with something so prescient you could rely on it to shift around millions of dollars of television or to decide where you were going to schedule events, dragging the whole presidential campaign traveling circus with you. Ask a pollster about it and they will say that's the beauty of statistics, that you can average together enough nonsense and suddenly it will be brilliant.

But you have to trust something, so you trust tracking. Our tracks—the Bush campaign's—had been good. We liked our tracks. We had mostly happy tracks.

Then the call came from Mark McKinnon. Outside it was raining and inside everything was a pleasant blur. That morning I'd been to an eye doctor in preparation for having laser surgery two days after the election, and the drops had thrust me into a fuzzy but not unpleasant world of vague shapes. I was also wearing sunglasses inside, which no doubt made me look like the biggest asshole in Austin. Major league, as we like to say. My best hope was that people might think I was actually blind and show a little pity, which was working pretty well, I think, until I realized I had been staring for half an hour up at the bank of televisions where CNN was dueling with MSNBC and Fox. That blew my blind thing and I just went back to being some jerk in sunglasses at the gym.

Then Mark called and I'm surprised people didn't start hurling dumbbells at me. I would have. A jerk in sunglasses *talking on a cell phone at the gym.* Death.

"Tight," Mark said.

"What?"

"Tight," he said again, sighing.

"Like how tight?"

"Like tied in the popular."

Tied in the popular? I thought. How could we be tied in the popular vote? We were going to win this thing by three or four points.

"How's Pennsylvania?"

"Down four."

"Michigan?"

"Down four or five."

"Florida?" I realized my heart was pounding and I was holding the cell phone so tightly, I'm surprised it didn't shatter like a martini glass. If we were losing Pennsylvania, Michigan and Florida . . .

"Not so good." Mark sounded incredibly depressed but Mark could get that way and then bounce back sixty seconds later. "Down four," he sighed.

I literally shivered. Maybe it was just standing there soaking wet on a rainy cold day in Austin in a gym that seemed to have the air conditioning cranked to high.

"I'm coming over," I said to Mark, who was at campaign headquarters.

"Fine. I'm leaving," he said.

"Where you going?"

"I'll think of something."

☆　　　　☆　　　　☆

But Mark was still at the campaign thirty minutes later. Our whole crew was huddled together in Matthew's office looking like a suicide hotline group therapy session.

The "crew" was the Maverick crowd—Matthew Dowd, Russ Schriefer, Laura Crawford. For over a year and a half we had been working together as Maverick Media, which had been created as the Bush campaign's in-house ad agency. We had separate offices at two production facilities in town but over the summer Matthew had begun coordinating polling and set up shop in an office next to Karl Rove's in the strategy department of the campaign. (Or "strateregy" as everybody started to call it after *Saturday Night Live* mocked Bush for his tendency to mangle a "sylalable" or two, as he put it.)

Matthew, like Mark McKinnon, had been a Democratic political operative, the whiz kid who, as communications director for Ann Richards, had engineered the last big win Dems had in Texas, the 1990 sweep. Mark and he had worked together at Public Strategies, Austin's powerhouse lobbying and PR firm, which Matthew had cofounded. When Mark signed on for the Bush presidential, he brought over Matthew to be chief financial officer of Maverick and plan the television buys for the campaign. Matthew loved numbers and it was easy to peg him at first glance as a quiet numbers guy with a pencil fetish. There were always razor-sharp pencils arranged neatly on his desk and if he was wearing a sports coat, usually there would be two or three pencils sticking up like lances from his handkerchief pocket. I always figured if he was running through an airport and tripped, there was a high likelihood he would fatally impale himself. I mentioned this to him once and he seriously considered it for a second, then shrugged and said, "I need my pencils. It's worth the risk."

Truth was, underneath the quiet front he presented to the world, Matthew had the soul of a wild Irish rogue, voluble and passionate. He loved to laugh, drink, smoke cigars and was one of the few people in the Austin operation who seemed to appreciate the joys of arguing for arguing sake. He was also married to a wondrous, funny woman whose father had once managed the Sex Pistols. This you had to like.

"Have they surrendered yet?" I asked.

No one laughed.

"If we win every state we currently are leading in or are close, we win with just over two hundred and seventy votes," Matthew quietly announced.

"Are we including Washington and Oregon in those numbers?"

Matthew nodded.

I hated this. I'd done Senate and gubernatorial races in both of those states and though we were doing better than most Republicans, when the day was done, it was hard for me to imagine George W. Bush winning Washington and Oregon. The Nader vote was inevitably going to collapse. Some votes are "hidden" and tend to show up in greater strength on Election Day. This happened with David Dinkins's first win as mayor of New York City. His vote was always underreported in polls and every pro I knew agreed it was because he was African American and either pollsters weren't reaching his voters or there was still some element who were reluctant to admit they were voting for a black man.

But Nader's vote was largely a protest vote and it was a lot easier to answer the phone and say you were going to vote for Ralph, hell yes, screw the system, than actually to go through the motions of voting. Even in a state like Oregon that had carried the idea of voting by mail to a truly nutty conclusion. You could *only* vote by mail in Oregon, one of those "good government" reforms that managed to accomplish two things at once: undercutting one of our few remaining national civic functions and making it easier to cheat. Why was it such a terrible idea that on one day every four years, everybody in America would emerge from their self-contained little worlds and go down to a fire station or schoolhouse and participate in a national ritual with their fellow citizens? If you didn't care enough to go to the trouble, maybe it wasn't the worst thing in the world that you just took a pass.

Anyway, the first exits weren't a pretty picture. So we did what came naturally to people like us—we started to spin ourselves.

"You know, these guys are wrong all the time," I said. Of course, if the numbers had been good, I would have been defending the exit polls like Martin Luther arguing for the Reformation. "Don't forget, they called Wisconsin for Mo Udall and Carter still won."

Everybody looked at me like I was utterly mad. "We got an example this century, maybe?" Russ asked.

"Who's Mo Udall?" Laura asked. She was Maverick's top producer, twenty-six, Texas homegrown, a woman who looked like a professional tennis player and seemed to do everything in the production world at a very high level.

"They had Dole in third place in Arizona behind Forbes and Buchanan and he only came in second!" I blurted out.

"Now I feel better," Mark mumbled. "Wahoo." He paused for a minute, then, "Can we start drinking now?"

"I think they may be modeling this thing wrong," Matthew said.

Ahh. This I liked. The "they" Matthew was referring to was Voter News Service, or VNS. In a little-noticed—that was about to change in a hurry, thanks to Florida—cost-cutting arrangement, all the networks and major news organizations used one service to provide exit polls. In essence, this was like every news outlet in America depending on one reporter to file a story. Each of the nets or newspapers put a slightly different spin on their numbers but in truth they were all drinking out of the same glass. If there was something nasty in the water, everybody was going to get sick.

"How long has it been since Republicans voted with any kind of intensity?" Matthew asked no one in particular.

"How are they modeling the Nader vote?" Russ wondered.

Karl Rove burst into the office. "VNS is saying they may have problems with their models."

We laughed. A nervous death row sort of laugh but it was better than screaming.

"What?" Karl asked.

"We were just on the verge of convincing ourselves that their models were all wrong," Russ explained.

"There's voter intensity," Karl said.

"Right," Matthew said.

"And the Nader vote."

"Got it," Russ said.

"Give us a minute and we'll come up with some other theories," Matthew promised.

"Good. But don't go too far out there. The next wave may improve."

"We should allow for the possibility they may correct their mistakes," I said.

Jan van Lohuizen, a Washington-based pollster who had been part of the campaign's polling team, hovered in the doorway. It was a small office, like all the offices at the campaign, and it was getting crowded. Jan was born and raised in Holland and was given to the boisterous swings of emotion one normally associates with those wild and crazy Dutch.

"I don't believe Florida," he announced. The way he said it, it was a declaration of fact, not an expression of disbelief.

"Good," Russ said. "Why?"

"We are not going to lose Florida by four points. This isn't going to happen."

We were all so desperate for good news, you could feel the mood shift.

"We might lose by one, but not by four," Jan insisted.

"Anybody want a drink?" I asked. "I'm buying."

☆　　　☆　　　☆

By the afternoon, the numbers had improved slightly. Florida had tightened to down two and Michigan and Pennsylvania were getting within striking distance.

"It's in the bag," Mark was saying. "Just a pretty thin bag."

Of the black arts of polling, exit polling was one of the most suspect. We kept questioning the "models" Voter News

Service was using because modeling was everything to exit polling. The theory was fairly simple and potentially wildly dangerous: By selecting certain key precincts that had previously proven to be reliable indicators of overall voting and interviewing a sampling of voters after they had voted, you could extrapolate the numbers and predict the overall vote.

The problem with the theory was that it assumed the past would predict the future. This worked great until the future introduced unpredictable messy elements—like a significant third-party challenge from the left a la Nader or exceptional turnout by one segment of the electorate, be it Christian conservatives, African Americans, or citizens outraged by the American League's corrupt use of the designated hitter.

We didn't like the results of the exit polls so we naturally began to challenge the polls. This is a human instinct no less ferocious than the need for food, shelter or sex. All bad polls must be disputed. Show me somebody who sees a nasty bit of polling and doesn't immediately begin to calculate how these terrible numbers are a crock, and I'll show you a person who's lost their lust for life. It would be like finding out you had cancer and saying, "Oh, good, I needed that."

There are three waves of exit polling on Election Day—morning, afternoon and the final numbers. Everybody knows this and everybody knows there is only one source of information for the exits—Voter News Service. But somehow this doesn't stop us from talking about the "ABC numbers" versus the *"Washington Post* numbers, which look better in Florida." Particularly when you don't like the numbers, you want to believe that if you just hear from a different source, somehow the numbers will change, which is sort of like buying different copies of the same newspaper in hopes that magically the front-page, above-the-fold piece you hate will morph into an obscure item on page D27.

All during that rainy Election Day, we traded phone calls
with the hotshot political reporters who had been covering us
for over a year and a half. It was just more of the horse trading
that went on constantly, bits of information bartered back and
forth through the now endless news cycles of cable and online
news. We spun the not-so-great exit polls partially out of habit
and reflex—we'd been spinning for so long, it was as natural
as breathing and often easier—and there was also one final
endgame of spin that was absolutely critical: Election Night
coverage.

We were fighting fiercely to delay any negative calls—
calls for Gore, that is—as long as possible. We knew by now
that our hopes for a comfortable win—the three hundred plus
electoral votes and three-to-five-point margin that we'd hoped
for—was never going to happen. We were, at best, in a death
struggle where every vote was critical. When states in the East
started closing their polls, there would still be millions—*millions*—of potential votes uncast in the rest of the country
where the polls were still open for business.

There's long been a debate in poli-sci circles as to whether
or not voters are influenced on Election Day by knowing that
their candidate is losing or winning. This is silly. How could
they not be? Why don't third-party candidates ever get any traction? In part, because nobody thinks they can win. So if you are
a mildly interested West coast voter with a busy day and you
turn on the television before voting and see that network map
covered with the other guy's colors and the pundits babbling
on about how hopeless it is for your guy, of course it is going to
affect you. You find something else to do, like floss your cat's
teeth. If by 8:05 P.M., the on-air spin was how hopeless it was for
the Bush campaign, we would start shedding voters in Arizona,
New Mexico, Nevada, Oregon, Washington State, all critical,
tight-as-hell states. Not to mention California, which we didn't

really expect to win unless we were having a landslide night, and the odds for that weren't, shall we say, looking too hot.

So by early afternoon on Election Day, we were banging on every news organization we could reach, trying to raise doubts about the exiting polling in key states that looked bleak but still winnable. Our best weapons were arcane, detailed bits of turnout information, numbers we had from contacts on the precinct levels in each state, a level of specificity no news organization could ever match.

Karl was the master at this because reporters understood that he had an amazing mind for numbers and a feel for the political terrain like no other operative in the Republican party, and probably the country. And he didn't lie to reporters.

"This is what we're hearing about the Fall River Valley," he'd tell a Bigfoot reporter. "In precinct thirty-eight, in 1992, Clinton won it by two hundred and twenty votes, in '96, four hundred and thirty votes. Got it? But as of three P.M., we were down only twenty-eight votes. Hey, and look at this, in Green Bay . . ."

We never came out and said, "Don't call these races early." That would have been too clearly self-serving and a direct challenge. "We'll call 'em like we see 'em," would have been the inevitable huff and puff back. Plus they *hadn't* called any states, so it was hard to yell at them for screwing up (that would come later). All we were trying to do was raise doubts that might keep a network analyst from pulling the trigger sooner rather than later based only on the VNS modeling. Be careful, was the message we were trying to deliver, you might end up looking stupid. Better to wait until some real votes are counted—this thing is close and could be confusing as hell.

☆ ☆ ☆

"Stevens! Fergie here! Where the hell are you? I don't like this! Get your ass over here and cheer me up."

Fergie was Jim Ferguson, creative director of Young & Rubicam, which made him the head creative guy at the largest ad agency in the world. "What were they thinking?" is what he says one of his daughters asked when Young & Rubicam installed him as the Grand Poo-Bah. Fergie was from Hico, Texas, and when we were looking around for someone to head up a possible team of Madison Avenue superstars to help with the campaign, my next-door neighbor in Manhattan, something of a legend in the ad world himself, described Ferguson as "goddamn brilliant. Big one. You know all that great McDonald's stuff, the Michael Jordan and Larry Bird stuff? That was Fergie. He's crazy too. You'll like him."

All of which sounded good to me. So I called him up out of the blue and he quickly agreed to have lunch with McKinnon and me during our next trip to Manhattan. He had a deep voice and a blunt manner—"What do you want with me?" was his opening on the phone. He didn't sound creative or crazy, just all business with a slight Texas twang.

We met at Tropica in the old Pan Am building that straddles Park Avenue at Forty-second Street. Fergie was a big guy with long hair who looked like a cross between a very successful pirate and a retired rock promoter. He'd brought with him a young woman who headed PR for Young & Rubicam, just "to make sure I don't screw up too badly, you know." So we sat down and the first thing Fergie said was, "So if I do this thing, I'm not going to wake up to pictures of me with a corkscrew up my ass in the papers, am I?"

I sputtered—literally—into my designer mineral water.

Fergie had this way of cocking his head and looking at you with a slightly mad glint in his eye, as though drawing you into a little conspiracy he was having with the rest of the world.

"I mean, look, I want to help, I just don't want to be way out there, you know?" Fergie continued. "I'm an ad guy and I don't want a bunch of attention."

I thought about this later when I saw a copy of *Advertising Age* with Fergie on the cover riding a horse down Madison Avenue.

"I don't want Geraldo howling at my door. You know I live in Elizabeth Taylor's old apartment, pretty cool for a guy from Hico, huh? Robin Leach lived there too but they swear it's been disinfected a bunch. Hope so."

McKinnon and I loved the guy. You had to.

"I don't want to get paid and I don't want any sons of bitches working with us who want money. We make more money than God already. The hell with the money. Okay?"

How could we say no?

"You want some ribs? We got ribs," Fergie shouted into the phone. It was late afternoon on Election Day and I was looking for a good reason to get out of headquarters, which was beginning to feel like the waiting room in a cancer ward.

"Get over here. We're in the Davy Crockett suite."

Fergie and the core of the Park Avenue Posse (so named for Fergie's Liz Taylor–Robin Leach pad) had flown down for election night and were staying at the Driskill Hotel, a couple of blocks from the campaign. It was an old hangout of Lyndon Johnson's where John Connally was famed for handing out cash during Johnson's first statewide race against Ralph Yarborough. (This was the race in which Johnson took to spreading rumors that Yarborough had sex with pigs. Literally. Connally told him to knock it off, nobody would believe it, to which Johnson replied, "Yeah, but I just want to hear the son of a bitch deny it once," which, you could argue, is pretty much the basis for all negative advertising, God love it.)

In the lobby of the ornate Driskill, I asked which room

number would be the Davy Crockett suite. The woman behind the front desk stared at me. She was Italian, for some reason.

"You are looking for Mr. Crockett?"

No, no, I explained, the *Davy Crockett suite.*

"Mr. Crockett, he is a guest?"

"Not very likely but if he is, I'd love to meet him."

She stared at me, no doubt contemplating the deep eccentricities of Americans.

"He's dead," I tried to explain, but her eyes just widened.

"A dead man?" she whispered.

Finally I gave up and called Ferguson on his cell phone.

"Don't be so goddamn literal, Stevens," he barked when I told him there was no Davy Crockett suite. "And hurry up, the ribs are going fast."

That was a lie. When I finally found the room, there were enough ribs piled up along the windows overlooking Austin's famous Sixth Street to feed the Dallas Cowboys. Fergie was lying on the bed with a Shiner Bock beer, the local brew, in his hand, gnawing on a huge rib, yelling at the television.

"You ridiculous fool! You knave!" Geraldo Rivera was on the air.

"Jim wants to hear from you, Stuart, that we're not going to lose," Janet Kraus explained. She was a Young & Rubicam superstar writer who had dazzled us from the very first time we met her in Fergie's apartment.

"We're not going to lose, are we?" Fergie groaned.

"Okay, we're not going to lose," I said.

"Do you believe that?" Ed Ney asked me. He was sitting on the window ledge next to the massive order of ribs, dressed neatly in a tie and sweater. At seventy-something, after heading Young & Rubicam for twenty-five years and serving as President Bush's ambassador to Canada, Ed was now chairman emeritus of Young & Rubicam and had "living legend" written all over him. He looked out over the amiable chaos of Fergie's suite like a benevolent headmaster who had seen it all.

I actually thought about it for a moment. "Guys, I've always said we had a forty percent chance to win and I'm sticking by it."

"I don't have a problem with that forty percent," Fergie groaned, "it's just the sixty percent I hate. This sucks."

"Alex says if we lose Michigan, Pennsylvania and Florida, it's probably over." Alex was Alex Castellanos, who had made the RNC ads and the guy talking was Harold Kaplan, another Y&R heavyweight who had worked with Alex. Harold wore tortoise-shell glasses and looked like a hip high school teacher.

"We are not going to lose all three," I promised. "It's just not going to happen." All three were close in the exits but I was convinced that one would break our way. Our tracking numbers had shown us slightly ahead in Michigan and trending upward, one or three behind in Penn and four up in Florida. The odds of all three breaking against us seemed like a piece of bad luck that was out of character with this campaign. When we needed luck, we'd been lucky. But if we did lose all three, Alex was right, we were probably goners.

"I just want you to know, Stevens, the Hico Tigers do not like to lose," Fergie declared.

"Jim, now that I know that it's important to you, I'm really going to get focused on this campaign. I promise."

"Well, it's about time somebody took it seriously." He eyed the piles of barbeque. "You try the brisket?"

☆   ☆   ☆

Kentucky came in first. All the nets agreed. It was a relief—if we lost Kentucky, we might as well start jumping out the windows real early. But Kentucky was a must win, hardly a reason to start working on an inaugural address.

Parties were going on all over Austin but we were hunkered down at 301 Congress, the campaign mother ship. Much of the two hundred plus staff were working at the elaborate stage setup that had been erected at the end of Congress Street. With bad weather predicted, there had been a debate up until the last minute as to whether or not to have the event outdoors or inside a University of Texas arena. The plans had been for a giant outdoor celebration, sort of a block party on steroids, with local talent like Jimmie Vaughan revving up the crowd before President-elect Bush gave his speech. Finally Brian Montgomery, the unflappable head advance wizard who probably could have planned the invasion of Normandy without breaking a sweat, made the call forty-eight hours before Election Day: We'd go outside, the hell with the weather.

It had turned into a nasty night by Austin standards, rainy and cold, but thousands had still turned out on Congress Street to listen to the music and watch results on a pair of huge screens. Inside headquarters, there was a strange end-of-term feeling. People were dressed up and girlfriends and boyfriends and spouses were suddenly hanging around. It was startling, like walking into the locker room before a game and discovering someone had set up a piano bar. It was supposed to feel like a party, except it didn't—and couldn't, not with these exit polls.

Every network kept announcing that the polls would close at 7 P.M. EST in nine states—Florida, Georgia, New Hampshire, South Carolina, Vermont, Virginia, North Carolina, Ohio and West Virginia.

"Wrong, wrong, wrong." Karl was sitting behind his antique wooden desk shaking his head. His eleven-year-old, Andrew, was playing with his computer, and people were wandering in and out of his office. "Can somebody tell these guys that the Florida panhandle doesn't close till eight P.M.?" Karl yelled out to no one in particular.

"They're not going to call Florida before eight," Chris

Henick said. "It's too close. They can't." Chris was from Yazoo City, Mississippi, and had joined the campaign after the primary as Karl's top deputy. Years earlier, we'd worked together on Haley Barbour's failed campaign for the Senate in Mississippi. He was one of the best operatives in the party and also the only one who was a regular at the annual Faulkner conference in Oxford, Mississippi.

Most of the Maverick crew was hanging out in Matthew Dowd's office next to Karl's. Matthew had set up a computer program to track the results as they were fed to us from each state. In every key state, we had people at courthouses and the secretary of state's office to call in vote totals, so we expected to have a more accurate and faster count than the networks. Back in the summer, Matthew had predicted that there was an 80 percent chance we'd win, a number we often kidded him about during September when nothing seemed to be working. He was, like most of the Austin crowd, a natural optimist. I was always the guy saying we had a 40 percent chance— which I thought was pretty good, considering the givens of peace and record prosperity—but now our roles were reversed.

"Matthew, we're going to win," I told him, based, of course, on absolutely nothing.

"I'd say we've got a forty percent chance," Matthew answered. "You are always such a goddamn optimist."

"Eighty percent," I countered.

He hurled one of his ever-sharp pencils at me. His wife, who was dressed for an elegant evening on the town, moved a cluster of pencils out of reach.

"Boys," she scolded.

Behind us on the television screen in Matthew's office, the nets started calling states. It was 7 P.M. EST.

Dan Rather: "Bush gets South Carolina; Gore gets Vermont: part of our CBS News Election Night headlines of the hour. Bush picks up his first state in the South; Gore gets his first win in New England. But no call yet in what both campaigns say may be the key to this election, Florida. Florida could turn out to be the decisive battleground state tonight. The polls just closed in six states, with sixty-six electoral votes, including Florida's big twenty-five."

Chris Henick yelled at the screen, "The panhandle is still open, Dan baby! Get a life!"

"These guys," I said, "have nothing to do but get ready for this for four years and they still can't get it right." It was comforting to have somebody to blame for something. It made me feel a little less helpless.

"It's an East Coast Liberal Establishment plot," Janet Kraus said. She wandered in with the rest of the Y&R crowd.

"This comes from a woman who lives on Manhattan's Upper West Side," I reminded everyone.

"Just across the park from you," she teased.

"Have we won yet? I am ready to win this goddamn thing right now." Jim Ferguson filled the doorway of Matthew's office. He was holding a beer in one hand and a cigarette in the other.

Dan Rather was promising, "Let's get one thing straight right from the get-go. We would rather be last in reporting returns than to be wrong. And again, our record demonstrates that's true. If you hear someplace else that somebody's carried a state and you're off, as you shouldn't be, watching them, then come back here, because if we say somebody's carried a state, you can pretty much take it to the bank, book it, that that's true."

Chris Henick stuck his head in the door. "Judge in Missouri just ordered the polls to stay open for three hours in East St. Louis."

"Is that good or bad?" Janet asked. When she saw our

faces, she answered her own question. "It's bad, I guess. Like real bad?"

Ben Ginsburg, the campaign's lawyer, was in Karl's office explaining the situation and Karl was on the phone to two different people in Missouri. Ginsburg, as ever, was calm. He was on the verge of becoming a familiar face on television but right now he was doing what he always did for the campaign, translating a confusing situation into language we could understand. The polls that had been ordered to remain open were in heavily Democratic precincts.

"A judge can just decide he wants Election Day to go as long as he wants?" Henick asked.

"The Missouri Democratic party filed a lawsuit requesting it and the good judge, in his infinite wisdom, has granted their request. Now we go in and appeal."

Bill Clark, one of the campaign's young research experts, walked in with a fistful of paper.

"Oppo dude!" Karl greeted him. "Oppo" was short for opposition, as in opposition research, which is campaign speak for what someone like Bill did.

"This judge in St. Louis who ordered the polls to stay open was formerly Dick Gephardt's chief of staff."

"Gambling?" I said. "There's gambling here. I'm shocked."

"I think maybe we will try another judge," Ginsburg said dryly.

"Florida goes for Al Gore," Dan Rather suddenly announced. "Now, folks, the equation changes. CBS News estimates when all the votes are in and counted, the Sunshine State will have plenty of sunshine for Al Gore."

"Kristen," Karl shouted to his assistant, "get me Randy!" Randy was Randy Enwright, the former executive director of the Florida Republican party.

"Have you seen the hard count in Florida?" Matthew

Dowd asked. He and Mark McKinnon crowded into Karl's office. The room was small and it was getting crowded. "We're ahead by something like seventy-five thousand votes. Where are they getting this?"

"Are these people ever wrong?" Fergie asked me.

"They called Wisconsin for Mo Udall over Carter," I started to explain.

"Mo Udall?" Fergie paled. "Are you kidding? That's it? One mistake in a hundred years?" He turned to Janet Kraus. "We're screwed. Let's go across the street and have a dozen margaritas immediately. As the head of your agency, I consider it a priority."

"What about Pennsylvania and Michigan?" Janet asked.

Within the hour, we'd lost both.

Bush's lead had "been melted faster than ice cream in a microwave," is how Rather called it.

"You know, when we are ahead, I find this guy amusing," Russ Schriefer said, nodding toward Rather on the screen, "but when we're losing, he is really, really annoying." We were back in Matthew's office, along with about fifteen other people. Everybody was trying to look at Matthew's computer, where he had the actual vote count from the Florida secretary of state's office on the screen. Our lead kept growing.

"This doesn't make sense," Matthew said.

From every source—the networks to the secretary of state's office to our own individual reports from various counties around the state—we were winning Florida with a growing lead.

Karl and Ed Gillespie in the press shop were calling every network and banging on them to retract their Florida prediction.

"I can't tell you we're going to win Florida," Gillespie said, "but I can sure as hell guarantee they can't predict Gore is."

I was in the bathroom when a great cheer went up. You

probably could have heard it down on Congress Street. The nets were pulling Florida back.

But we weren't convinced we were going to win Florida, we just thought we had a shot.

In Karl's office, everybody was working on different Electoral College strategies to get us over 270 votes. It was like some kind of parlor game with the presidency as a prize.

"Don't forget that Maine can split its electoral votes," Karl reminded us. "We could pick up an extra vote in Maine."

For a few minutes a little group of us furiously worked on our different formulas. If we lost Oregon but won Iowa and New Mexico, adding in the one vote in Maine, then we could get to 270 if . . .

I heard Karl chuckling and looked up. "One vote?" He laughed. "This thing may come down to one lousy electoral vote?" We joined him in a tired, giddy laugh.

Karl's office had a large interior window, and I suddenly realized that a crowd was peering inside the office. "This is like waiting outside the delivery room to see if the baby has two heads or not," Fergie said.

States were coming in that were incredibly close—we were a few hundred votes behind in New Mexico, a couple of thousand behind in Iowa. And there were stories pouring in of lost ballot boxes and voting machines breaking down, requiring ballots to be counted by hand. It was as though the fog of war had settled over the entire electoral process.

By 12:30 A.M. we were pretty certain it would all come down to Florida. There was still an outside chance we could win even if we lost Florida, if we carried Oregon, New Mexico and Iowa, although it looked like we would miss by the smallest of margins. But at least we'd won Arkansas and Tennessee. When they came in, the entire headquarters exploded. People were standing on their desks and cheering. How could anybody who lost his home state expect to win?

"You know," I said to Karl, who was frantically getting numbers from Florida, "nobody has ever lost their home state, lost Missouri, lost Ohio and still been elected president. Never in the history of the country."

"I'm sure Gore will withdraw as soon as this dawns on him," Karl said. "Dade County? What percent is in?" he yelled into one of the dozen or so lines that we had open to various places in Florida.

Standing next to Karl's desk, Matthew Dowd was working through a complicated formula to determine whether or not it was possible for Gore to make up the number of electoral votes he was behind given the number of electoral votes that were outstanding. It was like the algebraic logic problem from hell: If two trains leave the station at the same time and one train is traveling at two miles an hour but stops for five minutes while the other train travels at three miles an hour . . . except you weren't really sure what time the trains left or even whether there were two trains or three.

I was sure we'd win Florida by at least ten thousand or so votes. With only one hundred thousand votes left to be counted, we had, according to the nets, a forty-seven thousand vote lead. How could we lose?

"Fox called it for Bush!" Chris Henick suddenly shouted.

We were stunned. Nobody really cheered. We all looked at each other.

"It's only Fox, don't forget," somebody said.

Matthew was still working his numbers furiously and Karl was on the phone to Florida. "What does Fox know we don't?" he demanded from someone down in Florida.

Brokaw interrupted an interview with Doris Kearns Goodwin. "George Bush is the president-elect of the United States. He has won the state of Florida."

The headquarters exploded in one long scream. I looked

over at Karl and he was hugging his wife and son. He looked utterly exhausted. Matthew was still working his numbers but was smiling now. Everybody had tears in their eyes.

Karl's "bat phone"—the one to which only George W. Bush had the number—rang. He grabbed it.

"Mr. President!" he shouted.

Karl led the way as we poured out of headquarters. It was raining and a strange mist hung over Congress Street. A traffic jam suddenly appeared on Congress Street, horns blaring, people hanging out the windows chanting, "Bush! Bush! Bush!" I felt mostly relieved and incredibly tired. Karl was surrounded by people who were trying to lift him up and carry him but he wouldn't let them. Music poured out of the huge stage set up at the end of Congress Street.

As we neared the stage, one of our advance team emerged from a command trailer. I hugged her. Everybody was hugging everybody.

"I spent the whole night with Wayne Newton and Bo Derek," she said, looking dazed. "Wayne always said we'd win."

Forty minutes later we were soaking wet, still waiting for President-elect Bush to make his speech. Henick and I looked at each other.

"What's taking him so long?" I wondered.

Chris was talking into a cell phone.

"Florida is down to three thousand votes," he mumbled.

"Jesus Christ," I moaned.

"Now it's nineteen hundred," Henick corrected, still on the phone.

"Is this thing ever going to be over?" I asked.

2

Austin Heat

KARL LAID IT ALL OUT ON A NAPKIN.

We were in one of Austin's many coffee shops, a place called Java that was next door to Lance Armstrong's cancer foundation. It was full of the usual multipierced and tattooed Austin hipsters and across the way the musician Bob Schneider was trying to wake up. He was a Big Deal in Austin and played somewhere almost every night, either by himself or with his pickup band of Austin all-stars, the Scabs. But really he was most famous because he'd had sex with every good-looking woman in Austin, or so they said, including Sandra Bullock, who was his current girlfriend.

It was April 1999 and the Bush campaign was just taking shape.

Java was an unlikely place to be plotting a Republican takeover of the world, but that's what Karl was doing. We were part of a political phenomenon and we all knew it. More Americans wanted George W. Bush to be their president than anyone else. A recent Pew poll showed Bush leading Gore by 54 percent to 41 percent, even though Clinton's job approval was at 62 percent. Hell, the *Boston Herald* even had Bush beating Gore in *Massachusetts,* 44 percent to 37 percent. And as far as the rest of the Republican field was concerned, Bush was trouncing them. These guys might as well have been in the witness protection program for all the attention they attracted.

Bush was in the middle of the only successful presidential draft since Eisenhower. Successful in the sense that Bush was actually planning on running, and he probably wouldn't have run if the numbers hadn't indicated he could win. Colin Powell had faced a similar draft in 1996 and 2000, racking up huge popular numbers in every poll. Basically all you had to do was throw him onto a poll and he would crush anybody. But part of his appeal was the knowledge that he probably wouldn't run. Bush's numbers were all the more impressive since people saw him as a realistic choice, not just a wish list kind of candidate.

At Java, we talked about why Bush was beating everyone.

"What do people know about him?" Karl asked, keeping his voice low so that the couple next to us with matching purple hair wouldn't hear. "He's a Bush. They like that."

"They like the Bush brand," Mark said.

"You should tell him that," Karl teased, knowing how much Bush would intuitively resist the notion of his family being "branded."

"He's a successful, big-state governor," Karl continued. "Most people don't know much about him but they do have a sense of this."

"He's not Clinton," I added.

Karl nodded. We all felt that the public was longing for a change. Even if you *liked Clinton*, you were exhausted from the trauma of the Clinton years.

"And he's a different kind of Republican. Compassionate conservatism." Karl scribbled on a napkin. He was drawing little boxes—one was labeled BUSH, another BIG STATE GUV. He made COMPASSIONATE CONSERVATIVE a big box that overlapped the others. This was what Lee Atwater would have called "the ditch we were gonna die in." If compassionate conservatism "worked," the campaign worked; if it didn't, we would probably lose. We'd certainly lose the ability to control our own destiny and actively win the campaign.

We had to face reality: The Democrats had been wildly successful in painting the Republican Party as a natural home for right-wing lunatics and nutballs of all stripes. And the party hadn't helped itself with antics like shutting down the government or failing to denounce the wackos who were busy circulating pictures of Clinton behind the grassy knoll in Dallas. "Compassionate conservative" was the shorthand that would signal to the world that Bush was different. We wanted people to hear it and think that yes, Bush was a conservative, but he cared about education, cared about the poor and lower middle class, cared about finding new solutions to vexing problems of inequality. There had been a lot of back and forth over who actually coined the term but there's no question it was Rove and Bush who had latched onto it and wrapped the Bush candidacy around the concept. If it worked, compassionate conservatism would be the way to cut the Gordian knot that was holding back the Republican party. Like the Democrats in the 1980s, the Republican party's growth was bounded by its extremes. It wasn't as though everybody didn't know it, it's just that nobody had come up with a way to get out of the box. If you ran from the left like Bill Weld or Christie Whitman, you were dead meat as a national candidate. You might win a crowded primary or two by being the only moderate in the group, but once you got one on one with a more conservative candidate, you were a goner. Plus, to satisfy the left part of your support, you probably had to take positions that guaranteed you were unelectable, like supporting partial birth abortion. In his 1996 Senate race, I had tried to dissuade Weld from supporting partial birth abortion but I lost the argument because the feeling among the Massachusetts crowd was that if he was less than 100 percent pure on the pro-choice front, he would get his brains beat out as just another Republican. In the end, his "moderation" left room for the entrance into the race of a conservative, pro-life, pro-gun independent candidate, who siphoned votes we desperately needed. It was a classic lose-lose.

Jack Kemp had tried to position himself as a "bleeding heart conservative," but he had never been able to get beyond his own eccentricities, like loving the gold standard and thinking anybody remotely cared about the Bretton Woods Agreement. Still, there were a ton of people who knew the problems of the party and had been drawn to Kemp only to be disappointed by his performance at the ballot box.

Bush was in another class. People liked him. Which was not insignificant. His fav/unfav—pollster speak for those who had a favorable opinion of him versus those who didn't—was 47 percent to 14 percent (Gore's was 40 percent to 33 percent). Of course that would change. At some point in the not-so-distant future, Bush's unfavorables would climb into the twenties, then thirties, and, ultimately, on Election Day of November 2000, we'd be lucky if his fav/unfav was ten points to the good.

I'd seen it happen again and again and few candidates or campaigns were ready for it. It goes like this: An attractive candidate runs for office and starts out with something of a clean slate; people don't know a lot about him or her, but what they know they tend to like. Every candidate and campaign is convinced on some level that if the voters just get to know the candidate—the *real* candidate—then victory is assured. It's a natural, very human instinct. Most everybody around the candidate likes the candidate, so it's only reasonable to assume that the rest of the world will too.

So you start the campaign with high hopes and low negatives and, for a while, everything goes great. People respond positively. They *do* like your candidate. Your numbers improve, which means that your fav/unfav ratio only increases to the good. This is *fabulous*.

Then two things start to happen. First, the other side starts to realize that you aren't on their team. At some point, as more people tune into the race, it dawns on them that, hey, you're a *Republican* and I'm a *Democrat* and that means I don't like you. It happens first with the most partisan slices of the electorate. For Republicans, that means union members, African Americans, single women and people with postgraduate degrees. It's not as though they were in love with you before; they just didn't have much reason not to like you. But now it dawns on them that you're a skin and they're a shirt, so your negatives start to rise.

This seldom troubles a campaign. You see your unfavorables rising but reassure yourself that it's only happening with people who aren't going to vote for you anyway. Which is mostly true. You get the pollsters to start breaking out hardcore Democratic groups, so that you can see numbers that don't include, say, African American women or labor households that haven't voted Republican since the Civil War. When you drop those folks out of the samples, your numbers instantly improve. You feel better. Soon you have convinced yourself that the world only includes the voters you want to include. "Hey, among married women, our numbers went up three."

Then the other side attacks. Or you attack first. Instantly your negatives rise. It's not complicated. You're now in the middle of two things humans hate—you're being attacked, which means that bad stuff is being spread around, and you're fighting back with counterpunches. Either one is going to shoot your negatives skyward, and now you're in a race to see who can beat up the other guy more effectively. You resolve to endure pain to inflict pain. It's Serb vs. Muslim, Hatfield vs. McCoy, Spy vs. Spy. You wake up every morning and read the overnight tracking with a sense of dread, heart racing. Media markets become battlefields and the tracking provides casualty reports: *Jesus, we're dying in St. Louis with thirty-five to forty-five women. Just dying! But hey, look at this, in Springfield we've knocked the other guy's negatives up to fifty with white men over thirty-five. Killing his ass! Yes.*

You design spots like smart bombs. *Let's see now . . . if we attack on school safety, we appeal to men and married women, don't alienate moderates and energize our base. That's it. Film a school with metal detectors and kids with backpacks being searched and . . .*

At the time it all seems perfectly normal. It's only later that you look back and wonder, Lord, we said that? *He voted to pardon a killer who shot a sixty-eight-year-old woman **in the** face.* In the face? Nice touch.

And if you're lucky, really lucky, and maybe a little smarter and tougher than the other side, you win. But you win with high negatives. It's like any war—you begin with parades and bands and banners and high hopes, convinced God is on your side, and end up bloody and battered and beat to hell. But by God, you won. And those other poor bastards, you ought to see what they look like.

Later, you forget how bad it was, or you mostly forget, enough to get ready to do it all over again. You forget how your hand was shaking when you read the tracking, how it felt when you realized that ad you just put on the air was the dumbest mistake you ever made in your life, what it's like to know that you can win this thing if you just come up with the right spot, but *you can't think of the right spot.* It's out there, just beyond your reach, floating around. It's been two months since you slept more than four or five hours at a stretch and you find it utterly impossible to even talk to anyone who isn't involved in the campaign. *Civilians*. Who has time for them? God, don't they know what's going on? Somebody asks you innocently if you want to go to a movie and you want to laugh and tear their head off at the same time.

But you do forget and you do tell yourself that next time it will be different. Next time you'll be able to run a positive campaign, debate the issues, do it the way you want to do it, not the way it was last time.

That's how it was that spring morning in Austin at Java.

With one of his elegant fountain pens—Karl had better taste in pens and paper than any man she knew, my wife maintained—Karl diagrammed the campaign structure. Karen Hughes would run the press and speech operation, traveling with the governor. That was a no-brainer—she'd done it since he ran in '94 and Bush had said publicly that he wouldn't be running for president if Karen wasn't onboard. Joe Allbaugh would be campaign manager, handling logistics, watching the money, overseeing scheduling, making sure all the pieces fit together. Karl would head up strategy, media and polling. Josh Bolten was putting together the policy shop.

When he told me that Mike Gerson was going to be head speechwriter, I was surprised. I didn't really know Gerson but he'd worked for Senator Dan Coats, whose campaigns I'd handled. Coats is one of the most decent and genuine people you'll ever come across in politics but I'd never fancied him an orator. "Wait until you read this guy's stuff," Karl promised. McKinnon, who was with us at breakfast, weighed in as well. "Big gun," Mark said. "Big gun."

As we sat there drinking coffee surrounded by the morning mating rituals of life in a hip college town—the lesbian couple holding hands over organic oatmeal, the guy in the

U of T swimming T-shirt and his girlfriend who looked like they'd just spent their first night together—it struck me that there hadn't been a modern Republican presidential campaign, at least not a big-time, might-actually-win campaign, that had been structured and staffed like the one Karl was describing. At its core was a group of people who wouldn't have been in the presidential race were it not for their involvement with George W. Bush.

This may seem like a simple notion until you contemplate the stranglehold the consultant culture had gained over the top talent in both parties. Clinton was the perfect example. When he decided to run for president in '92, he went shopping for help and except for an Arkansas pal or two like Bruce Lindsey, all his top players—Stephanopoulos, Carville, Begala—were just that, players, guys who could have worked for any other Democrat in the race.

But Karl, Karen, Mark McKinnon, Joe, they were all Texans. (Well, Joe was actually from Oklahoma, but that's close enough.) It was such a slap in the face to Washington that *you had to love it*. They were going to run this thing right here in Austin, and if you wanted to be part of it, you moved to Austin. None of this flying in and being smart and then flying back to D.C. and dinner at the Palm.

Of course, I wasn't a Texan. And like it or not, I was more a part of the consultant culture than anybody else in the campaign. It put me in a position a little like my boyhood hero Natty Bumppo of *The Deerslayer:* He was in love with the wilderness untouched by White Man America, but wherever he went, as a white man he began the ruin of what he loved. Yes, I hated what consultants were doing to the political system and yes, I hated the Washington scene and did everything I could to avoid it, refusing to live there, developing a counterlife as a writer, but there was no escaping that if the revolution came and they started lining up political consultants to be shot, I'd be right up against the wall.

I also couldn't pretend that there wasn't something about being a media consultant that I loved, or had loved in years past. The very notion that I could sit in a dark editing studio in New York and make a spot that might change the outcome of a big election, change the minds of hundreds of thousands, even millions—this was great stuff. And I loved the combat of it all, loved the late-night adrenaline rush of charging into the studio to defend my guy at all costs, loved the clarity of winning or losing. I loved to attack, counterpunch, outthink 'em, outfight 'em. I had even done campaigns overseas, parachuting in with a team of highly trained specialists—or so I envisioned it. I was a *specialist*. Gunslinger? Loved it.

For me, it began with a bulletproof vest at a high school football stadium. I was fifteen, young enough to drive in my native Mississippi, and I was spending the summer driving William Winter, who was running for governor, all over the state. He was a college friend of my parents, with a daughter my age, and he was facing a one-armed congressman named John Bell Williams in the Democratic primary. In those days, there wasn't a Republican party in the state, so winning the Democratic nomination was the same as getting elected governor.

The race had started with a field of five or six candidates, all hoping to be in the top two and make the runoff, which state law required if no one received 50 percent or more of the vote. It was a system common in the South, designed to stop blacks from winning races. The idea was simple and deadly: If a bunch of white guys and one black ran for the same office, and if the black candidate was lucky enough to run either first or second, he was sure to lose the runoff, when the white voters would coalesce behind the remaining white candidate.

There wasn't a black in this race but it was still all about race. It always was in those days, one way or another. William Winter, though hardly a screaming liberal, was the moderate on race and John Bell Williams, the one-armed congressman, was the states' rights, stand-in-the-schoolhouse-door, protect-our-way-of-life candidate. Winter did well in Jackson and some of the bigger towns along with the Delta, where Hodding Carter published the *Delta Democrat-Times,* which strongly backed Winter. John Bell—that was what everybody called him—romped and stomped everywhere else, from the piney woods of south Mississippi to the hills of north Mississippi. "Let him have Hinds County [Jackson]," John Bell liked to say, "I'll take the rest."

Of course it wasn't as though Jackson, Mississippi, was some liberal hotbed likely to be confused with Berkeley. My hometown was the place where they beat the hell out of Freedom Riders, shot students at Jackson State, and set off bombs in front of the rabbi's house with such regularity it was easy to think that being Jewish involved arcane rituals requiring high explosives.

I loved William Winter. He was good-natured and tough and, to my eyes, a warrior for good. What else would you think about a guy who when told of death threats—very specific death threats—if he dared appear at a night rally in a south Mississippi high school football stadium, had merely shrugged. There was no formal security in those days—no mags, no ticket-only events, no plainclothes agents, no bulletproof podiums or Plexiglas shields that can bounce a magnum. If he had already been governor, Winter would have at least had a pair of burly state troopers who could have swelled up and looked tough.

But he was just a candidate for the Democratic nomination for Mississippi governor, and candidates didn't get protection.

Somebody came up with a bulletproof vest. I think it was

an off-duty cop. I remember there were a surprising number of law enforcement types supporting Winter, men—and they were all men in those days—who didn't like a lot of what was going on in the state, although there wasn't much they could do. Except help William Winter in their off-time.

The vest was big and bulky. This was August in Mississippi and you started sweating as soon as you stepped outside for your first event—6:30 or 7 A.M. at the latest. Winter worked like a fiend. And you just sweated through the day so that by eight or nine at night, you felt like you had been walking around in old gym towels all day.

When they were putting on the vest, Winter had a bemused look on his face, as though he was humoring a friend telling a not-very-good joke. His wife, who traveled on her own a good bit, couldn't be there. But I knew he wouldn't have wanted her there anyway. She always stood or sat right next to him onstage.

He wore a white shirt over the white vest, with one of those skinny dark ties everybody had. We were in the visiting locker room of the stadium. There were motivational posters, hand lettered: "You can't soar with the eagles at day and play with the owls at night." The senior campaign aides, the guys I wanted to be, huddled in the corner, talking quietly. They seemed a lot older but thinking back, none of them could have been more than thirty-five. Outside we could hear one of the candidates for lieutenant governor really jacking the crowd up with the states' rights pitch that everybody loved that summer.

"Who's gonna tell 'em the feds got the bomb?" somebody cracked. It was a joke we batted around a lot that summer. States' rights was great and glorious, but when it came time to stand up to the federal government, who was going to tell Mississippi the feds could nuke them off the planet?

"It's time, William." One of the senior aides opened the

door. The crowd was going crazy. Winter stood in the doorway, silhouetted against the stadium lights. He stepped for-
ward, through the door.

My hero.

So I fell in love with politics. Who wouldn't? It had all the
fun of combat but nobody died, or at least not very often. (No
one shot Winter, but he lost, ran again and lost, and then finally was elected and turned out to be the best governor Mississippi had in fifty years.) It was simple—your guy was good,
the other guy was evil, and every day you woke up trying to
beat the crap out of the other guy.

I loved it.

But I never figured I'd make a living at it.

Then a friend called just as I was finishing film school. He
was running for Congress in Mississippi against Senator John
Stennis's son and couldn't afford to hire anybody to make ads
for him. So he asked me to do it. I explained that I didn't have
the slightest idea how to make commercials and when he
protested that I had just been to two of the fanciest film
schools in the country, I tried to tell him that mostly what I did
was watch old films and write little essays and listen to people
like Vincente Minnelli tell us how it used to be. (Minnelli wore
a blazer the color of a canary yellow Post-it note. Perfect.)

But my friend was insistent. This would be great fun. We
wouldn't win but we could shake up the Known Order and
maybe, just maybe, scare the hell out of 'em. And, oh yeah, he
was running as a Republican.

Republicans were a new phenomenon in Mississippi.
There were only two Republican congressmen (out of five) in
the state and no statewide officeholder was a Republican. The
congressman from Jackson, my hometown, was Thad Cochran
and he was running for the Senate, opening up the seat my
friend was trying to win.

It wasn't as though I had a lot of offers after film school

and I had to admit it did sound like fun. So I went back to Mississippi and somehow we stumbled our way to victory in what was seen as a major upset. Then I discovered other people would pay me money to make commercials for them.

So I became a media consultant.

Why not? It's a profession of charlatans. You want to be a media consultant, just say you're one. To drive a cab in New York, at least you have to take a test, know how to get to Kennedy. But media consulting? No way.

At first it was like migrant labor work, seasonal and very intense. In the off-season I could write and I enjoyed the fact that campaigns were everything writing wasn't—you worked with other humans, not just in a room by yourself, and the results were unequivocal. You either won or lost and when it was over, it was over. Somebody blew the whistle, added up the score and if you had more votes than the other guy, you won. Very simple.

A friend of mine who's a famous pollster says he went into politics because he saw himself like a Jedi knight, fighting for good. Me, I fancied myself more of an angry linebacker type, running around looking for somebody to hit. That was the fun of it.

By 1998, I'd pretty much had enough. The people who handle PR for my firm like to say I'd elected more governors and senators than any other Republican consultant and it might even be true. I'd always respected and most often liked the people I'd worked for, but like an aging bachelor who had dated too long, it was becoming harder to fall in love.

But there was one thing I'd never done—worked for a winning presidential campaign. And I knew that if I worked for anyone in 2000, it would be George W. Bush.

☆　　　　☆　　　　☆

I'd met him for the first time at Karl Rove's house in the Austin hills. This was the spring of 1997 and nobody was really talking about him running for president. Not yet, anyway. It was the kind of evening that makes you understand why so many people love Austin—an exploding sunset behind the hills, lots to eat and drink with low-key, smart people who didn't feel obligated to impress one another. Karl cooked quail in the wonderful old Texas farmhouse he had saved from destruction. Outside, it had a big porch with sweeping views and inside it was jammed with books. Hunting quail, politics, his family, and collecting books were Karl's passions and they were all part of the evening.

Bush spent most of the evening on the porch, laughing and smoking cigars. There was talk of the Texas Book Festival, a celebration and promotion of Texas writers that Laura Bush had started. Not surprisingly, writers loved it.

"They might not all like you, Governor," somebody teased, "but they love Laura."

"I'm used to that," Bush said.

Toward the end of the evening, Bush was helping wash dishes, which seemed to be something of a running joke between him and Karl. "Is there anything else, Mr. Rove, I can do around the house? Maybe clean some quail for you?"

"Actually I've got some killdeer that need cleaning."

They laughed. In 1994, when running against Ann Richards, Bush had mistakenly shot a protected songbird, a killdeer, while on a quail hunting trip. "Good thing it wasn't a deer hunt, or I might have shot a cow," he'd quipped at the time.

"I know Karl is trying to set the two of us up," Bush said to me in the kitchen. "One of his arranged marriages."

"Not true!" Karl protested.

"He does this all the time," Bush whispered loudly. "I

don't know what we're going to do with the boy." It was, I'd learn, the sort of thing he loved to do—take the subtext of a situation and spell it out, tease people with it, have fun. He was a governor, I was a political consultant and we'd been brought together at our mutual friend's house and he couldn't let it pass without letting us know he knew exactly what was going on.

"Well, I just want you to know," he said, winking, "that even though Karl has terrible judgment, occasionally he gets things right. Like Darby here," he said, throwing his arm around Karl's wife.

I liked him. Of course I did. He was funny and unpretentious with a touch of mischievous irony that is rare in the self-serious world of politics. And he seemed to enjoy himself, which is even more rare.

The next time I saw him was three years later. The world had changed. George W. Bush was now the leading candidate for president. Clinton was hanging by a thread. Bill Bradley had mounted a threat to Al Gore that looked like it might kill Gore's candidacy in the crib.

It was June 1999 and I had just moved to Austin to work as a media consultant to the Bush campaign. In a couple of weeks, Bush would fly to Iowa and announce his candidacy. It was all just beginning.

We met in a hotel in Dallas where he was speaking to a group of donors. The press was buzzing about how much money the campaign had raised and how much more would be needed to mount a serious challenge for the nomination. This was how the press and political industry kept score before there were votes to count. Money was the easy yardstick.

In 1996, $20 million had been seen as the amount needed for a serious challenge. This number had basically been made up by Senator Phil Gramm. He figured he could raise the dough and nobody else could, except Bob Dole, so he sold the press on the idea that if you couldn't raise $20 million, you weren't a serious player. When the day was done, Gramm raised $28 million and still ended up dead meat even before the Iowa Caucuses, humiliated by Pat Buchanan in Louisiana. So much for the inevitability of money.

Nobody knew how much the Bush campaign could raise. But the campaign faced a key decision—whether or not to reject public financing for the primary. The law went like this: Under a complicated formula, the feds would match individual primary contributions up to $250, provided a campaign agreed to limit their spending to an overall figure of $37 million.

There was one other catch. The FEC—the Federal Election Commission—required that if you took public financing, you had to limit the amount you spent in each state based on a convoluted scheme that no one really understood, including the FEC. This was a monumental headache and, if enforced, potentially fatal. The danger was that if somebody else had a ton of money and rejected public financing, it freed them up to spend as much as they wanted in a given state and left you vulnerable. In our case, that somebody was Steve Forbes.

In 1996, as media consultant to Bob Dole in the primary, I'd been forced to watch Steve Forbes pummel us with millions of dollars of television we couldn't answer. Forbes, who chose his parents well, was spending his inheritance at a furious rate. And having rejected public financing, he had the ability to spend unlimited amounts of money in any state. Forbes transformed himself from a quirky editorial writer with a goofy smile and a rich dad into some kind of political death star, slaughtering all in his path. At one time in Iowa, he had ads attacking Dole, Lamar Alexander and Phil Gramm, who was already dead (Forbes was the only guy who didn't realize it). Forbes could have established himself as an interesting intellectual gadfly raising the level of debate, much as he had tried to do as an editorial writer. Instead, for reasons only his shrink could answer, he decided that for once in his life, he would be the toughest kid in the schoolyard.

Eventually he flamed out, but in 1999 he was back. And once again he had rejected public financing, setting the stage for him to spend his seemingly unlimited family fortune whenever and however he desired. The word was that Forbes actually thought he could win this time, a testament to the powers of human self-delusion.

"Stevens," Bush yelled, "get in here and let's bond!" He was standing in the hotel room door with a wink and an unlit cigar in his mouth. His eyes were bright and intense, his mouth cast in that slightly ironic but friendly way I'd get to know well. The look said, "I know this is a bit silly and you know it is, but let's go along and do what we're supposed to."

Inside the room, Karen Hughes and Karl were on the phone. I was with Mark McKinnon, who had arranged the meeting to give me a chance to spend some time with the governor.

"You moving to Austin?" Bush asked.

"Already have, Governor. Moved down just two days ago."

He nodded. This is how he wanted the campaign to be run—everybody totally focused on one thing—winning. Mark McKinnon had left his public affairs company, PSI, and Karl Rove had sold his direct-mail company. Normally I would work on ten to fifteen governors' and senators' races but for the next eighteen months, I'd have only one client—George W. Bush.

"You ready to win?" he asked me. He was looking at me very directly, almost staring. This was something I'd learn he did a lot. It was an open, almost innocent look, focused and blunt.

His question surprised me and made me chuckle. What could I say? Of course I was ready, as much as anybody can be. I mumbled something in the affirmative and we looked at each other for a beat and then the moment passed and we chatted like any two people getting to know one another. He asked about my wife and where we were living in Austin and was she going to get a job in Austin. Just stuff.

Karen handed him a cell phone. Ron Fournier of the Associated Press was on the phone. Fournier was always on the phone; he was somebody everyone respected, a no-nonsense, hardworking guy who played it down the middle.

"Fournier?" The governor looked at us and winked. He lowered his voice. "I want you to be the first to know that I've decided not to run. No, I'm not kidding. Go with it, Fournier, it'll make your career."

Mark and I had to leave to get ready to film his speech at the fund-raiser. When we left he was still on the phone, laughing.

"I gave you a scoop, Fournier, what else do you want?"

3

The Phony War

HE WAS WEARING JEANS, BLACK BOOTS and a tight white
T-shirt. The total effect was more early Paul Newman than a
guy leading in every presidential poll. Outside it was 103 degrees, but he had just gone running and was chuckling over
how the DPS (Department of Public Safety, the Texas guys,
this was before Secret Service protection) officers were complaining that he always had to run in the hottest part of the
day. Lately they had taken to following him on a bicycle rather
than trying to keep up in the heat. He was fast—seven- to
seven-and-a-half-minute miles.

We had been shooting commercials all morning and had
taken a break for lunch. The governor had used the break to
go for a run. I'd tried this running in the middle of the day stuff
when I first got to Austin and by the end of four miles, my skin
felt like it was on fire. And my pace was considerably slower
than Bush's. Only McKinnon, who had body fat lower than the
sales tax and ran like a deer, could keep up with Bush.

It was August 1999 and we were preparing our first package of commercials. It was a great relief to actually be doing
something rather than just planning and thinking about doing something. This was the phony war stage of the campaign
in which we seemed to spend a lot of time parading up and
down in neat formations. The latest *Wall Street Journal* poll—

one of the few public polls worth respecting since it's conducted by two of the best political pollsters in the business, Peter Hart (a Democrat) and Bob Teeter (Republican)—had Bush ahead of McCain by 59 percent to 3 percent.

That's right—59 percent to 3 percent.

A fifty-six-point lead falls under the "comfortable" heading pretty much any way you slice it. We had never been behind in the primary and the only time any number was ever published showing us in second place was when pollsters put Colin Powell on the ballot. A year earlier in July '98, a Harris poll had Powell at 24 percent, Bush at 20 percent, Elizabeth Dole at 10 percent and Quayle at 7 percent. McCain wasn't even in the race at that point. But that was it—every poll with the actual cast of characters had us leading by at least twenty-five points.

When pollsters threw Bush up against Gore, we won that in a walk as well—the ABC/*Washington Post* poll had us up 53 percent to 36 percent, the CNN/*Time* poll put it at 56 percent to 38 percent. Piece of cake.

Then there was the small matter of money. In part because of the fact that we were ahead in every poll, the campaign was raising unbelievable amounts of money—$33 million for the first reporting period. The number was so big, reporters literally gasped when Don Evans, the campaign finance chairman, announced the total. The campaign had decided—thank God—not to take public money. This freed us up to do battle with what we figured would be a forty-million-plus assault from Forbes.

But I hated this stage of the campaign. It felt like we were tiptoeing through a lion's den in porkchop panties, just waiting for somebody to rip a big bite right out of us. Everybody was out for us. That's just how it was when you were a front-runner.

The press was bored to death with the same story line—Bush leads. What the hell could they do with a 59 percent to 3 percent race? They had to do anything they could to ding us; "get a little blood in the water" was how more than one of them put it.

Which is exactly what had happened over the past few days.

I heard about it for the first time when Mark called around 11 P.M. This was odd—Mark was a go-to-bed-early, run-ten-miles-before-dawn kind of guy, which put us on precisely opposite schedules. He was traveling that week with Governor Bush, stepping in for Karen Hughes, who was jamming away on the book that would become *A Charge to Keep*.

Mark started right in. "Is it fair to ask if a president should be able to answer the same questions about past drug use as his staff?"

"Fair?" I felt my heart pick up a few beats. This is how it always was in politics—a late-night phone call and the world shifts a little. Sometimes a lot.

Mark sighed. He sounded exhausted. "Attlesey asked the governor if he could answer the same drug questions as the White House staff. Have you used drugs for the last seven years? Do you think we have to answer that?" Attlesey was Sam Attlesey, a *Dallas Morning News* reporter who had covered Texas politics since the Alamo.

I thought for a moment. It was a clever question. Not to answer it would imply that you believed in some double standard. And make it sound like you were afraid to answer it. Seven years wasn't ancient history. People could see it as a relevant question worth answering.

"I guess," I said. "Hard not to."

Mark sounded relieved. "That's what I told the governor. He answered it."

"What was the answer?" I asked Mark.

"What? Are you—"

"A joke. Look, Mark, I think you did the right thing. I really do."

I felt for the guy. Mark had a deep and abiding affection for George W. Bush. They both had teenage daughters, ran together, were passionate about education—they were good friends. Apart from any political considerations, Mark hated the idea of giving the wrong advice to someone he cared about very much.

I hadn't known Mark long but considered him one of the most decent guys I'd ever met. We shared a mutual dislike for the way politics had evolved—the pretensions, the bitterness, the people who wanted to be something more than do something. But while I still reveled in the sheer combat of campaigns, the smell of napalm in the morning and all that, Mark had gotten back in the game for one reason—to help Bush. And every time something happened like this blind side hit on White House drug screening, it reminded him of exactly why he had the good sense to get out of politics in the first place.

We talked about it some more, playing out different scenarios for how long it would take for the story to flush out of the news cycle and whether or not there was any lasting damage. I couldn't predict how the story would evolve, but I was absolutely convinced that, in the long run, this whole drug thing would be a nonevent.

The reality was there was no reason to believe George W. Bush had ever used cocaine. No one even suggested that they had seen him at a party or been at a party or heard this or heard that. Zero. There was only one red flag—his refusal to answer questions of that sort about his past.

"This is all Ann Richards's fault, you know," I told Mark. "It's Ann Richards's revenge." Mark laughed. He knew how I liked to tease him about working for Ann Richards.

But I was serious. The whole "did you or did you not" cocaine story had started with Ann Richards, which most of the national reporters just covering Bush for the first time never realized. It goes back to when she was running in 1990 for the Democratic nomination for governor against Jim Mattox, one of the meanest, wildest characters in Texas politics, no small achievement.

I actually knew Mattox in a vague sort of way. When I lived in D.C. during the early 1980s, he was a young congressman and lived in my neighborhood. One of his campaign consultants was a pal of mine. He liked to tell the story of how Mattox called him up one night and told him that a reporter had just found out that Mattox had been running a secret rump poll trying to determine if people would be less likely to vote for his Republican opponent if they thought the Republican's wife was either Hispanic or African American (she was, in fact, Hispanic). My friend had to laugh—this was so typically Mattox—and commiserated that it was a shame he had been caught. But Mattox didn't seem concerned and assured him that the story wouldn't hurt him.

"Yeah?" my friend asked, "why's that?"

"Because," Mattox told him, "I just told the press that it was all your idea and I didn't know anything about it."

That was Jim Mattox. In 1990 he found himself in a death struggle with Ann Richards. Mattox did not like to lose. He hired Bob Schrum—the same Bob Schrum who was working for Al Gore in the 2000 campaign. Richards had been at the epicenter of the wild and crazy seventies around Austin when the conventional wisdom was that just about everybody from musicians to politicians were partying like there was no tomorrow and for a lot of them, there hadn't been. She had been public about her former drinking problem, but the rumors were hot and heavy that she had also been in rehab for cocaine addiction. This she had neither confirmed nor denied.

So Schrum made a commercial for Mattox with an Ann

Richards look-alike—an actress with a wig just like Richards's trademark cone of white hair—with her back to the camera engaged in an activity that looked a lot like cocaine sniffing. The script went like this:

> ANNOUNCER: Did she use marijuana, or something worse like cocaine, not as a college kid but as a forty-seven-year-old elected official sworn to uphold the law?

A nasty piece of work and, not surprisingly, it backfired. Richards continued to refuse to answer any questions about cocaine, jumped all over the high road and beat the hell out of Mattox for going too far. Mattox lost, while Richards won and went on to beat Republican Claytie Williams.

In 1994 when Richards ran for reelection, reporters took another crack at trying to get her to answer questions about cocaine use. She stuck to the same position—none of your business. And, of course, it was only fair that reporters ask the same question of her opponent—George W. Bush.

Bush backed up Richards's right not to answer the cocaine question and it was then he laid out his own position—that when he had been young and irresponsible, he was young and irresponsible. It was coupled with a reiteration of what he had been saying for years, that when he was forty, he quit drinking because, "I thought I was drinking too much."

So, yes, it was true that George W. Bush had refused to answer questions about cocaine use. But the only reason the question had ever been raised was the Ann Richards situation.

The next morning the phone rang early. It was Mark, calling from the road. "This is a disaster," he said. "Listen to this. Here's the AP lead: 'Governor says he hasn't done drugs in seven years.' "

Of course. We should have realized how it would play. It

was precisely the danger of getting into this kind of silly, "bigger than a bread box" incremental answers. Bush's instinct not to answer any of this stuff was the right one. Once you started, how did you stop?

"It gets worse," Mark said. "It seems like when you work at the White House they don't really ask about seven years, it's more like seventeen or eighteen years."

"What does the governor want to do?" I asked Mark.

"I don't know. If he refuses to answer, then we get headlines saying that Bush won't deny drug use. We're into this, we just have to get out of it. It's so goddamn stupid."

That day it seems like every political consultant I knew who wasn't working for another presidential candidate called me, all with one message: Bush should answer the questions. All the questions. Whatever they asked, just answer it yes or no. Get it over with.

As political advice went, they were probably right. But on a gut level I admired what Bush was trying to do. Running for president was such a grueling, humiliating, debilitating process and he had seen it up close starting in 1979, when his father ran for the first time, then in '88 and '92. When he decided to run for president, he'd made a decision to try and do it on his terms as much as possible. There were certain things he wouldn't do and if that hurt him, so be it. He wasn't going to play twenty questions about his past. He would protect his daughters as much as possible—they would not be filmed, they wouldn't campaign. And he refused to use polls to craft policy.

This last point was, in the political world, pure heresy. I'd never seen anything like it.

The Bush campaign had assembled a powerhouse policy team lead by Josh Bolten. He had a team of Rhodes scholars and former Supreme Court clerks, your typical brilliant policy wonks. Then there were groups of policy advisers—Condoleezza Rice led an all-star group in the foreign policy world; Larry Lindsey in the economic area; Steve Goldsmith, former mayor of Indianapolis, headed up domestic policy. There had really never been anything like it in the Republican world and as the campaign went on, the policy staff's ability to generate interesting ideas and impressive policy proposals was a huge advantage.

In the normal course of campaign life, polls would have been used to develop the policy. Detailed, very specific options would have been tested over and over. On tax policy, questions probing for the exact size of the ideal tax cut would have been asked. On Social Security reform, campaign pollsters would have been used to design the most politically pleasing plan. This was just how campaigns did things.

But it was forbidden in the Bush world. Believe me, I tried. It wasn't that the campaign didn't poll and it wasn't as though Bush didn't pay attention to polls, at least the head-to-head numbers. He watched those like box scores. But when it came to writing policy, polls and focus groups were never used.

When I first got down to Austin and asked Karl Rove for the polls being used to develop policy, he handed me two books, Myron Magnet's *The Dream and the Nightmare* and Robert Samuelson's *The Good Life and Its Discontents*. I thought he was kidding.

"That's it," Karl said. It took a while, but like the dumbest guy in the world, I slowly came to realize that he was dead serious—there wasn't any polling being used for policy decisions and there wouldn't be any. We could use polls and focus groups to try and determine the best way to present policy proposals, but that was it. (Later, when the campaign wanted to focus-group our television spots, a process I hated, I reminded everybody that we didn't focus-group when we decided to start hugging the third rail of American politics by reforming Social Security or rolling out a $1.3 trillion tax cut or using faith-based organizations for the next step in welfare. I lost. The spots still went before focus groups whenever we had time.)

"Not going to happen," Karl said. "Nonstarter." That was the term people most frequently used when describing something that Bush had specifically ruled out. Like when I asked whether I could film his daughters' graduation from Austin High School. "Nonstarter." Like when I wanted to attack McCain before he went up with television commercials (I was joking about this, but would have done it in a heartbeat if allowed). "Nonstarter." There were a lot of those nonstarter ideas. More than in any campaign I'd ever known, it was generally acknowledged that this was the candidate's campaign and there were certain things that wouldn't be done and, hey, get used to it. Like when I was pushing to launch a particularly nasty attack against Gore and Don Evans finally said in his Gary Cooper kind of West Texas way, "Uh huh. And when you run for president, Stevens, *you* can do it."

☆　　　☆　　　☆

We were filming the commercials in what looked like a small Italian palazzo near downtown Austin. With its ornate ironwork, high arches and dark tapestries, it would have been the ideal setting for some Renaissance sitcom.

I'd spent days driving around Austin looking for the right place to shoot. We knew we wanted to do three things—film Bush in a relaxed interview setting, shoot some scripts in the same setting direct to camera and then shoot some other scripts using a solid white backdrop.

The interview and the first set of scripts were the kind of

things I loved to shoot outdoors, using lots of natural light and greenery. But Mark was partial to an interior look.

"I like it pretty," he insisted. "Let Wayne light the hell out of it. Make it gorgeous." Wayne was Wayne Forster, a director of photography from Dallas. He had this ability to take something that looked ugly as a car wreck to the naked eye, throw up some lights and by the time you got it back from the lab, it was beautiful.

"It'll look great outside," I said, half believing it.

"Are you kidding?" Mark asked. "It's August in Texas. You die if you shoot outside."

He was right, I had to admit. Even if you started early, by the time you added a couple of lights and ran through a couple of scripts, even a guy like Bush who loved the heat would probably look half-melted.

So while Mark was filling in for Karen out on the road, I tried to find a place to shoot. I knew exactly what I wanted—something open and handsome that looked like middle America, maybe a glimpse of a yard and trees out the windows, a neighborhood that could be like any neighborhood. It should have been easy to find.

It wasn't.

Austin has all sorts of houses, from fancy, new imitation French chateaus to classic Texas limestone cottages. All I needed was one house that had the right look and was large enough to let us set up lights and get some distance from the camera. And whoever lived there had to be willing to let their house be trampled by strangers for a full day . . . and it stood to reason they needed to like George W. Bush.

Nothing seemed right.

"Try Daddy-O's," Matthew Dowd finally suggested.

I thought he was talking about some hip club or restaurant. We were also looking at commercial spaces.

"He lives up on Mt. Bonnell. Cool house, kind of south-western."

"Daddy-O is a person?" I asked. "A pioneer, I bet. Went to Yale with the governor." A "pioneer" was someone who had pledged to raise $100,000 for the campaign.

Matthew laughed. "You know the giant armadillo at the Lone Star Cafe in New York?"

I actually did.

"That's Daddy-O."

I nodded, having no idea what he was talking about.

"Take Laura," Matthew suggested. "That will help."

Daddy-O had a salt-and-pepper goatee and longish white hair pulled back behind a receding hairline. His eyes twinkled. We shook hands and introduced ourselves.

"You're a good one," he said right away to Laura Craw-ford. "You work with McKinnon, right?" Laura nodded. She was wearing jeans and a white tennis shirt and carrying a little silver video camera. She had this way of looking very put to-gether without doing a thing.

Daddy-O's real name was Bob Ward and he had grown up in Texas, gone to U of T, then moved to Santa Fe, where he had become a successful artist. "I like 'em big like the ar-madillo," he said, pointing to a photograph of the giant ar-madillo that adorned the Lone Star Cafe. "Or like the Bonnie and Clyde mobile." That was a bright orange laundry van he had machine gunned.

"Then I do these things with photographs." He showed us a long wall with old photographs he had hand-tinted and colored. They were wonderful—five cowgirls sitting on a fence swirling lariats or a south Texas hunting party, every-body holding rattlesnakes.

His house felt like Santa Fe, low slung and filled with leather furniture. It wasn't what I had been looking for but it might work.

"This would look more like what we shot at the governor's lake house," Laura said from behind her video camera. She was taping all the different angles. "Very western."

"I'm Roy Rogers's second cousin, you know," Daddy-O told us. "I like western. You want me to sit in? I'll be the governor." He plopped down in a large leather chair we had been looking at as a possible place to film. "You want a pardon," he growled, "you better start being nice to me right now." Then he thought for a moment. "This chair's too big. It'll swallow him."

We agreed. While we were moving a chair in from the kitchen, Daddy-O said, "I can tell you why he's going to win this thing. It's like this," he explained. "People like Clinton. They think he's a lying son of a bitch but they like the guy. They want a president they can like. George W. people like. So they get that part they like about Clinton. But they want somebody who isn't a lying bastard. Bush ain't. They just know he ain't. So they get to keep what they like about Clinton and get somebody new. It's gonna happen, trust me."

He sat down in the chair. "This is too stiff," he said. "I feel like Al Gore, got something jammed up my butt, you know? Let me tell you one other thing. People are gonna just fall in love with Laura Bush. My writer buddies who are all Communists and crap, they love her." He moved around in the seat for a while. "You need a different chair. You been to Ranch Six-sixteen yet? I've got a giant rattlesnake on the outside with a neon rattler. Very cool. Got to see it."

"What's Ranch Six-sixteen?" I asked. Laura and I were still trying different angles. My fear was that any way we shot it it would still feel too western, too hacienda. These spots had to play in Iowa and New Hampshire. We didn't need to advertise the fact that Governor Bush was a Texan. They knew that. And some probably still remembered the bumper stickers that sprouted up in Texas during the last energy crunch: DRIVE 90. FREEZE A YANKEE.

"The ranch?" Daddy-O asked. "You don't know the ranch? New place on Nueces just above the Star Bar. Laura Bush has been there a couple of times. You ought to put her in commercials. Hey, maybe I could put one of my little iguanas in the background. You don't have any idea how powerful the iguana vote is."

We were scheduled to shoot in a day. We convened a Maverick meeting at the Club de Ville to talk about our options. The de Ville was a club partially owned by McKinnon and our regular hangout, a cinder-block affair that looked to have been constructed by a bunch of hip survivalists, complete with multicolored shards of glass embedded in the concrete wall out front. We gathered regularly in the club's courtyard, a patch of dirt littered with old lawn furniture. Mark had just gotten off the road, where he had been in the eye of the cocaine/White House clearance storm, and was feeling glad he didn't have Karen's job every week. We were in the courtyard of the de Ville, drinking beers and a drink named for Mark that was some diabolical tequila martini. It was terrible.

People love to drink outdoors in Austin and have been doing it forever. Twenty years ago, the beer gardens of Austin were famous, places like Scholtz's, where the real work of the state legislature took place. Now it happens more in hip enclaves like the de Ville or the Cedar Street, a jazz bar which, inexplicably, is on Fourth Street.

In the summer in Austin, sunset is always a time for celebration. During the day, the sun attacks with the ferocity of an enemy bombardment so that when it finally gives up and slips behind the western hills, there is a natural instinct first to seek relief, then to do a bit of gloating. *See, we survived another day.* Rushing outside to jeer at the departed sun and having a few drinks seems like perfectly reasonable behavior.

We ran down the locations we had as options. None were perfect, though probably Daddy-O's was the most interesting. It was decidedly warm, masculine and a setting in which Bush would look at home.

"What's not right about it?" Lucy asked. Lucy was the woman who always did the governor's makeup and part of the independent film and music scene around Austin. She was also a professional fitness trainer and amateur bodybuilder and most impressive to behold. Originally she was from New Jersey and had a tough Jersey girl persona that was very handy in the production world. Call it a way of getting what she wanted.

"Too western," I said.

"If you don't want western, I know a place that is fabulous. It's got a lot of looks."

"Looks like?" Mark asked. He hadn't been worried about finding a location. "Something will turn up," he kept saying.

I was learning that the Austin production world operated much more casually than in New York, where I had practiced my evil trade for years. There was something about the Austin way that I found highly appealing though occasionally terrifying. The terror usually involved reassurances that everything would work out. People seemed to believe that in Austin, whereas in New York the assumption was that the world was about to end and only immediate and extreme action might save it.

"An Italian look," Lucy said.

"Italian Italian or Tony Soprano Italian?" I asked.

"This is not Tony Soprano," Lucy insisted. "I know Tony Soprano. I went out with Tony Soprano."

"That explains a lot," Matthew said.

"Hey, be careful," Lucy said, giving him a playful slug.

He winced. Lucy was a strong girl.

☆　　　☆　　　☆

It was an odd house, no doubt about it. Dark, velvet tapestries, stone floors, a fountain or two, very northern Italian—all within spitting distance of a dozen restaurants where they would laugh at you if you asked for anything other than barbeque.

Mark loved it. Wayne, the lighting guru, could have a field day.

"We're really going to shoot a candidate for the Republican nomination for president in a baby Italian castle?" I asked. "Maybe we can dress him like a Renaissance prince."

"You didn't want western," Mark reminded me.

"Does he have some velvet pants he can wear? And one of those velvet hats, what do they call them?"

"Wayne can make this beautiful."

"I'm not saying it won't be a very attractive Renaissance look."

"We can shoot him on the couch and bounce light in through the windows." Mark was getting excited.

"The leaded glass windows," I noted. "On the plush velour sofa."

"Wayne can fix all that," Mark promised. "Don't worry."

"I can get a different sofa cover," Laura suggested.

"What do you have against leaded glass?" Mark teased. "It's a nice touch."

We were planning on shooting a ridiculously large number of spots—basically almost everything we might run during the fall campaign. Or at least everything that would feature the governor straight to camera. In most campaigns, this would have been impossible even to consider if for no other reason than most campaigns would have counted on weekly polls to determine what spots would run. Personally, I always find it hard to predict on a Monday what spot should run on Friday. But Karl had a different style and approach. He was a master planner who had a rare ability in politics to map things out months ahead—and actually stick to the plan. The few times I had felt compelled, or been compelled, to draw up a long-term ad plan, it always ended up on a shelf like abandoned launch codes for a war that never happened. It wasn't so much that I was against planning, it was just the idea of sticking to it that seemed unnecessary.

Not Karl.

About a month earlier, Karl had come over to our Maverick Media offices "to kick some ideas around about the ads." Our offices were separate from the regular campaign headquarters, in the basement of a formidable-looking building on North Lamar Street that appeared to have been designed by Albert Speer. All stone and harsh angles, it would have looked perfect with an eagle and twin lightning bolts on top. From the beginning, we called our offices—located in a windowless basement—"the bunker." Later we discovered that it had in fact been built as a fallout shelter in case, God knows why, somebody was in a mood to nuke Austin. Perhaps some mad Russian general who hated Willie Nelson or had become a devout University of Oklahoma football fan. I said to Mark when we first moved in that we should get some survival food to decorate the place and within a day or two, he had dispatched interns to the army surplus store down the street to load up on canned goods.

All of us—Matthew Dowd, Mark, Russ Schriefer, my partner who had also moved down from Washington—had ideas on the right message and approach. We were strongly predisposed to use Bush as much as possible direct to camera. This was the format Mark had used when he did the spots for the reelect in 1998 and focus groups had responded well when shown footage of Bush speaking to small groups or to the camera. Focus groups are the only time you get thirty amateurs to tell professionals what to do, as Roger Ailes used to complain. But I have to admit they can give you a sense of whether or not a candidate can carry a message himself, or whether you are better off using an announcer. People liked Bush on camera.

We sat around in the Maverick conference room surrounded by a half-dozen televisions and ate barbeque. In the Bush world, lunch meetings usually involved ingesting large amounts of barbeque, a tendency I always encouraged.

We figured at the time that we would spend between $15 and $20 million on television for the primary. Most of it would be spent in a few states: Iowa, New Hampshire, South Carolina, Michigan, possibly California, though we were counting on having the nomination wrapped up by California. If we didn't, we'd be in trouble.

After the primaries, we hoped to have left a considerable sum that we'd be able to spend on ads in key general election states. The period after securing the nomination and before the convention had proven deadly for Dole, who was broke and at the mercy of a Clinton assault on television. This time we wanted to be the ones taking advantage of a wounded Gore while he was still recovering from his battle with Bradley.

While the fall ad campaign was obviously intended to win the nomination, we were also aware that it would get a huge amount of press scrutiny and send a message about the kind of campaign we intended to run. Because there wasn't much really going on in the campaign at this point and Bush was such an overwhelming favorite, everything we did was overscrutinized. The spots would have an inordinate ripple effect beyond the markets in which they were aired. They'd air on news shows and be discussed on cable chat fests and written about in every paper in the country.

We wanted to design a campaign that would appeal to primary voters but lay a base for winning the general election. It made sense—why spend $20 million just to appeal to primary voters if you are ahead by fifty points? And some of these early primary states would be important swing states in the general—Iowa, New Hampshire, Michigan, Illinois. A Republican presidential candidate hadn't carried those states since 1988 and we wanted to win, and thought we could win, all of them against Gore.

And we were convinced that we would be running against Gore, despite the hot streak Bradley was enjoying. It was all but impossible for Gore to lose. There were basically four pillars to the Democratic nominating apparatus: party activists (which is French for "liberals"), minorities (predominantly African Americans), labor and the party establishment (meaning other officeholders). Bradley had yet to crack any of those groups in a significant way.

In looking at the primary campaign, we were facing a strange paradox. Though Bush had a huge lead at the moment, this would not only shrink, the entire dynamic of the race was likely to change. There would be three or four defining moments of the primary and we would be lucky if we controlled one or two. And none of them could be predicted.

Russ Schriefer and I, having gone through the Dole primary campaign, were the most concerned about the damage Forbes could inflict.

"It's not the first thousand points that hurt," Russ said, "it's six, seven, eight thousand points of negatives that keep adding up. He'll take one or two obscure things and pick at 'em."

Karl was skeptical. He and Steve Forbes had once been friends and he was still in contact with people who were close to Forbes. The word he was getting was that Forbes wanted to do it differently this time, that he realized he had hurt himself in '96 with his unrelenting negatives and he was determined not to make the same mistakes.

McKinnon was worried about McCain. "He gets that outsider thing going, fight the system, it's powerful stuff."

No way, I told him. "The guy is the quintessential *insider,* chairman of the Commerce Committee, been in Washington for two decades. How is he going to run as an outsider against a guy who has been governor for five years? And what's he going to run on?" I asked. "Campaign finance reform? In a Republican primary? Gimme a break. That's crazy."

Mark shook his head. "He's just got something that scares me."

We teased him that he thought McCain had appeal because he'd spent his life in Democratic party politics and McCain was much more appealing to Democrats than Republicans. And McCain was making it clear that he didn't intend to participate in the Iowa Caucus.

"This process has rules," I insisted. "They may be arbitrary, silly rules but you don't show up at the Super Bowl and ask, 'Why is the field one hundred yards long?' You cannot disrespect this process and expect to win." I was convinced that by staying out of Iowa, McCain was making a critical mistake.

But Elizabeth Dole did concern me. In 1996 I had seen her work some magic in front of Republicans and I had a tremendous amount of respect for her discipline and the way she prepared for any challenge.

"Democrats won't even nominate a woman, you're telling me Republicans will?" Mark asked.

He had a point. But in theory, Elizabeth Dole was a formidable threat. With her genuine evangelical convictions, she had the potential to appeal to conservatives, including Christian conservatives. In the worst moments of the Dole campaign, she would often retreat to a quiet corner and read the Bible. But she also could appeal to moderate voters who loved the idea of voting for a woman, and she had the ability to mobilize new voters who wouldn't normally be drawn to the process. In that way, she could change the rules of the game in her favor and redefine a race.

"Look," Karl said, "there's a limit to what we can control. Things will happen and we will deal with them when they do. What I want us to focus on is designing the perfect campaign. Not a good campaign—the perfect campaign."

He was right, of course. Campaigns have a tendency to worry far too much about the other side and not enough about their own. It was a hell of a lot more fun to sit around and bullshit about the other guys than deal with the problems that were staring you in the face. It was a classic management problem. And though campaigns are a billion-dollar-plus industry, they are probably, as a group, some of the most mismanaged, inefficient businesses in the world.

We'd been kicking ideas around for fifteen minutes when Karl got to the point and simply asked, "What are the basic goals we want these first ads to accomplish?" He then proceeded to outline the foundation of an entire campaign's worth of spots. Mark wrote it down on a sheet of poster board hanging on an easel that we had set up to make it look like a real meeting. The goals read something like this:

- Future not past. Focus more on what he will do than what he's done in Texas.
- Build Credentials. Bush = successful, big-state governor. Leader.
- Win Education. Capture Bush passion. Make education a defining issue.

- Win Taxes. Appeal to economic conservative base; use taxes to define compassionate conservative approach.
- Rebuild military.
- Change the tone in Washington.
- Social Security reform. Back up the Bush plan once announced.

There wasn't a silver bullet in the bunch, but that didn't bother any of us. What Karl laid out were the basic building blocks of the entire candidacy. The plan didn't touch on every issue, or even every major issue—health care was the most obvious missing item—but you would get a sense of what he had done, what he wanted to do and why he wanted to do it.

But would it be good enough? We had no way of knowing. One of the dirty little secrets of political media is that positive ads will only get you to a certain point and then they begin to lose effectiveness. There comes a time when voters want to hear why you are right and the other guy is wrong. Positive ads work best when they are used to set up attacks or contrasts.

But we didn't have any plans to attack or contrast. Not that the campaign hadn't consistently reserved the right to counterpunch or "set the record straight," as we often put it. Forbes was the most likely to attack and if he did, we'd hit him back. But that was it. There would be no first use of attacks.

I loved this and I hated it. Loved it because there was something honorable about it, a genuine effort to play by a higher standard. But I hated it because it was a form of disarmament and reduced our chances to control our destiny. I'd been in races where the only reason we won was going after the other guy before he went after us. If we had waited and counterpunched, it would have been too late. There was always a chance we could get through the primary with just positives. But it had never happened before and I couldn't see any reason why this year would be any different.

☆   ☆   ☆

After the meeting with Karl, we drafted scripts and went out to the governor's newly purchased ranch to finalize them with him. The Bushes had bought the ranch a few months ago but none of us had been there yet and I had no idea what to expect. It was west of Waco and all anybody seemed to say was, "That was near the Branch Davidians, you know," as though that explained everything.

Mark and I liked to ride our bikes near Lyndon Johnson's ranch south of Austin on the way to Fredericksburg. That was the image I had in my head—a green expanse on a river, rolling hills, plump cattle grazing. I'd ask the governor if there was water on his ranch and he said, "We got water. Even waterfalls in the right time of year. And I'm building a pond for bass."

Waterfalls. That sounded intriguing.

It takes two hours or so to get from Austin to Crawford. There's still a core of Austin that feels like someplace specific, someplace special, but driving north or south through Austin, you are very quickly immersed in generic Sunbelt sprawl that could be anywhere or nowhere. There's a sense that what you are seeing is very much a work in progress and once they finish with it, odds are it's going to be pretty awful. Towns like Round Rock or Pflugerville, once small communities with a curious mix of German and Swedish farmers and a few African Americans, now were crowded with malls and tract housing, feeding off the high-tech boom that had transformed a once-funky student town into a Silicon Valley–like place of supercharged prosperity.

Crawford, Texas, is always the byline on any story about the Bush ranch but in truth, the ranch is miles from Crawford, down a road surrounded by nothing but Texas that probably doesn't look much different than it did fifty years ago. Fields that are green or brown, depending on the time of year, a wood frame house on the crest of a modest hill, a church steeple in the distance. It's a pleasant, relaxing drive, and it's easy to see why if you were looking for a part of the world to remind yourself that there was more to life than the problems sitting on your desk or the emails in your in-box, this would feel like the right place.

There are fashionable places to have a ranch in Texas, like the hill country below Austin. But outside of Crawford, Texas, isn't one of them. If you buy a ranch or some land around here, you do it because you like it, not because you expect somebody at a cocktail party to look impressed when you mention your new place near Crawford.

There was a metal fence, a long dirt road surrounded by flat pasture and a small and simple house of maybe one thousand square feet.

"We're going to fix this place up a little," the governor said, "while we're building a new house over there." He gestured across the pasture. "I'm digging a big bass pond. Come on, let's go." He was wearing jeans and work boots and a Texas Rangers T-shirt. There was an architect with him, a couple of guys I took to be construction foremen, and somebody who seemed to be an expert on pond construction.

Mark, Matthew Dowd and I had driven up in Matthew's Chevy Suburban, a vehicle that is to Texas what Land Cruisers are to Africa. We formed a little caravan of four-wheel-drive vehicles and headed out to the site of the new bass pond.

There's an image of George W. Bush in the media as a relaxed guy, not very driven. To the extent I ever really thought about it, I suppose that's what I expected.

But that wasn't the George W. Bush I was getting to know. He hated delays, couldn't stand wasting time and was always the one urging everybody to move faster, get it done, let's go. He ran fast, worked fast, got up at dawn and had a restless energy that seemed irrepressible. Sure, he liked to joke around and loved to laugh and tease anything or anyone even vaguely pretentious. But show up at 8:10 A.M. for an 8 A.M. meeting or talk about something in vague generalities when he was expecting specifics and you'd find out how laid-back he was.

"It's leaking. We've got to fix this," Bush said. We were all standing around by the edge of the bass pond-to-be. It looked like the crater of a very large bomb into which hunks of concrete had been dumped. The concrete was for the fish. "They love that stuff, bass do," Bush said. Right now his concern was the amount of rain—there hadn't been much—and the slow leak, the combination of which was delaying the day he could be casting into the pond. That's what he did—cast. He wasn't a fancy fly fisherman. He was a bass guy.

"You know what that is?" Bush asked us. He was pointing at a cluster of trees in the middle of the field.

We looked at one another. Was this a trick question?

"Trees?" Mark finally said.

"You guys got to get out of Austin more. It's a mot. Even a windshield rancher like me knows that."

"You know what that is?" He pointed to some cattle grazing.

"Cows?" Matthew suggested.

"Good. There's hope yet."

He went back to talking to his pond guys. Mark wandered over with one of the digital video cameras we always carried around, if only to feel like we had some useful purpose. It was shady by the side of the bomb crater pond and when the breeze picked up for a moment it was possible to forget that a few minutes earlier you had been melting. The scene felt familiar in a vague way and then as I leaned back against the warm metal of the Suburban, it struck me—Africa. It was the last time I'd been surrounded by a sea of grass stirring gently in a hot breeze with clusters of trees outlined against a sky so bright it hurt.

The governor led us all over his new property that morning. He joked that when his daughters first came out to the ranch, they had been appalled, asking "What have you done?" But when he showed them the hidden canyons, the land by the small stream that became more of a river in the spring, the way the trees looked silhouetted at sunset, they began to understand why he'd fallen in love with the place.

It was lunchtime when we sat down to go over the scripts. We sat on old folding metal chairs on the concrete slab floor of the small house and ate peanut butter and jelly sandwiches, one of his favorites. He rocked back in his chair, reading glasses perched on his nose, and peered intently at the pages.

"What are we trying to say here?"

"It's about your priorities," I said, forgetting that the word "priorities" was slashed in bold letters across the piece of paper he held.

He looked at me for a beat over his glasses and said, "Now I get it.

"My top priorities will be to strengthen the military and Social Security and improve education," he read aloud. "I believe that government should do a few things and do them well."

He slapped the script against his knee. "This isn't right." He pulled out the cheap black felt pen he liked to carry and started editing. "I believe that government should do a few things and do them well," he read again. "That's got to go on top, doesn't it? Don't we want to make the big point first and then get into the specifics?"

"That might make it too clear," Mark said.

"We'd hate that," Matthew added.

Bush made notes on the script, holding it against his blue-jeaned knee to write.

"What about Medicare? Why aren't we talking about it?"

We nodded. Fine.

"I believe that once top priorities have been funded, we should pass money back to the taxpayers," he continued to read. "That's what I've done in Texas. I signed the two largest tax cuts in Texas history." He paused. "Lot of Texas in here." He made some notes and tried it again. "I signed the two largest tax cuts in our state's history."

"Does it bother anybody that it sounds like that if it's not Medicare, Social Security or defense, it won't get funded?" I asked.

"I thought that was the point," Mark said.

"What are you worried about?" Bush asked.

I shrugged. "That it makes you sound like that if you're president you'll pay for these three or four things but that's it."

"Republicans love this stuff, don't they?" Mark said. "Isn't that what they want?"

Bush laughed.

"Are people going to think that you won't pay for roads or airports or—"

"Roads?" Bush teased. "You want roads in here?"

"No, I mean—"

"You want some roads, we can put some roads. 'As your president, I promise to finish I-Thirty-five, so help me God.' "

"You know what I mean."

"Don't count on it." Then Bush continued, "It's an ad, not a budget. We can write the budget later."

"What if we put something in here about Texas not having an income tax?" I asked. "You've cut taxes and Texas still doesn't have an income tax."

Bush looked at the script and made some notes. "I can't imagine what you're thinking about." New Hampshire and Texas were two of the few states not to have an income tax. They didn't even have a sales tax in New Hampshire.

"How would you say it?" Bush asked. Then he answered his own question. "We don't have an income tax in Texas but I still cut taxes twice . . . no."

We suggested several alternatives, realizing each wasn't very good as soon as we said it aloud. Bush concentrated on the script with his scribbled notes. He pulled a cigar out of his briefcase and fiddled with it while he stared out the windows of the little house.

"You're not going to recognize this in a couple of months," he said, gesturing around the house.

"Some good places to run around here," Mark said.

"Some great places. You go along by that bottom where the creek is." He looked out the window, then down at the script. " 'I signed the two largest tax cuts in our state's history, and we still have no personal income tax.' That works, doesn't it?"

It did.

He read the final line of the script. " 'I believe we ought to cut tax rates to continue economic growth and prosperity.' We should change this. It makes it sound like all I want to do is continue what Clinton has done. We can do better than that and we ought to say it. The whole idea of the tax plan will be to eliminate taxes for people at the bottom of the spectrum."

In a thirty-second spot, you can comfortably get in seventy-five to eighty words, depending on the speaker's natural cadence and accent. That's it. There's a terrible tyranny and a forced efficiency to trying to convey complicated ideas with so few words. It was both a discipline and an art, a form of poetry if executed properly. There's a reason great copywriters make a gazillion dollars a year and end up in the Copy-writers Hall of Fame—which actually exists and is not the punch line to a nasty joke about failed writers. So what if the spot is about *mouthwash* or *deodorant,* that's not the point any more than, say, tennis is about hitting a little white ball over pieces of string or chess is about little stick figures on a checkerboard. The demands of the process—arbitrary, diffi-cult, without meaning—are what make it admirable and, ulti-mately, if you get it right, rewarding.

Maybe three or four times in my life have I felt like I nailed a script, captured lightning in a bottle. That day it wasn't hap-pening.

"Broaden," Bush said. "That's what we want to say. 'I be-lieve we ought to cut tax rates to continue economic growth and broaden prosperity.' "

We went through a dozen or so scripts and by early after-noon were headed back to Austin. As we passed a house not far from the ranch gates, a family in the front yard waved at the little procession of vehicles. The governor stopped and chat-ted for a while. When he got back in, he was smiling. "We're going to have a big barbeque as soon as we get the place fixed up. Invite all the neighbors."

We drove toward Austin.

☆   ☆   ☆

After spending so much time on the scripts, we put them aside when we started shooting.

Mark and I were in total agreement on this—we saw scripts as a necessary evil but, in most cases, we preferred to have the same sentiments expressed *without* scripts. There were two classic ways to get this done—conduct an interview of the candidate in an informal setting or film the candidate documentary-style as he or she interacts with voters.

I loved the documentary approach and tried to use it whenever possible. Sometimes a candidate just wouldn't be very good at it for one reason or another—not articulate on the issues in an informal setting, uncomfortable with the camera, annoyed at the whole idea. But when it *did* work, you could get magical stuff, the kind of thing you never could have scripted in a million years. Maybe it was a candidate hugging a woman in tears as she talked about her son dying in Vietnam or a moment when the candidate and an elderly man sitting on a city stoop talked about how crime was ruining a once-great neighborhood. But it's a terribly inefficient way to operate that requires shooting hours of film, invariably most of it junk, looking for that one golden moment.

Technology was helping though. Now there were inexpensive digital cameras no larger than a VHS camcorder that captured a phenomenally good image. You could shoot hours and hours of footage at almost no cost. Just run and gun, looking for the moment. At Maverick, we had two of these and somebody—usually Laura Crawford, our MVP production whiz—was always shooting Bush whenever he was on the road.

But the problem was that in a presidential campaign with a candidate who is leading in the polls, you are constantly surrounded by press. Scores of press in every flavor—national and local print reporters (scribblers, as they are called by political press flacks), shooters (still photographers), network producers, network and local correspondents and their cameramen. Throw in security and you've got the makings of a real mess. It's crazy. Every time a front-runner went out the door, he was at the center of a seething scrum of media pros starved for any tidbit. The kind of thing that would be easy to do in a Senate or gubernatorial race—say, have a candidate walk down Main Street and talk to voters—becomes an exercise in crowd control. Whatever poor voters are unlucky enough to find themselves in the way of this information-sucking mass are immediate celebrities, interviewed by *The New York Times* and ABC, their every response and exchange analyzed. "Did he ask you about tax cuts? Who are you voting for? What do you think about his Social Security plan?"

Getting a real moment on film is about as likely as having an intimate moment on the field in the middle of a Super Bowl halftime show.

So though we kept our digital or film cameras cranked, we didn't have much hope that we'd come up with something that was going to change the world. That left us with the inter-view format as the best for capturing an unscripted, com-pelling moment.

We wanted to do the interview first thing, before filming any of the scripts. Once you got into a rigid script mode with lights and TelePrompTers, it was hard to recapture a free-flowing mood.

The governor showed up the morning of the shoot right on time. He was always on time. Just as he would every time we filmed him, he went around to each of the crew mem-bers and introduced himself. He'd ask where they were from, joke around a little, tease the guys about their earrings—big with film types, of course—and thank them for helping out. Then he grabbed a donut and said in his typical way, "Let's get with it."

Mark asked the questions. He and Bush had been through this process in the last governor's race and were comfortable with each other. Mark and I had talked about what we wanted to get out of the interview and what we really needed was some different way to talk about the Clinton scandals. There was a standard line that Bush used at almost every appear-ance: "And when I put my hand on the Bible, I'll swear to not only uphold the laws of the United States but the dignity and honor of the White House, so help me God." It never failed to bring down the house and one of the scripts included a voice-over of the line over a close-up of his upheld hand against a white backdrop.

But we wanted something different, something fresh. We hadn't been able to come up with it—all our takes were far too heavy-handed and obvious. Nobody wanted to be hit over the head with the Clinton contrast, and the worst thing would be to put some spot up that sounded self-righteous and conde-scending. Which is exactly how Republicans sounded so often when talking about Clinton.

Bush sat on the newly reupholstered couch at an angle, his arm resting on the arm of the couch. He looked relaxed but still engaged. Wayne's light spilled through the windows like the most gorgeous morning sun you ever saw. Mark sat on a box to the right of the camera lens, which would make it appear that Bush was looking just off camera. Viewers wouldn't see Mark but they would assume Bush was being interviewed—it was the same set-up they were used to seeing in countless tele-vision interviews.

Everybody has a different interview style. Mark's was very relaxed, with an elliptical way of working around to the good stuff. It suited Bush well. You would never get him to open up by asking a direct, personal question or anything that verged on the pretentious. The trick was to lead him into areas and let him work through a subject at his own pace in his own way. It would either work or it wouldn't, but it was definitely the best shot we had.

Mark started out with some general questions about growing up in Midland. We weren't sure how we would use this, but it was familiar terrain and a way to start a conversa-tion. Bush loved Midland and you could see his eyes soften and his whole body relax when he talked about what it was like to grow up in a place with few trees and a ton of oil wells.

They moved on to the standard issues, tax cuts and then the military. When talking about how important it was for America to be respected around the world, his tone shifted and he looked off camera for a moment and for a beat I thought he might tear up. It surprised me. *What was he thinking, feeling?*

"You know," he said, "everywhere I go in America, everywhere I've gone on this fantastic journey so far, people walk up to me with pictures of their children and say, 'Governor, I want my child to look at the White House and be proud of what he or she sees.' "

Then he stopped and a hint of tears did come. The room was utterly silent, with only the faint hum of the 35-millimeter film running through the camera.

In the editing room a week later, we used what he said in a spot we called "Pictures." It was always my favorite.

4 Losing While Winning

WE STARTED OUT WITH A FIFTY-POINT LEAD in New Hampshire and by the end of October, we were dead—we just didn't realize it.

Blame it on me, it's only fair. I was the guy down in Austin who had the most New Hampshire experience. I'd done the last two successful Republican gubernatorial races in the state and I never understood what was happening until too late. For years I've preached to campaigns that the worst thing you can do is fight the last war instead of the next war. But if I hunker down and get really honest, I have to admit that's what I did in New Hampshire.

I should have realized we were going to lose New Hampshire when I was standing on top of Mt. Washington. That was in August, back when the numbers were still good, before Elizabeth Dole got out of the race and when McCain was still wandering the state trying to draw a hundred people to his town hall meetings. Back when George W. Bush couldn't walk across a street in New Hampshire without being swarmed by people trying to get his autograph. Back when almost no elected officials were backing McCain and Governor Bush had the active support of the most powerful Republican figure in the state, Senator Judd Gregg.

I'd snuck away from the 102-degree heat of Austin to

New Hampshire to scout some locations for future film shoots. And to hike up Mt. Washington. On my way to Mt. Washington, I stopped for gas. It was sixty-five degrees and everything was a lush green, both of which you don't really appreciate until you spend a summer in Texas. I was aggressively not thinking about the race.

It was a little country store gas station, the kind of place you still find quite unselfconsciously thriving in out-of-the-way parts of northern New England. And there on the make-shift bulletin board, right next to a notice about a bake sale for the volunteer fire department and Fourth of July parade notices no one had removed, was a flyer announcing a town hall meeting for Senator John McCain. It shocked me, actually, like an unexpected reminder of another life. It read: "Come hear Senator John McCain, an American hero and the next President of the United States."

For a moment I felt a twinge of pity, not so much for McCain but for his campaign, where I had a number of friends working. This is what it was like when you were buried deep in the polls. You drove around to remote gas stations and put up flyers and hoped somebody would show up. How many of these town halls would he have to do to make an impact? Fifty? One hundred? The guy was running for president, not state rep.

I wasn't thinking about John McCain when I was working my way down Mt. Washington hours later. I was hiking with a friend from New York and we stopped for lunch at Lake of the Clouds hut, one of a system of huts, each built at a different time with a unique feel. My friend Chuck was proudly wearing lederhosen he'd recently bought in Bavaria.

"Chuck," I'd said to him that morning, when he'd turned up looking like he was answering a *Sound of Music* casting call, "you're not really going to wear that, are you?"

"Why not? I was hiking in Bavaria and everybody wore it."

"Bavaria, yes. But we're hiking in New Hampshire."

"The stuff is great. Super comfortable."

Chuck is a big, athletic guy and it made for quite a sight—a six-foot four-inch male in lederhosen. On the hike up, we fell into talking about Vietnam, where Chuck had served two tours as a Green Beret, and I discovered that when people see a six-foot four-inch male in lederhosen hiking up a mountain discussing different ways of setting ambushes, they get out of the way.

At the Lake of the Clouds hut, Chuck's outfit was a big hit. We were chatting with two young hikers, and he was explaining the benefits of lederhosen when, out of the blue, one of the hikers asked me what I thought of John McCain.

This was startling. Why, I asked, were they interested in McCain?

The reason, it turned out, was that a friend of theirs from Dartmouth was volunteering for McCain and they had gone to one of his town hall meetings. They were shocked by how much they liked him.

"You're not going to believe what I did afterward," one of them said with a slightly sheepish tone, as though he had pulled some prank. He had long hair and was wearing a bandanna sweat band, a popular look on the mountain. "I went out and registered to vote." He and his friend exchanged "can you believe that" looks.

"Really?" I asked. "And what do you like about McCain?"

"They played Fat Boy Slim when he finished talking," one said.

"And he was funny. And kind of nasty."

"Nasty?" I asked.

They laughed. "Some jerk asked him how come he didn't support still looking for prisoners in Vietnam and he just ate the guy up. It was great. Everybody cheered."

"He's different, you know?" his friend said.

I nodded. On the way down, I had a vague sense of unease but hardly panic. I ran through in my mind all the reasons McCain wouldn't get off the ground. He couldn't raise the money. His main issue, campaign finance reform, excited about ten people in America who weren't editorial writers and of those ten, nine were already voting for Bill Bradley. He had no natural base within the Republican party. He wasn't competing in Iowa. I was feeling better by the time I got down the mountain. Then my pal Chuck had to go and say, "You know, I like the hell out of McCain too. You worried about him?"

So driving back, I explained to Chuck what I called McInturff's Law. It was named after one of the smartest pollsters in America, Bill McInturff, and it went like this: The Republican party has basically four slots for a candidate to fit into. There's the Establishment slot, the Economic Conservative slot, the pro-life/Christian Conservative slot, and the Businessman/Outsider slot. To win the Republican nomination, you had to fit into at least three of those slots. Bush fit into all four. McCain? He really only fit one—the Businessman/Outsider slot. That limited his appeal such that he could never really get traction.

Chuck thought about this for a moment and agreed it made sense. "This guy McInturff, he sounds smart. Who's he working for?"

"McCain," I admitted.

"I think I'd be worried."

☆   ☆   ☆

In the early fall of 1999, the numbers stayed good. Ridiculously good, actually. We were winning everywhere, even beating John McCain in his home state of Arizona where we had a ten-point lead. We loved this and talked it up with every reporter in America. "Can you believe this? McCain can't even carry his home state. Can you imagine if Bush was losing to McCain in Texas? You'd laugh us out of the race." One of the whiz kids in the office came up with a chart plotting the margin by which past candidates had won their home states. It looked great on paper. For days I carried it around and showed it to random strangers.

Every campaign has a story line, a plot that is constantly evolving. At that moment the story line was pretty much what it had been all summer: Bush campaign on a roll, raising tons of money, looking unbeatable. Howard Fineman of *Newsweek* and NBC proclaimed at the end of September that "the Bush campaign couldn't be any closer to where they wanted to be . . . right now I think they're finding it hard to believe even themselves how good it's going. There's no race on the Republican side right now." The real race was on the Democratic side where Bradley threatened Gore.

We liked this story line. It had a happy ending for us.

In October we launched our first spots in Iowa and New Hampshire. I flew to Iowa to unveil the ads at a low-key press conference in the home of a supporter. At a press conference in Des Moines, I played the spots and Lionel and Kathy Sosa, who were handling the part of the ad campaign aimed at Hispanic voters, distributed copies of a radio spot in Spanish we were running in Iowa. In part it was symbolic—we wanted to lay down a marker that we would actively pursue Hispanic voters in the primary—but it was also a fact that in Iowa there was a segment of Hispanic voters who could potentially be mobilized to turn out in the caucus. And in a world in which you only needed forty to forty-five thousand votes to win the caucuses, an edge of even a few hundred votes was important. (Orrin Hatch kept talking about winning Iowa with Mormons and chiropractors. There was actually a certain mad logic to his thinking.)

Everybody seemed to love the spots but that never really means very much. It's fairly predictable that nine out of ten "normal" people—nonpolitical pros, civilians—will like almost any spot that is positive and pretty. It's one of the great dangers of focus-grouping spots—often the stuff that works best will test the worst, just because people in test groups like to dismiss any spots that they feel are overly manipulative, especially any that make comparisons between candidates or feel negative.

The governor was campaigning in Iowa and I drove from Des Moines to Sioux City to meet him and the traveling road show. He gave a speech to a lunch crowd of about four hundred people and afterward, I ran into David Yepsen, the *Des Moines Register*'s lead political reporter. Every four years Yepsen becomes a familiar face on television, being generally recognized as the guy who knows more about the Iowa Caucuses than anyone else alive. Which might even be true.

"So what did you think?" I asked him outside the small auditorium.

He shook his head. "Not a great crowd, you know." Yepsen has that permanently rumpled look that reporters probably think makes them look like Dustin Hoffman playing Carl Bernstein in *All the President's Men*.

"No? Anybody draw better at noon in Sioux City?" I knew the answer to this. He ignored the question.

"I just don't see anybody getting excited here."

"Excited? In October? What do you expect, old ladies tossing hotel keys? This is Iowa, David. When do you people ever get excited?"

"I just don't know if Bush has the organization to win big." Ahhh . . . I knew it would come down to this. Organization. Yepsen was obsessed with the notion that organization rather than paid media was the key to winning the Iowa Caucuses. This had become the conventional wisdom ever since Jimmy Carter put the Iowa Caucus on the map by outworking and outorganizing the field in 1976. George W. Bush's father reinforced this in 1980, when Rich Bond moved to Iowa from New York and led the Bush campaign to a huge upset of Ronald Reagan through meticulous organization.

Of course Yepsen loved this theory since it meant that any campaign that wanted to win had to spend months and months on the ground in Iowa trying to put together networks of potential caucusgoers. This made life much more interesting for Jepsen and guaranteed he would be sought out by every prominent national reporter, or Bigfoot reporters as they were known, for the inside scoop on what was really happening behind closed doors across Iowa. Essential to this view of the world was the idea that paid media—television and radio—would not carry a candidate to caucus victory. If anybody was ever able to rely more on media than organization and pull off an Iowa victory, it would go a long way toward reducing the value of an insider like David Yepsen. Then the Iowa Caucuses would become just like any other big statewide race, with the likely outcome determined by media buys and easily digestible polls. The voodoo of the caucus systems would be exposed as, well, voodoo.

"I just don't know how good the Bush organization is," Yepsen intoned solemnly.

I tried to look concerned. "Well, David, we all know that's the key, don't we? I mean, this is Iowa, right?"

He cocked his head and looked at me. Was I teasing?

"I saw you're going up on television," Yepsen said.

I nodded. "Yeah, but I don't know how much it's going to help us."

He eagerly agreed. "Don't win it in Iowa on the tube. No way."

We had three more days in Iowa before we were scheduled to fly to North Dakota. Our last overnight was in Dubuque, in far eastern Iowa on the Mississippi River. Dubuque
is the sort of town that exists all over America but is basically
ignored by the media except when something particularly
gruesome befalls either the town or its citizens—a flood, a
double murder, a school bus that turns over on an icy road on
the way home from the away game. These towns are fighting
just to stay the same size, forget about growing, and if anybody is getting rich in the new economy, they are doing a
good job of keeping it to themselves.

Earlier in Dubuque, Bush had visited a volunteer organization that helped unwed and poor mothers. It was run
by Catholics, though not connected to any church, and the
women who volunteered there were all strongly against abortion. But it was the kind of place where the harsh rhetoric of
the pro-choice and pro-life debate seemed shrill and almost irrelevant. The main function of the organization was providing
clothes and other necessities—one shelf was filled with do-
nated disposable diapers—to mothers who couldn't afford
them. It gets cold in Dubuque, with a wind off the river that
cuts through you like a jagged icicle, and what they needed
most was warm clothes and coats.

When you work for governors and senators in Iowa,
South Dakota, Nebraska, as I have, you find yourself spending a lot of time in towns like Dubuque. I find these places
strangely affecting. At first it's reassuring to know that people
still have lives centered on family and church and jobs that are
not glamorous in the least. But the longer you stay, the harder
it is not to feel the claustrophobia that must affect some of the
residents, especially those who are young and ambitious. It's a
struggle between the disappointment of limited possibilities
and the comfort of a life lived on a manageable scale. As a

friend of mine from Mississippi says, "It's both depressing and reassuring that if I dropped dead tomorrow, the church would be filled with people I went to the third grade with."

On the flight to Fargo, North Dakota, we talked about Dubuque. I said that I found the visit to the charity for poor mothers depressing.

"Depressing?" the governor asked. "Those are wonderful people."

"It just reminds me that there are people out there who need this stuff." I shrugged. "I don't think about that very often."

"I know, you're one of those bury-your-head-in-the-sand guys," he teased. "If you don't see it, it doesn't happen."

"Exactly," I agreed. "Pure yuppie trash."

"Liberals want to give them everything and old-fashioned conservatives don't think government should do anything. Where do you come down?"

"I'm in the confused middle."

He laughed. "We'll do well with you guys."

"Part of our base, no doubt about it. Give me your tired, your poor, your confused."

"I don't think there are many confused souls in Fargo," Karen Hughes said.

"It's too cold to be confused," Bush agreed.

"Did you ever see the movie *Fargo*?" I asked.

"You betcha," he said, in a perfect imitation of the characters in *Fargo*. "Ahh, the statie doesn't look so good," he continued, repeating one of Frances McDormand's lines from the movie. He reeled off several more lines from the movie.

We were coming in to land at Fargo. There was snow on the ground and the pilot announced it was twenty-five degrees.

"Ahhh . . . looks chilly," said the governor. "Welcome to Fargo."

The next day at a press conference primarily for local reporters, when asked what seemed like an endless series of
questions about free trade and grain prices, the governor answered, "You betcha, we're going to support free trade. You
betcha." It was his *Fargo* voice. For a panicked moment I
thought for certain the reporters would balk but then I realized that to them it sounded normal. How nice to have a president without an accent. You betcha.

☆　　　☆　　　☆

The dynamic in New Hampshire started to go sour when
we skipped the "first" debate in New Hampshire on October
28, 1999. In truth, it wasn't the first debate, as we'd had scores
of offers to debate, from Rotary Clubs to local news shows in
primary states. But it was the first one everybody took seriously because it was sponsored by WMUR-TV in Manchester
and because every candidate accepted—except Bush.

There's a dirty little secret about debates. What actually
happens in the debates is often less important than all the ma-
neuverings surrounding them. *Will you debate, won't you debate, how should you debate, where should you debate*—all
that can dominate news cycles for days, even weeks, while the
event itself has maybe a forty-eight-hour shelf life. What happens in debates? Nothing usually. Especially in primary debates with a lot of candidates.

Do the math. With five candidates in an hour-long debate
and, say, two minutes to answer a question plus a minute each
for closing statements, each person might get five questions,
but more likely four. That's it. And there is almost never a pro-
vision for direct follow-up to a question, so nobody gets
pressed to explain what he meant when he suggested alien intelligence should be utilized to help the CIA.

With Bush so far ahead, the debate strategy for the other
candidates was easy—debate all the time. Accept every de-

bate invitation. Why not? It was the stage in the campaign when everybody but Bush was getting the same kind of press attention Triple A ball clubs get on national television. Not much. If Bush showed up at a debate, the other candidates would get a huge dose of publicity. And if Bush turned down the debate, they could use his no-show status as a nice club with which to beat us over the head.

We thought we had it figured out just right. Debating too often seemed dumb—it only increased the chances for some kind of ambush from another candidate. Plus, debating was a terrifically time-consuming process. When his father was running, George W. Bush made the observation that debates "paralyze a campaign" and he was right. You have to prep for every debate, take at least a day off to be rested and if you're way ahead in the polls, it's almost impossible that a debate will increase your lead. It's a victory if you wake up the day after in the same position you were in when you walked into the debate the night before.

But of course you have to debate some, if only because you can't look like you're afraid or arrogant. The perception of arrogance was always a huge danger for the Bush campaign. On the one hand, we very deliberately created the impression that Bush was playing the game on a different level than his primary competition. Part of it was just the way the campaign operated. We had the most sophisticated advance teams: Bush—like most governors—traveled with security, which meant motorcades, cops, flashing lights; and there were always scores of press in pursuit. It was an impressive road show that swept people up in its excitement. At its center was George W. Bush, a celebrity, a leading presidential candidate, a big-state governor. When it worked, it resembled a shadow government in motion. We'd hit a town and it was like nothing they had ever seen.

Okay, that was the good part. The flip side was that we came across sometimes as an arrogant bunch of Texans who acted like, well, a shadow government. And there was the awkward reality that not one person in America had yet voted for George W. Bush for president.

We had two problems with the October 28 debate. It was too early—we wanted the whole process to begin in late November or early December—and it fell on the day that Laura Bush was to be honored as a distinguished alumna of Southern Methodist University. The fundamental flaw in our logic was that we were looking at the world logically. This is often a bad thing in life and almost always in campaigns. The fact is that we were planning to debate more than any other Republican candidate had debated before in a presidential primary—at least five or six times before New Hampshirites went to the polls. We thought that might be good enough to stop people from thinking we were ducking debates.

Talk about naive.

Oh, we also thought that people might like the notion that George W. Bush was putting family, specifically his librarian spouse Laura Bush, promoter of books and reading, over crass political gain. Turn it around: Surely, we thought, if he stiffed his wife on a truly special and significant night just so he could spend quality time with the likes of Alan Keyes and Gary Bauer, every woman, if not man, would run screaming from the room in disgust.

Yeah, we were naive.

The day before the October 28 debate, a *Boston Herald* poll came out showing McCain with higher favorables than Bush, though Bush was still leading 44 percent to 26 percent. But McCain's favorable/unfavorable ratio was 67 to 12 while Bush's was 64 to 19 percent.

At the Maverick bunker, we felt the first twinges of helplessness. None of us liked what was happening in New Hampshire but we weren't sure what to do about it. There was only one thing I knew for certain would work.

"We should attack McCain," I said. "Right now. Torch him." I was joking, since I knew it was out of the question, but it was a wistful kind of joking.

"Attack him for what?" Mark asked. "And do we run the attack spot before or after the spot we have up pledging to stay positive?"

"Let's attack him for not attacking us," Russ Schriefer suggested.

Everybody loved that idea. "John McCain," Russ improvised dramatically, "he hasn't even attacked. In New Hampshire, we know what it means when a man doesn't have the guts to attack."

The race had to tighten. Everybody knew we weren't going to win by the fifty-point lead we had going in to New Hampshire. But that inevitable tightening wasn't being treated as inevitable, it was being embraced as a McCain surge. And the worst part of it was that there was some truth to it.

McCain was surging and if it wasn't a full-fledged tidal wave, it had the makings of one. He was spending two or three times the amount of time Bush was in New Hampshire, running around holding his town meetings everywhere. The McCain campaign knew their candidate was a long shot and had embraced his very improbability, playing up his image as a maverick, as the outsider who was challenging the system.

It was the last bit that was so damaging. From before Bush even announced, the major story line of our campaign had been "The Guy from Texas Taking on Washington," with a nice undercurrent of redemption. Redemption from his father's defeat, redemption from all the sleaze and nastiness of the Clinton years, even redemption from the overzealous mistakes Republicans had made. But there was only room for one Outsider in this plot. If McCain became the Outsider, that made Bush the Establishment. The Insider. And our campaign would effectively be neutered.

The rationale for going up with some kind of spot about McCain was simple: People were just getting to know him and he would never be more vulnerable.

"How many people in New Hampshire," I asked the Maverick crowd as we sat around the bunker, "know that John McCain, Mr. Outsider, is chairman of the Commerce Committee and has been an elected official in D.C. for two decades? How many know that John McCain, Mr. Campaign Finance Reform, is raising money like mad from people he regulates on the Commerce Committee? How many people know that his campaign is run by a lobbyist? Or that he was one of the Keating Five? How many of these nice New Hampshire moderates know he's pro-life, pro-gun, wants to pave the wilderness and bomb Belgrade back to the Stone Age?"

"That's the spot Bradley should run," Russ said. "He's bleeding voters to McCain because they think he's moderate and they like him more than Bradley."

"How many pro-choice voters for McCain think he's pro-choice?" I asked. "I'm betting north of seventy-five percent."

We toyed around with the spot that Bradley should run. "Pro-choice? Not John McCain. Pro-gun control? Not John McCain. Pro-environment? Not John McCain. Want somebody to clean up the system? John McCain was part of one of the worst fund-raising scandals in modern history and still continues to raise money from companies he helps regulate. If you're pro-choice, support gun control and the environment, and want a true outsider—Bill Bradley."

There was a morbid joy to sitting in our windowless bunker coming up with spots that would never see the light of day. It was sort of like when cops let off steam at the firing range shooting at paper targets. At least that's what they do in the movies.

As much as I would have liked to put up some kind of spot—a funny one would have been perfect—tweaking McCain for his inconsistencies, it wasn't an option. McCain first had to make the mistake of attacking us or misrepresenting some position Bush had taken before there was any chance that Bush would let us respond. The ads we had up would help build Bush's positives and reinforce support, giving people who were already for him more reasons to support him. But they were unlikely to change the dynamic of the campaign, and it was looking more and more like that's what we needed to do.

In the past, any candidate who sat out Iowa and tried to begin the campaign at a time and a place of his own choosing had failed. That's how Gore flamed out so spectacularly in 1988, when he tried to begin his campaign on Super Tuesday, basically because it would have been more convenient for him. There was an arrogance to thinking you could bypass the rules. The conventional wisdom had long been that there were three tickets out of Iowa and if you didn't win, place or show, you were doomed.

Our hope was that increasingly press coverage would focus on Iowa and that by skipping Iowa, McCain would not be part of that story, forcing him into a press blackout at a critical period. Then we'd win Iowa and get a bump and ride that bump to victory in New Hampshire. That's how it usually worked.

Except of course there really aren't any rules to the whole process. Iowa was never important until Carter won it and used it as a springboard to the nomination, and remember how it was impossible to lose New Hampshire and still get elected president? That was one of the rules until Clinton did just that in 1992. The gods of politics seemed to enjoy lulling you into a false sense of order, then unloosing chaos.

☆   ☆   ☆

The first debate we had accepted was scheduled for December 2, in New Hampshire. We could spin it a dozen different ways, but there was no escaping that this debate was going to be seen as a referendum on George W. Bush.

It would be followed by a lot more debates—more than had ever been held before in the Republican nominating process. The debate on December 2 in New Hampshire would be followed four days later by a debate in Arizona, then a week later by the first debate in Iowa on December 13. The candidates wouldn't be together again until January 6 with yet another debate in New Hampshire, this one sponsored by the *Manchester Union-Leader* newspaper, then another debate in Iowa on January 15, and one preprimary debate on January 26. All of which would take place before the New Hampshire primary. And there could be others down the road in South Carolina, Michigan and California.

Publicly, the campaign was doing a good job of lowering expectations for Bush's debate performance. Karen and Karl really went to work on this, driving home the message that McCain was a skillful, experienced debater given his years in the Senate. Which had the double benefit of being actually true, while reminding people that McCain was a career politician. (Not that the last bit got much traction. This was when the press was right on the verge of falling completely, totally, head-spinningly in love with John McCain. We might as well have been telling a teenager who just landed a date with Ricky Martin that Ricky really didn't do so well on his SAT scores.)

What could we accomplish in the debates? Our first goal

had to be to reassure people that Governor Bush was up to the job. That didn't mean that viewers needed to walk away from the debate thinking that he should be president—no one was really examining each of these candidates that closely. It would be enough if he came across as capable, confident, smart. If he didn't achieve that much, then the debates could seriously jeopardize his chance to become president. Everybody in politics remembers the interview that CBS's Roger Mudd did with Ted Kennedy when he was launching his campaign against Carter in 1979 and Mudd asked Kennedy why he wanted to be president. And Kennedy completely booted the question, mumbling and ahhing and awwing and not even remotely coming up with a rational explanation of why he should be the most powerful man in the world. If Kennedy had any chance to knock off Carter, it ended with that interview.

But there was a second, more remote goal and that was a chance to dominate the debates in a way that would damage the other candidates. This wouldn't be easy given the simple math of five people answering questions. It was hard for anyone to dominate and that's why the also-rans loved it so much—how else could Gary Bauer end up on the same stage with George W. Bush and get equal attention? It was forced parity at its most crude, like what the NFL tries to do with salary caps and draft rules.

Preparing a candidate for a debate is one of these critical tasks in life for which there really is no road map. Over the years, I'd helped conduct scores of debate prep sessions and every candidate responds differently, just as players do to different coaches and coaching styles. But I'd come to believe that the best strategy was a rigorous combination of mock debates, candidate briefing and rapid drills. Not everybody responded well to this kind of structure, but I'd never known

anyone who went through it who didn't come out at least a
little better.

"I don't think that'll work," Mark said, when I outlined the
steps I thought we should take. It was after the morning press
meeting, held at the painful hour of 7:30 A.M. and before the
11 A.M. message meeting, which Karl chaired. The morning
press meeting was devoted to talking about the message of
the day and how we should respond to overnight events. We
sat around the Bush campaign conference room drinking coffee and reading clips like a slumber party book club. The
young press aide Mindy Tucker, known within the campaign
as Xena the Warrior Princess, usually ran the meetings. Someone from the road, usually Karen Hughes, would call in, so
that we could try to coordinate headquarters and the traveling
campaign, always one of the hardest things to do in a presidential campaign. Inevitably the road, as it was always called,
developed its own culture and saw events differently than
headquarters. It was kind of like those scenes in the astronaut
films when mission control is talking to the astronauts. There's
always a feeling that the astronauts are heroic, dealing with
the minute-to-minute crises, but also a suspicion that they are
under a lot of stress and probably not thinking entirely clearly.
This, of course, drives the astronauts crazy, since they believe
mission control is filled with a bunch of people who are sitting
around all day eating donuts with no idea what it's really like
to float around in space dodging asteroids.

We did eat a lot of donuts at the morning press meetings.

After the press meetings, which lasted about half an hour,
the Maverick crowd—Mark, Matthew, Russ and I—would retire to Karl's office. He always had a stash of some kind of pas-
try he picked up either downstairs at the little coffee shop or at
Starbucks. Mark and I started out avoiding the goodies as we
were training for various triathlons, but as the primary got

tighter and tighter, we started devouring them at a ferocious, mindless rate, searching for some kind of reliable pleasure. By the time we got to the South Carolina primary, Karl had progressed from coming in each morning with a small sack of pastries to a large box of donuts, enough to feed a whole shift change of cops.

In Karl's office, we'd go over poll numbers and talk about what spots we had on the air, what the other guys were running and generally discuss the state of the political world. It was at one of these meetings that we started talking about debate prep.

"I can tell you, a mock debate won't fly with the governor," Mark insisted.

I protested that we had to have mock debates—how else could we prepare?

"Alan Keyes? Gary Bauer? Orrin Hatch? We're going to get people to play all these characters?" Karl asked skeptically. "I want to play Keyes," Karl said. "He has the most fun."

"I'll play Bauer," I said. "I agree with him completely on the Chinese. It's terrifying but I do, I swear. I want to send gunboats up the Yangtze." We were laughing.

"He'll hate it," Mark said, meaning the governor. "It just won't work. It'll be a circus."

"We ought to have three or four of these things," I insisted. "With critiques. Videotape them and go over them with him."

Karl and Mark looked at each other, bemused. "George Bush is going to sit through three or four mock debates with five people playing Gary Bauer, Alan Keyes, et cetera," Mark said, "and then we're going to have these penetrating little critiques afterward, sure to be insightful, and then we review the videotapes of each one." He paused. It did sound improbable. "You are out of your mind. Never gonna happen."

"We've scheduled debate preps, they'll just be a different format," Karl said.

"Like?"

"Mainly substance. He wants to get together with Josh and some of the propeller heads"—that was Karl's term for the policy staff—"and go over issues."

"We can't rent a studio and arrange it just like the WMUR and—" I sounded pained.

"You just want to play Bauer," Karl accused.

"The Chinese!" I shouted. "Red Army money! Trilateral Commission! See, I've been practicing."

"Look," Karl continued, "everybody should write questions and we'll have a good session. It just won't be a big production and goat rope. Substance, baby, substance. That's what this campaign is about! Are you going to eat all of that?"

I was nervously picking off little pieces of a juicy cinnamon roll on Karl's desk.

"No," I protested, "I—"

"Finish it! Then go to work on questions. Write some tough ones. You'll feel better."

I tried.

☆　　　☆　　　☆

It was, as billed, an informal affair. We met midmorning at the governor's mansion. It was the first Monday in December, three days before the New Hampshire debate. Condi Rice was there and Larry Lindsey, Josh Bolten, and a couple of his propeller heads, along with Karl, Karen, Mark and Mike Gerson, the speechwriter. No outside debate coaches or speech pros. Just the usual campaign crowd.

The governor was wearing jeans and a polo shirt. He had been on the road four to five days a week since June and you could see the first hints of the deep fatigue that would sink in over the next couple of months. As always, he was waiting when we arrived, amiably impatient. Josh was carrying briefing books specifically for the debates, along with the two notebooks he used to organize his life, one labeled *Something* and the other *Nothing*.

"Who's going to say it first?" the governor said, seeming annoyed. We looked at each other.

"First, Governor?" Condi Rice asked.

"I know what's on your mind," he said and you could see a hint of a smile, "so just go ahead and say it."

"Some coffee would be nice?" Josh ventured.

"Just be myself!" Bush exclaimed. "That's what everybody is telling me about this debate. Don't get overprogrammed, just be yourself." He laughed.

"I think we've avoided the overprogramming danger," Josh said. Josh, who worked until midnight every night, was not sympathetic to the dangers of entering any situation overprepared.

There was no agenda, nor did one person run the meeting. We sat around a table in a parlor of the governor's mansion and Bush dove right in with detailed questions for Josh and Larry Lindsey about the tax package he would unveil the following day in Iowa. It had been billed as one of the half dozen or so major policy speeches of the primary season, in the same category as the foreign policy address he had given at the Reagan Library two weeks earlier and September's national defense speech at the Citadel in South Carolina.

The precise sequencing and venues of these speeches had been hotly debated and calibrated as finely as possible. In most campaigns, there is a gulf between strategy/tactics/media and policy, with each side viewing the other as a necessary evil. Media guys like me tended to look on policy as that stuff you had to have a little of to be credible but too much was either distracting, consuming valuable time and resources without attracting votes or highly dangerous, exposing the candidate needlessly to positions that might alienate potential voters. Policy wonks see media consultants and campaign operatives as nasty and brutish tools regrettably required to get through that awkward stage of actually getting elected so that the world can embrace their brilliant ideas.

In the Bush campaign world, Karl bridged the gap. He was actually interested in the details of policy, a trait which I might have found suspect if I didn't know that he was also completely committed to the messy business of getting elected. Karl even read the briefing books prepared by the propeller heads, which is a bit like finding a fifteen year old who actually read the articles in *Playboy*.

As early as June, a schedule of policy initiatives had been drafted by Josh Bolten and Mike Gerson, which was then hashed over by the message meeting crowd. Each of the major speeches was a product of a process that involved outside advisers like the foreign policy experts known as the Vulcans and led by Condi Rice, the domestic policy teams headed up by former Indianapolis Mayor Stephen Goldsmith or the economic policy team, chaired by Larry Lindsey. Each speech was backed by lengthy policy position statements with a level of detail unheard of in a primary campaign.

As I settled into the Bush world, I was astonished to realize that there was an assumption throughout the campaign that the policy would actually be used to govern once Bush was elected. This struck me as highly admirable and terribly unnecessary. For a while I tried to point out to Josh and his crew that once a candidate was elected nobody really expected that campaign policy proposals would be used to govern any more than promises made in a courtship were expected to be the guiding principles of a marriage when suddenly both partners are working and kids are running around the house.

No Republican primary candidate had ever gone as far as Bush had in laying out a governing framework of serious proposals involving the work of some of the leading talent in their fields. But it also may be true that no candidate had ever *needed* to go through this process as much as Governor Bush.

He was the leading presidential candidate and yet most Americans had little idea of what he actually wanted to accomplish. He'd only been an officeholder for five and a half years, had never run for public office before that and had never been on the national stage except as a presidential son. There was also every reason to believe that Bush would be running in an environment in which people generally felt good about the country. If voters are angry and believe the country is going to hell, they are much more willing to take a chance on an unknown. People didn't know much about Jimmy Carter but they were sick of Watergate, furious at Nixon, upset with the man who pardoned him and looking for change. After twelve years of Presidents Reagan and Bush, voters were shopping for change and willing to risk Clinton.

George W. Bush wouldn't have the luxury of being just an alternate for a dissatisfied electorate. Voters had to not only be comfortable with him, they had to believe that he had good ideas, that he was running to accomplish specific goals and had plans to reach those goals. It was this realization, combined with his natural instinct for the bold stroke, that pushed the campaign into certain policy proposals which in turn pushed the envelope of conventional political thinking. The tax cut plan he was about to unveil, the Social Security plan that would come later, the education reforms—all of these were efforts to send a signal that Governor Bush would be an activist, aggressive president with a bundle of bold proposals.

We were in the toughest kind of race to win. Years ago, I had learned that the secret to success in political consulting is to work for candidates who were going to win anyway. Then all you have to do is not screw it up too badly. And the single greatest determination of that likelihood was the political environment. Okay, money too. But given adequate money—and in the general election, both Democrat and Republican would have the same amount of money, all federally funded—who won and lost was usually determined less by the individual candidates, their personalities or positions, but by what we call in politics the right track/wrong track environment. Incumbents tended to win when the country was perceived as going in the right direction and lost when people believed things were headed in the wrong direction. And if there was no incumbent, the person who most came to represent the incumbent, usually a member of the same party, went up or down just like an incumbent. In 1990, I had handled Bill Weld's campaign in Massachusetts, where only 14 percent of the voters were registered Republicans and on any given day, about a third of those were mad at Weld because they thought he was too liberal. No Republican had been elected governor of Massachusetts in twenty-five years. It was like running as a Hindu in a Muslim state. But the voters were so pissed off at Michael Dukakis and the Democratic party that they were willing to take a chance on Weld.

The tax speech was timed to set the agenda going into the New Hampshire debate. We wanted taxes and education to be the dominant issues in New Hampshire and we believed that we were on the winning side of both issues. I'd handled the last two winning gubernatorial campaigns in New Hampshire and I was convinced that at the end of the day, the race would be about taxes. It had been that way since before Reagan ran against George Bush in 1980, and though there would be other distracting issues, if you played your cards right, you could drive the message stream of the race onto taxes. We knew McCain didn't really have a tax proposal—he had almost no substantive policy proposals except campaign finance reform—and I would have bet everything I owned that a good tax message would beat campaign finance reform in a New Hampshire Republican primary. I reiterated this that morning at debate prep.

"You know," I said, "this tax message tests far better than the campaign finance stuff. Nobody really—"

The governor cut me off. "But if campaign finance tested better, I'd be for McCain–Feingold, is that what you're saying?" He was smiling but annoyed.

"I'd want to test it first," I joked.

"To see if it would be good for the brand. I understand."

His eyes flashed the way they did when something got on his nerves. He *hated* the concept of testing positions and policy more than anybody I'd ever known. It seemed to strike him as demeaning, an insult to his intelligence. I wondered if he had always felt this way or whether it was the Clinton obsession with polling and testing every word that had driven him in the other direction.

"Governor," Condi jumped in with the first question, "if Saddam Hussein continues to develop weapons of mass destruction, can you please tell us the exact steps you would take as president?"

"We have to send Saddam Hussein a strong message. Unfortunately, the current administration has allowed sanctions to completely collapse. As president, I will send none other than Larry Lindsey to deal with Saddam face to face. Five minutes with Larry and Saddam will crumble, begging for mercy."

He loved to throw these kinds of curveballs. Then he would continue, dead serious. "Sanctions have failed . . ."

We spent about an hour hitting him with our roughest questions. Most were much more detailed and much tougher than he would ever get in a debate, as if we were trying to outdo one another by proving who could ask the hardest question. Karen had the best sense of what was most likely to get asked as she dealt with the press every waking hour. "You will get asked about Social Security, some question playing off the Russert comments," she predicted. Bush had just appeared on *Meet the Press* and Tim Russert had pressed hard on Social Security, after which Steve Forbes, who was looking for any opening to attack, had lashed out at Bush for threatening to raise the retirement age. Which Bush hadn't said, though he had made it clear he believed the system needed reform. That in itself was a provocative statement by the old rules of politics, which considered any tinkering whatsoever with Social Security to be suicide.

"We found something, Governor," Josh said, "that might be helpful if Forbes attacks on Social Security. It's in your briefing book."

Bush put on his reading glasses and flipped through the thick binder. "I'll have this memorized by this evening, Josh, I promise."

"We'll have a pop quiz," Condi said. It had been only a couple of weeks since a Boston television reporter had surprised Bush with a so-called pop quiz of the names of foreign leaders.

"Very good, Ms. Rice," the governor said, not looking up as he flipped through the briefing book. "Vladimir *Putin, Victor,*" he started reeling off foreign leaders' names, deliberately mispronouncing each one.

"It's from an editorial Steve Forbes wrote advocating raising the retirement age," Josh explained. " 'At last, the unaffordable promises have to be scaled back,' " he quoted from the editorial. " 'And the best way to do that is to gradually raise the age at which one may collect his full benefits.' "

"Steve wrote this?" Bush asked, smiling.

☆   ☆   ☆

To read the press accounts, the debate went fine for us.

"Having finally been pressured into debating his Republican rivals, Governor Bush calmly and skillfully fended off their attacks last night on everything from his tax cut plan to Social Security," said David Bloom, who was the NBC lead reporter on the Bush beat. "Bush appears to have emerged unscathed from last night's debate despite sharp attack."

Which was true. There were no blunders and the only dramatic moment was when, just as Karen predicted, Forbes hit Bush for raising the retirement age on Social Security and the governor pulled out the Forbes editorial and stuffed him with it.

But nobody was writing that Bush had dominated the field or raving that he had clearly demonstrated that he was head and shoulders above the competition. Given the format, nobody could dominate. The format had worked as we feared, putting everybody on an equal, not very illustrious plane. It was ten minutes into the thing before Bush got his first question, and at one point there was almost a half hour when he was up onstage without a question being thrown his way. "I think we've all seen more exciting police lineups," Chris Matthews said and even Brit Hume, who was one of the moderators admitted, "We were sitting here kind of dying. This was not an explosive series of encounters."

As a campaign, we could spin victory because we hadn't lost. Our line was basically that we entered the ring the champion and nobody took away the title. So we left the champion.

"What did you think?" McKinnon called me right after the

debate. He had gone up to New Hampshire and I was in New York, dealing with some film production issues.

"Not great," I said. "Not terrible but the format didn't give us a chance."

Mark laughed. "You're just a glass-half-empty guy, Stevens. It was fine. What about that Forbes thing?"

"That was fun. I don't know, Mark, it's just an overall sense, like he wasn't comfortable. He seemed too tentative. How's he feel?"

"Relieved. Glad to get one under his belt."

That made sense. Of everybody up there, he was really the only one with anything to lose. All the pressure was on him.

"One thing's for sure," I said, "I don't think we won or lost New Hampshire tonight. This is going to seem like ancient history in two months."

"Don't get positive on me, Stevens, it throws me off."

"I'll keep it under control."

"Arizona next, baby, then Iowa. Here we go."

☆   ☆   ☆

Back in Austin, the governor asked me how I thought he did. We were standing around, waiting to start another debate prep session and he just threw the question my way. "What do you think, how'd it go?"

It caught me by surprise. I knew that Karl and Karen had talked with him about the debate and I didn't want to send mixed signals. The worst thing you can do to someone in the middle of a debate cycle is offer up a lot of contradictory advice, like one coach telling a quarterback to pass and another to run. But I didn't want to tell him I thought he had hit it out of the park—he could see right through meaningless compliments and what good would it do anyway?

"I didn't like it," I simply said. "It was okay, no disaster or anything, but—"

"I can do a lot better," he nodded. "I've got a feel for it now."

"Don't worry about the time limits. Just talk right through them, make them ring the bell to stop you."

"You mean be obnoxious."

"Absolutely."

"You know what I really need to do?"

I shrugged.

"Just be myself," he laughed.

The funny thing was, he was absolutely right. One-on-one or in small groups, the governor was charming, quick and funny, eager to challenge anyone whose opinion he disagreed with and never hesitant to probe for more information from someone who might know more than he did. He wasn't the type that always needed to prove he was the smartest person in the room nor was he threatened by those who were more knowledgeable about a given subject. George W. Bush was a fundamentally confident person with great faith in his own judgment.

It made for an impressive combination. This was the Bush his fellow Republican governors knew, this was the guy who consistently wowed the various business, political and policy leaders who had come down to Austin trying to see if there was anything to this Bush guy or if he was just all hype. But we had not been able to capture it with any consistency in the campaign. And this failure had led to a growing drumbeat of dissatisfaction among those who knew Bush or had seen him at his best. It came from other Republican governors, from his longtime friends, from Iowa and New Hampshire operatives—we weren't capturing the real Bush.

They were right—we just weren't sure what to do about

it. At the Maverick bunker we spent a lot of time watching the news coverage of Bush, trying to analyze exactly what was broken that we could fix.

The contrast with McCain was most vivid. He seemed to be having the time of his life, riding around on his bus, surrounded by reporters who had been so beaten down with lack of access that they were having journalistic orgasms finding a candidate who would talk to them all day long about anything, all of it on the record. It was turning into one long donut rave, as the press bounced across New Hampshire eating, quite literally, out of McCain's hand. Since they didn't really believe McCain might win, they were covering his race more as an act than as a serious presidential candidate and there was no denying it was a very entertaining act.

McCain was having more fun than us, maybe it was as simple as that. In person, Bush was informal and both fun and funny, but little of that was coming through on the campaign trail. We had become a prisoner of our own success, too big and cumbersome, surrounded by security, engulfed by a press that felt isolated and excluded. It wasn't Bush's fault—he hadn't undergone some transformation, he was the same person. It was the process: We were letting it define us, instead of using the process to define Bush. We were falling into a classic front-runner trap. This was the same rat hole into which Ed Muskie had disappeared.

Ed Muskie. Say it ain't so.

5

The Volcano Belches

THE SAME KIND OF THING had happened to me in Mongolia. It was three o'clock in the morning, freezing cold, and men with guns were demanding documents I didn't have. In Mongolia the men called themselves border guards, but they were really just shake-down artists. On the tarmac of the airport at Manchester, New Hampshire, they called themselves Secret Service agents and were working for Al Gore.

"I need some kind of official ID," the man said. He was young and did not look like he wanted to be standing out on a tarmac in the early morning hours.

I handed him my driver's license.

He stared at it as if I had handed him a ransom demand.

"This is a driver's license," he said accusingly.

"Yes," I sighed. It was very cold, I wasn't wearing a lot of clothes, and I hadn't slept in what seemed like a very long time. We had left Des Moines, Iowa, around midnight, after winning the Iowa Caucuses with 40 percent of the vote. The Bush traveling road show was still using two planes then, a small jet for the governor and a few staff and a larger 737 for the press. The two-plane situation didn't help our press problems since it only furthered the impression that Bush was isolated from the press, especially compared to McCain who was banging around on the great donut rave bus tour. After

New Hampshire, we planned to shift everybody to one larger plane, but in the meantime Karen had invited several reporters to fly from Iowa to New Hampshire on the governor's plane, and I'd been bumped to the press plane to make more room.

This I liked. The press plane was a combination flying bar and college dorm, altogether much more fun than the governor's plane, which was smaller and had more of an office feel, with either Bush or his staff members actually trying to work. Or sleep. Nobody cared about that on the press plane, where drinks were being downed before the engines started.

We landed at Manchester at 3 A.M. and I hurried off to reach a hangar where Bush was scheduled to give several interviews for the early morning network shows.

Until the Secret Service guy stopped me on the tarmac.

"I need something other than a driver's license. I want to see your press credentials."

All around me, the press crowd was flashing their official credentials and passing through the checkpoint the Service had erected. Apparently Vice President Gore was scheduled to land shortly and the Service was on point.

"I'm not with the press," I said, trying not to sound annoyed.

"No?" the agent said suspiciously.

"I'm with the Bush campaign."

"Where's your pin?" He was talking about the ID pins that the Secret Service gave out to campaign staff for a candidate they were protecting. The only problem was, I didn't have a pin because Bush didn't have Secret Service protection yet. No protection, no pin. I tried to explain this to the agent. Meanwhile, my pals in the press were passing by, enjoying my predicament.

"He looks very dangerous to me," Martha Brandt of *Newsweek* advised the agent.

"Can you vouch for this gentleman?" the agent asked Martha, nodding in my direction.

"I cover the Bush campaign and I've never seen him before in my life," she said somberly.

It was the start of the most important week in my political life and things just weren't falling into place.

☆   ☆   ☆

"No, I don't really think Governor Bush is a running dog capitalist swine. Honest, I don't."

I could hear McKinnon laughing. It was 7 A.M. in New Hampshire and I'd finally made it to the hotel from the airport around 5 A.M. For some insane reason, I had agreed to a radio interview by phone with Pacifica Radio, a niche network which markets itself to people who still hold a grudge that the Sandanistas lost. I was no more than half-awake, mumbling rebuttals to charges that ranged from the stunning accusation that George W. Bush had once been a baseball team owner—the horror!—to the vicious rumor that he was a Southern Republican governor who supported the death penalty.

Why in God's name had I ever agreed to do this interview? At 7 A.M.? As if one person listening to the Pacifica network would vote for George Bush even if you promised them free dinner for a year at their favorite macrobiotic restaurant.

"No, I don't think a governor who supports the death penalty is a mass murderer. Yes, I am familiar with the concept of ethnic cleansing."

McKinnon was howling. We were sharing what the Residence Inn in Merrimack billed as a "suite"—a room with two beds, one in a curious loft space. The Residence Inn was headquarters for the final New Hampshire endgame, home for the governor and all the staff. "The Alamo" we called it before it was over.

The day before, Mark and I had made what we thought

would be our final spot for the New Hampshire primary. We shot it in Iowa, on the campus of Iowa State using a local video crew. For complicated logistical reasons involving the governor's schedule, we didn't have much choice of location. At least that was my excuse for ending up shooting in the lobby of the student union building. The whole building felt more like Oxford than Ames, Iowa, with lots of high arches, flared valence lighting and windows with heavy ironwork dividing the panes. It was really an awful place to shoot, not helped by a distinct echo that bounced between the stone floors and the high ceiling. Naturally every student who happened to be wandering through wanted to watch.

The local video crew arrived. They had with them a camera that looked to have been borrowed from a museum documenting the history of video and a couple of lights of the sort I remember my father using with his Super-8 Brownie camera. When I told them we didn't have much time to set up, the cameraman shrugged and said, "Hey, we can shoot right now. Just throw up some lights. No biggie, man." I didn't know if I should thank him for cooperating or strangle him to stop a crime against aesthetics. The only reason we were shooting video instead of film was to reduce the turnaround time of the finished spot. By shooting video, we could edit the spot immediately after the taping, versus at least a twenty-four-hour lag while film was developed and transferred.

This seemed important at the time, though it's difficult to imagine why. The spot we were making was an appeal that relied on what were still Bush's strengths in New Hampshire. On the personal front, he was seen as positive and likeable and the best alternative to Clinton likely to win in November; on issues, we had to continue to push education and tax cuts. We were winning on both—the problem was, the race just wasn't about education or taxes.

We couldn't find a decent chair for Bush to sit in during

the spot and ended up with a formal upholstered chair with a high back. We had to elevate it on blocks to get it high enough so that the window would be visible behind the governor. At least there was snow on the ground and it would look like we were shooting in New Hampshire.

"You want me on the throne?" Bush joked when he hurried in and saw the elevated chair. Mrs. Bush started laughing. "Your Highness," she said. "Can we get some rose petals to sprinkle on the carpet before His Highness?"

He nailed the spot in about three takes. He was good but the setting was weird, and when we rushed it into the editing suite we couldn't believe how harsh and, well, cheesy it looked. We were accustomed to seeing Bush shot on gorgeous 35-millimeter film and this looked like a late-night car commercial.

"Maybe people will think we did it on purpose," I suggested, as we all stared bleakly at the video monitor.

"Just in case people thought that maybe he was too good-looking," Mark said. "Right."

To soften the look, we ran the spot through some kind of digital diffusion device which we thought made it look more like film. We shipped the spot that night to stations, and it wasn't until it had already gone that we looked at it again and realized that, instead of making it look like film, the diffusion gave it a gauzy glow of the sort popular with aging movie stars trying to hide wrinkles.

"Do you think that chair looks like a throne?" I asked McKinnon.

"It has thronelike qualities, I'd say."

But unlike the missiles that Ronald Reagan described in his first debate with Walter Mondale, our little missile couldn't be turned around in midflight. The spot was launched, and it would air. And, truth was, most people wouldn't be bothered by the stuff we were obsessing over. George W. Bush looked confident and was talking about restoring pride in the White House, cutting taxes and reforming education. That was our closing gambit. Maybe, helped by a bump from Iowa, it would work.

But I doubted it. Our ads, despite a massive buy, were simply getting swept aside by a tornado of free media coverage, none of which was really playing to our favor. We were caught in a down press cycle at a critical time.

For weeks we had been running ads that reinforced our overall strategy to drive the debate in New Hampshire on to taxes and education. Our strategy was simple: The tax argument would attract fiscal and social conservatives and the education angle would appeal to more moderate voters, particularly independents with a tilt toward female voters who are always more interested in education than men. For my money, it was a great strategy that, combined with a win in Iowa, should drive us to victory in New Hampshire.

There was only one problem: It wasn't working.

The failure of our tax strategy absolutely astounded me. It had been our greatest hope to get McCain to engage on taxes, to attack the Bush tax plan as too large. We never thought he would actually do it, since no one in history has ever won a Republican primary by attacking from the left on taxes. This was like running for governor of Mississippi on the vegetarian ticket.

But McCain did just that—he came over the hill screaming that the tax cut was irresponsible, didn't pay down enough of the debt and would leave Social Security "vulnerable." This was how Democrats attacked Republicans, not how you won a Republican presidential primary in New Hampshire.

We were delighted. In Austin we watched Bernie Shaw gravely report in his best "I'm in Baghdad and there are missiles coming out of the sky" voice that "McCain and George W. Bush haven't exactly taken the gloves off, but they are increasingly going after one another on the subject of tax cuts."

"We're going to win," I predicted to Karl at our morning donuts and coffee session. This was the middle of January, two weeks before the Iowa Caucuses. He looked a bit skeptical. "Karl," I insisted, "I wake you up in the middle of the night and I say that we've got two Republican candidates in New Hampshire and one is saying we can afford a tax cut and the other one is saying it's irresponsible, who do you bet on?"

Before he could answer, I hurried on. "And one is just coming off a lousy week where he looked like a hypocrite on his number one issue." McCain had endured his first run of bad press when the *Boston Globe* revealed that he had intervened for major contributors with the Federal Communication Commission, which, as chairman of the Commerce Committee, he could terrorize whenever he desired. It was exactly the sort of mess McCain had based his campaign on cleaning up and he was right in the middle of it.

For a few days, it looked like it might all come together quite nicely. McCain's credibility had been dinged on his key issue, he was on the wrong side of the tax debate and he wasn't competing in Iowa, which we were on our way to winning. I was actually beginning to feel good about New Hampshire.

But then McCain was able to move beyond the FCC contribution scandal by basically saying, "See, this proves the system is corrupt. We need to pass campaign finance laws to stop me from doing this kind of thing," which was a brilliant piece of spin right up there with killing your parents and pleading for mercy as an orphan. We could have easily attacked him and kept the issue alive, but our ground rules of no first use of contrast or negative spots still stood.

More troubling, the tax argument didn't seem to be working. It wasn't as though we were losing on taxes, but McCain was doing a very good job of fighting us to a draw. McCain had become a larger-than-life figure in New Hampshire—he was closing in on his hundredth town meeting—and the essence of his campaign was all wrapped up in stirring images of sacrifice and patriotism blended with his carefully cultivated persona as a guy who isn't afraid to tell you the truth, even when it hurts. This combination gave him a perfect platform to boast that cutting taxes was selfish and wrong. If any other Republican had said this kind of stuff, he probably would have been excommunicated, but McCain had attained such a cult status in New Hampshire that he could pull it off.

But there was one glimmer of hope in all this—McCain was saying things that simply weren't true, like, "Others have suggested that we should use every penny for tax cuts, forgetting that we have promises to keep and a fleeting opportunity to keep our word without imperiling the economic future of our children." That "other" he was talking about was George W. Bush, and it was more than just florid hyperbole worthy of Al Gore, it was flat-out not the truth.

The more McCain engaged Bush, the closer we were to being able to respond, if only to, as Bush had always said, "set the record straight." The McCain campaign was understandably full of itself, riding on an adrenaline high, starting to get that wonderful feeling that they were bulletproof. I'd been there and knew what it was like. It was a rich and heady experience, like reaching the top of a very high mountain. And it's usually when you are coming down from the summit that you make fatal mistakes.

☆   ☆   ☆

"Have you seen this thing?" Mark asked me. We were in our "suite" at the Residence Inn. Outside there was a foot of new snow and except for a debate prep session before yet another WMUR debate, we really didn't have a lot to do. Except watch television and act nervous, two activities we were close to mastering. A McCain ad was just finishing.

He changed channels and the same ad played again. Every station was wall-to-wall presidential ads. "There's one big difference between me and the others," McCain said, looking stern, "I won't take every last dime of the surplus and spend it on tax cuts that mostly benefit the wealthy."

"That's a total lie," Mark said. "The guy is attacking us and getting away with it not being an attack."

"That's what we want to do," I complained.

We had known about the McCain ad since it started, several days earlier. It was different, though, reading a script down in Austin and actually seeing it on the air. It was a much tougher spot on the air than it read.

"This is fabulous, he's attacking us. Let's go after the guy," I said.

"You always want to attack," Mark said.

"That's true. Why not?"

"Don't you think it's a little late to attack now?"

My first instinct was to say it was never too late to attack. But Mark had a good point. Any spot that was strong enough to really work would be accompanied by a press frenzy. We'd spend the next six days arguing over tactics, and everywhere he went, Bush would end up talking about the ad.

"You gotta ask yourself," I admitted, "is one spot going to turn things around here?" In most campaigns it would take a sequence of at least three or four spots to get across a point. Everybody likes to think the silver bullet spot, the one perfect spot, will win a campaign. But usually that one great spot you remember years later only succeeded because it was set up by two or three or four other spots that no one can remember. I've always thought of ads as arguments before a jury, and it was essential to lay your case out in a comprehensible, reasonable fashion. Jumping straight to your closing argument rarely worked.

"Don't be so pessimistic," Mark insisted. "We could win. Let's go for a run, I can't sit around here."

CNN was showing a McCain town rally. They had taken on a heady, celebratory quality where McCain was greeted as a cross between a rock star and Howard Beale, the newscaster character in the great film *Network,* who became a national cult figure by screaming, "I'm mad as hell and I'm not going to take it anymore!"

"You know what bothers me the most about McCain?" I said to Mark.

"I don't want to hear this."

"His confetti. This guy has the best confetti I've ever seen."

We watched in silence for a while, brooding.

"That *is* great confetti," Mark said.

The confetti was shooting out in great cannon loads, exploding at just the right arc, showering McCain and his wife in a blizzard of bright paper.

"If we had confetti like that this race would be over," I said.

"This is a character test," Mark said. *"Anybody* can win with great confetti. It takes a genius to win with so-so confetti."

We watched for a moment more. It was horribly painful.

"Let's go running," I sighed finally.

"At least ten miles," Mark said.

"At least."

When we left the hotel, CNN was showing yet another McCain rally. He waved triumphantly, showered in gorgeous confetti.

The polls were all over the place but nobody had us out

of reach. CNN had us down by ten points, the *Boston Globe* had it 38 percent McCain, 35 percent Bush, WMUR had McCain up by three. Had we been surging, we could have easily made up the point differences, but the whole thing just didn't feel right. There were times that week when we told ourselves we would win, but I don't think any of us really believed our own spin.

☆   ☆   ☆

The last week of the New Hampshire primary is to politics what the final few days before the Super Bowl is to the sports world. Every reporter, political junkie, lobbyist, and groupie descends on Nashua and Manchester, most with no useful purpose whatsoever but driven by a lust to be part of the action in a process that is intended to have an inordinate impact on the selection of the next leader of the free world. Every reporter is in search of a unique story to file or broadcast, but invariably only one or two themes dominate the coverage. For New Hampshire 2000, the Democratic story was a hapless Bill Bradley being worked over by a newly rejuvenated Al Gore. On the Republican side of the fence, it was George W. Bush trying to hold on against the triumphant insurgency of John McCain.

There was one final debate sponsored yet again by WMUR, and it had taken on a WWF quality. It was seen as the last best chance for the Bush campaign to stop the surging McCain express. Which is a terrible, unrealistic expectation for any debate. We did everything we could to lower expectations, just as we had in the past. But this time the response was, "So you guys are just planning to lose with dignity, is that it? Just roll over and let McCain ride that big bus right over you, right?"

Everybody wanted a blood fest.

The last debate prep was held just a few hours before

the debate in the governor's room at the Residence Inn. He had flown all night from Iowa, slept poorly and then started campaigning. Like all of us, he could feel that something just wasn't right with the entire campaign dynamic. Now he was exhausted and fighting off a nasty cold as he headed into a debate with supporters and the press demanding that he deliver a knockout blow against a man who had campaigned enough in New Hampshire to establish residency and had connected with an anti-establishment, independent current that is part of the New Hampshire political psyche.

"Well, you're a sorry-looking bunch," he quipped as we assembled in a small room.

We were a jumbled mess of jeans, sweatshirts and snow boots but what he was really talking about was our mood. Which visibly wasn't great.

"You guys know something I don't?" he asked. "Josh get caught in another scandal?"

"I didn't know how to tell you, Governor," said Josh, who was carrying his usual three or four briefing books.

It was a small group—Karen, Karl, Mark, Josh, Senator Judd Gregg and Russ. We sat around on the floor and talked about questions that were likely to come up. The governor was coughing and sniffling. We suggested he take some kind of decongestant like Sudafed, but he was reluctant to take anything before the debate. He sniffled loudly. "I don't see why you think there's any problem." He sniffed louder, dramatically.

Karen handed him some decongestant. "If you want to use it, Governor, it's here."

"You just want an excuse, so if this thing is really bad you can blame it on the drugs."

"Oh, we'd do that anyway," Mark assured him.

As if to make the debate more interesting, WMUR and

CNN, the joint sponsors, had developed an insanely compli-cated method of determining the order in which candidates asked and received questions. I was at the final briefing at WMUR and it became clear very quickly that no one, including the sponsors, actually understood the rules. Representatives of CNN, WMUR and each of the candidates sat around a con-ference table at the posh new WMUR mother ship—built, as they liked to joke, as a testament to how much money was spent in the New Hampshire primary—and puzzled over the rules. Everybody had different interpretations, as if we were arguing over a coded message and none of us had the key to break the code.

There were two rounds of direct candidate-to-candidate questions, and whoever wrote the rules—no one would claim authorship—had labored to create a formula that would guar-antee that not every question would be directed at Bush, which would have happened if the other candidates had had their druthers. Even though we were behind in New Hamp-shire, Bush was still the one walking around with the big tar-get on his chest.

"I think the first question you ask will go to Alan Keyes," I said.

"You think?" the governor asked.

"It's complicated," I said after a pause.

"How complicated can it be?" he asked. He was slumped in a chair with one of Josh's briefing books on his lap, his head tilted to the side.

Karen and I exchanged smiles. She had read the instruc-tions too.

"You'd be surprised," I said.

"You're right," he answered, raising an eyebrow.

"Let's assume it's Alan Keyes," Karen said.

"Glad you guys are on top of this," he said, shaking his head with a slight grin. Bush was an unfaltering optimist, not the type to give in to the kind of angry despondency that is easy to succumb to in a campaign that isn't going well. The kind of feeling a lot of us tended to get late at night when we pondered what might happen if we managed to blow everything and lost the nomination.

We discussed what kind of question to ask Keyes. Our first instinct was to think of a question that would give Keyes an opportunity to go after McCain. The most obvious question was something related to campaign finance reform. Keyes saw McCain's version of campaign finance reform as an infringement on free speech, and Keyes was a guy who liked his free speech.

"But what does that get us?" Karl asked.

Karen agreed. "All that does is give McCain a chance to talk about his favorite issue. Why do we want to do that?"

"I'm sorry I suggested it," sighed Bush, who had never mentioned it. "All this double bank shot stuff, why do we care about that? Why don't I ask Keyes a question that says something about me? A question I'm interested in."

"Such as?" Josh asked.

"Education. Or health care. He'll be great on Hillary-care. Or Medicare reform. Let's talk about that. After I ask Keyes a question, whose question do I answer?"

"McCain's," I said. "And in the second round of questions, you get to ask McCain a question."

"Good." He looked pleased for the first time since we had arrived.

☆   ☆   ☆

McCain gave us one opening in the debate. When Bernie Shaw asked him whether his tax plan looked too much like President Clinton's, he responded, "Well, I think maybe President Clinton's looks too much like mine."

Watching it, we literally gasped when he said this. "I can't believe that," said Joe Allbaugh, the six-foot four-inch campaign manager with the flattop haircut (not a crew cut, he always made plain). Joe is not an easily excitable guy. His email handle, Rock, offered a good indication of his unflappable style. "The guy just made our case for us."

There was a group of us watching in a conference room of an office building near WMUR. I turned to Senator Judd Gregg and asked, "Did he just free Poland?" referring to Gerald Ford's infamous remark in a debate with Jimmy Carter that Poland was not under Soviet domination.

"I'm not sure if McCain couldn't get away with freeing Poland," he said and smiled. He understood better than most what was happening with McCain in New Hampshire.

"Come on, he just said he had the same position as Bill Clinton on taxes. That's got to hurt," I argued, not really believing it.

"If the race is about taxes." Gregg had a laconic manner and a dry wit that was easy to miss. "This is New Hampshire. Who cares about taxes?"

We had to try to do something with the McCain tax clip, if only to make ourselves feel better. So Mark, Russ and I drove to an obscure editing house the next morning, one of the few video production places in New Hampshire not swarming with reporters and producers. By noon we had a spot produced using the McCain quote. To get it on the air by the weekend, we needed to deliver it to WMUR by 3 P.M.

By 1:30 we had assembled in an unused banquet hall of the Tara Sheraton, a huge hotel modeled, for inexplicable reasons, on a medieval castle. Senator Gregg was there with his top political aide, Joel Maiola, as were Karl, Joe Allbaugh, Mark, Russ and I. The banquet hall was the only place we could find to get away from the reporters roaming the hotel. A VCR and television were rolled in on a cart by a very curious hotel employee. *Why do these men want to watch television in the middle of the banquet room?*

We played the spot. This is always a terrible moment for a media consultant, that first time you show your work to a campaign. There was a long pause after the spot finished. Finally, Joe said, "Is that it?"

As responses go, "Is that it?" generally isn't the most powerful endorsement.

It's critical, I've learned, to defend your spots ferociously. Who else will? If the people who run the campaign have an inkling that you don't believe with all your heart that your spot will help their candidate (and how can you *know,* really?—it's almost always a crap shoot), then they're unlikely to throw behind it their hopes, dreams and credibility, along with thousands of dollars. It's the uncertainty that drives so many campaigns into the arms of testing and focus groups, which can, if nothing else, provide them with butt coverage should the spot turn out to be a a major bomb. *We tested it. It tested great.*

Mark, Russ and I looked at one another. None of us charged forth to defend the spot. Instead, I asked, "What do you think?" This is the equivalent of a lawyer standing before a jury and summoning up the defense of his client by mumbling, "Or whatever." Weak, weak, weak.

We looked at it several times. The message was clear— John McCain had clearly said, and meant it, that his tax plan was like Bill Clinton's. The question was, So what?

Karl hadn't said anything as the spot played several times. "It's awfully quick," he sighed.

It was. We had set up the McCain answer by putting Bernie Shaw's question on the screen with a graphic, read by an announcer. We were hesitant to use Shaw on camera, since CNN could raise hell and try to block the spot from airing, and with only a few days until the election, we didn't have any time to waste arguing with CNN lawyers.

Sitting in that big, empty banquet hall, I was coming to the conclusion that it would be a mistake to run the spot. The worst thing we could do was allow ourselves to be labeled as attacking—even if we were using McCain's own words—and then lose the primary and have the "attack" identified as one of the reasons we lost. That would be a disaster, potentially reducing our options after New Hampshire. McCain had found a way to attack us and not be seen as attacking. We needed to do the same but do it on more friendly turf—like South Carolina.

"What happens if we run the spot?" Karl asked.

"We probably lose," Senator Gregg said.

"And if we don't run the spot?" Karl asked.

"We probably lose," Senator Gregg said with something of a wistful smile."

"That makes it easy," Karl concluded.

☆　　　☆　　　☆

I was skiing when I got the first exits. Cross-country skiing, which is a curious passion of mine. Actually, cross-country long-distance racing, an obscure pursuit which is the racewalking of winter sports. I was at Waterville Valley, about eighty miles north of Manchester. Jacob Weisberg, who writes for *Slate* magazine, was with me. He'd heard through the incestuous grapevine of journalists and political operatives that I was planning to sneak away for a few hours on election morning and asked if he could come along.

"I was on the Yale cross-country ski team," Jacob told me, then added, "We were terrible, don't be impressed."

Driving up, Jacob started telling me about the first time he had met John McCain. "It was at Michael Lewis's wedding," he explained. "At my house."

"John McCain went to Michael Lewis's wedding," I marveled. That was perfect. Another journalist had told me that he had really enjoyed talking with McCain at Michael Oreskes's birthday party. This was part of the genius of McCain's candidacy—he was such an insider, that he could sell himself as an outsider.

I knew it was frustrating to Bush. On *Face the Nation* that weekend he had said, "My zip code is 78701; that's Austin, Texas, it's not Washington, D.C. If you were to call me on the telephone I'd be in area code 512, not 202. I come from Texas . . . I'm running my campaign in Austin, Texas. I'm not the chairman of a powerful committee like the Commerce Committee."

I told Jacob that I thought we were going to lose New Hampshire—he didn't disagree, I noticed—but that we would definitely win South Carolina.

"McCain beat Bradley in New Hampshire," I said, pounding the steering wheel in frustration. "He became what Bradley was supposed to be—the insurgent moderate fighting the system. He became in New Hampshire whatever hungry voters wanted him to be. If you're pro-choice, he's pro-choice. If you're pro-life, he's pro-life. If you believe in gun control, he's with you. If you're pro-gun, he's your guy. They were brilliant about fuzzing all these differences under the sheer power of his personality.

"Now in South Carolina, he's going to try and make himself into a conservative again. But it won't work. McCain's campaign is sheer emotion and energy. They'll probably have a big night tonight, but it will be their last." I think I actually believed this, though on the edge of a big defeat, it's always hard to sort through your own spin.

Jacob was looking like he was regretting getting in the car with some lunatic who apparently was going to rant all the way to Waterville Valley.

Russ Schriefer called me right after lunch. "It's ugly," he said. "Real ugly. Double digits and it could go as high as fifteen."

That night Karl, Mark, Russ, and Matthew Dowd and I had a quick dinner at a strip mall in Manchester. It was a beer-and-burgers place with cheery waitresses. We sat at a table in the bar area surrounded by televisions. It was a uniquely public form of humiliation, to see your own failures debated on every channel in America except possibly the Playboy Channel, and even they were probably interrupting some soft porn interlude to have Hugh Hefner discuss this remarkable victory by McCain. It was sort of like going to your own funeral and listening to everybody talk about what a moron you were.

Our cell phones were ringing every few seconds, mostly with reporters wanting to know the governor's reaction.

"He was unbelievable," Karl told me. "He was actually worried about how we felt, trying to buck us up."

"Every time a front-runner loses New Hampshire, they start throwing bodies out of the window," I reminded him. "Hell, Reagan *won* and fired people."

Karl shook his head. "Ain't gonna happen. He was incredibly steady. I've known the guy for twenty-some years and I always thought he was a leader but I tell you, tonight just blew me away."

"You know something," Matthew Dowd said, "I'm relieved. It's over, we lost, now we can get down to an environment that is much better for us."

I felt relieved too. New Hampshire had spun out of control, and there had been, at the end, nothing we could do. The time to win New Hampshire had been the previous fall, when we should have moved to stop McCain from defining us as the Insider. McCain had run in New Hampshire so hard and long that it was like he was running for governor of New Hampshire, not president of the United States. He had told New Hampshire voters he was in love only with them, not dating around.

The McCain campaign had proved once again that there is always some magic core of voter unrest waiting to be tapped into in every election. It's easy when the unrest is close to the surface, like when an incumbent party has become unpopular or there's a major national trauma—Vietnam, the civil rights movement, Watergate, the shame of the Iranian hostages— shaking the national psyche. But McCain had done something truly extraordinary in New Hampshire, tapping into an unrest that was so deeply buried as to be invisible. Once he connected with it, though, he was propelled upward like a feather on a geyser.

South Carolina would be different.

"The best thing about this," Karl said, as we listened to yet another pundit extol our stupidity, "is that now Bush can prove himself. If the big rap against him is that he's never been tested, this will be a test. We'll come out of this better off than if we had won New Hampshire and cruised to the nomination."

Personally, I would have been quite comfortable without this kind of test, but Karl was right. As long as we won South Carolina.

6

A Home Game

AT THE END OF OUR FIRST DAY in South Carolina, Mark, Karl and I found ourselves in a cab headed for the airport for a flight back to Austin. Twenty-four hours earlier, the polls had just closed in New Hampshire. Already it was starting to feel like some kind of bad dream, which I took as a positive indication of the powers of denial. The three of us were feeling about as good as you could after one of the more notable ass kickings in modern political history. On the radio was a local conservative talk radio show. They have a lot of them in South Carolina.

"You know that McCain," a caller was saying in a deeply outraged voice, "he could've gotten out of prison camp earlier than he did. He chose to stay in."

"He didn't want to take early release," the show's host said. "Not while others were still in prison. You got a problem with that?"

"Hell yes! He could've got out and gone back to fight! That's what he should have done! Instead of staying in that Hanoi *Hilton.*" He spat out the last word, as if there had been room service and a very nice pool attached to the prison.

The host started laughing. "You're crazy, man!" he shouted.

It was different in South Carolina. Right from the start, when we first stepped off the plane that morning into seventy-five-degree weather, everybody seemed to relax. It was the kind of gorgeous warm February day you could get down in Austin.

"This is more like it," Karen said, sighing, as we waited in the sun for Bush to greet the usual crowd of state politicians.

We hadn't felt comfortable in New Hampshire for months. Not since it turned cold and snow started falling. Something about tramping around in the snow just seemed to throw our whole Texas operation off-stride. It was like a constant re- minder that we were playing an away game on not-so-friendly turf. South Carolina would be a home game.

We got in the car and drove to Bob Jones University for our first post–New Hampshire event.

☆   ☆   ☆

The Bob Jones speech became one of the defining mo- ments of the primary, used throughout the campaign by critics eager to bash Bush as intolerant. The curious thing about it, given the later firestorm, was how inconsequential it seemed at the time. Bush gave a variation of his standard stump speech. When asked in a press conference afterward whether he agreed with the university's ban on interracial dating, he immediately said no. But he hadn't used the speech as an op- portunity to criticize the university's nutty prejudices on every- thing from race to Catholics, and it was for this omission that Bush later apologized.

It was no secret that social conservatives were a key group that both Bush and McCain were actively courting. In New Hampshire, McCain had run as a quirky independent and harvested a huge share of the independent votes from people who were basically social moderates or liberals. But in South Carolina, the McCain campaign understood that their only hope was to sell McCain as a conservative war hero with the guts to fight the system. They still played up McCain's independence, an appeal that cut across ideological lines, but it was no accident that in South Carolina McCain was running ads stressing his pro-life position, ads that had somehow never aired during *Ally McBeal* in New Hampshire.

It wasn't complicated. The John McCain who won in New Hampshire couldn't win in South Carolina, so the campaign was trying to make, if not a U-turn, at least a hard shift to the right. If McCain became the choice of social conservatives in South Carolina, he'd win and, arguably, capture the nomination as well. This was why he had turned over his South Carolina campaign to people like Richard Quinn, a $20,000-a-month political consultant who also happened to be a former editor of *Southern Partisan* magazine, which is sort of the *Paris Review* for the social conservative crowd. And his campaign was chockful of people associated with Bob Jones University, such as his South Carolina chairman Lindsey Graham.

After the Bob Jones speech, we met at the Hyatt Regency in Greenville with our South Carolina team, guys like Warren Thompkins, Heath Thompson and Tucker Eskew. It was a serious group of heavyweights and I felt better just seeing these guys. Between them, they knew as much as anyone about South Carolina politics. Warren was to South Carolina what Karl Rove was to Texas, a guy who had proven year after year he could win. Tucker, a cousin of Carter Eskew of the Gore campaign, was a smart-ass hipster who had a way of delivering a tough message with a smile that was very effective. Heath was a young operative with a good-old-boy manner that masked a type A-plus compulsion to win every minute of every day. All good guys to have on your side on a dark night.

I was still marveling that we were all there—no one had

been fired, demoted or publicly scolded. In a strange way, the crushing defeat in New Hampshire had played perfectly to George W. Bush's strengths. He was not a second guesser or a scapegoater. He had an interesting combination of confidence—he was one of the most confident people I'd ever known—and an ambition that wasn't haunted by desperation. The mix gave him a view of the world that was extremely useful in moments of high stress. On the one hand, he was convinced the problem of the moment would be overcome. In this case, the problem was a nineteen-point defeat in New Hampshire and the rocket-fueled momentum it gave to McCain. On the other hand, he was a man who genuinely enjoyed his life and didn't *have* to be president. This caused many political observers and pros to question his toughness and mettle. Was it possible for a man who seemed perfectly capable of being happy if he lost to go through what winning required? If you didn't have to win, could you?

Publicly, Bush was upbeat, and behind the curtain, when he was with us, he was exactly the same. It would have been normal to show a glint of anger and maybe a little fear. Anger because the people he had entrusted to run his campaign had somehow let New Hampshire get out of control and fear because he was surely on a precipice. If we lost South Carolina, the conventional wisdom was that the campaign would be finished. But Bush appeared perfectly relaxed, eager. As though he knew it was all going to work out.

There sure wasn't any reason to believe that looking at the polls. McCain was benefiting from what his pollster Bill McInturff called "the largest bump in modern history." Within the next twenty-four hours, everywhere you turned, somebody would be talking about how much trouble we were in. Brian Williams on NBC reported, "A bombshell out of South Carolina, where there is word John McCain has apparently turned the tide on George W. Bush. The New Hampshire bounce appears to be more of a boom." ABC's Ann Douglas told viewers that "McCain was way behind Bush in South Carolina but there is a poll now that shows that he's five points ahead of Bush . . . the Bush people say they are getting very nervous." And Lisa Myers informed NBC viewers that "in South Carolina, John McCain is riding what appears to be a huge wave, touched off by his victory in New Hampshire."

At that first meeting in South Carolina, we didn't know how bad things would get, but we knew that we were in for some nasty numbers combined with a virtual pistol whipping from every pundit in America. "We got a little rough period to get over here," Warren Thompkins said, "but then everything will settle down. We get our base secure then go after the suburban vote with education. But we can't let him beat up on us on taxes like he did up in New Hampshire. Are you ready to fight back?"

We were, thank God. Mark, Karl and I had written a spot on the plane coming down from New Hampshire. It was perfectly straightforward, more informative than inflammatory. It went like this:

ANNOUNCER: John McCain's ad about Governor Bush's tax plan isn't true, and McCain knows it.

John McCain's economic adviser says he'd support Bush's plan—$2 trillion to protect Social Security, pay down the debt and a real tax cut.

McCain's plan? A tax cut smaller than Clinton's—and not a penny in tax cuts for thirty million Americans. On taxes, McCain echoes Washington Democrats when we need a conservative leader to challenge them.

Governor Bush. Proven. Tested. And ready to lead America.

It wasn't especially elegant, but it was efficient. The opening line was a simple statement of fact. McCain knew that Bush didn't spend every dime on tax cuts, as McCain's ad maintained. The bit about McCain's own adviser was taken from an interview with Vin Weber, a former congressman and McCain adviser, who had said in an interview that he would vote for the Bush plan if he were in Congress, though he preferred McCain's plan. This was a useful way to jab McCain over his claim that the Bush tax plan would bankrupt Social Security and bring economic ruin—if it was so bad, how come his own adviser said he'd vote for it? Pointing out that McCain's plan was smaller than Clinton's was a no-brainer, as was the reminder that his plan didn't affect a huge hunk of taxpayers.

The last bit about echoing Washington Democrats cut a lot of different ways. We hoped it would remind people that McCain was part of Washington, reinforce that he was attacking Bush from the left on taxes, like a Democrat, and reestablish Bush as the conservative leader challenging the status quo.

Of course, most people wouldn't get all of this out of the spot. But they would get the point that Bush was fighting back and that they should not believe everything McCain was saying. It was a spot that wouldn't win the war, but that might start a battle that would allow us to win the war.

We made the ad when we got back to Austin, forty-eight hours after New Hampshire.

"You're not going to put a lot of those doom-and-gloom effects behind it, are you?" Karl asked. This was a running joke between Karl and me. In past campaigns, Karl had invariably hated the sound tracks in the spots I created. I love dramatic, eerie effects that make the hairs on the back of your neck stand up. Karl is more a just-the-facts kind of guy.

"No heavy effects," I promised. I was so damn happy to

be making the spot that I would have gladly used Brahms's lullabies as the sound track.

We emailed a copy of the spot to Karen on the road and she showed it to Bush. It wasn't a great way to demo a spot—invariably the video was lousy and it was hard to read the graphics, but it was better than nothing and we wanted to get his approval as soon as possible. No problem, the word came back, go with it.

We fed the spots to stations via digital uplink on Friday morning, so that they would air before the weekend. Releasing a new spot on Friday is a standard tactic in the campaign business, the theory being that you catch the other side by surprise, and they can't respond until Monday or Tuesday. This always made us feel exceedingly clever, though in truth no smart campaign airs many ads on Saturdays and Sundays since it's hard to find shows with large audiences of likely voters. The favorite slot for any political ad is next to a local or national news program, since watchers of news consistently vote more than any other group. At the other end of the scale would be, say, WWF wrestling, which tends to draw an audience that doesn't spend a lot of time reading *Foreign Affairs.*

In this case, getting a spot out before the weekend was important symbolically as well as tactically. Symbolically, because it was critical that we send a signal to the political world that we were fighting back. These were uncharted waters. No one had ever lost the New Hampshire primary by nineteen points and won their party's nomination, much less the presidency. Now we were trying to convince the world that we had what it took to come back from the dead.

Tactically, we hoped that getting the ad out over the weekend would allow us to start controlling the agenda of the race. It had been a long time since something our campaign did forced the other side to react. Our greatest hope was that the McCain forces would respond, and respond harshly. And our greatest fear was that they would do nothing. In order to change the dynamic of the race, we had to engage McCain— and it was tough to engage someone who didn't react.

It's always a strange feeling when you've launched a spot and are waiting for the response. My natural reaction is frantically to revise and rewrite the spot that has already been made, thinking of everything we didn't say that we should have, and better ways to say what we did. Once I've completed this futile endeavor, I usually try to find some means to exercise myself senseless.

Mark thought my tendency to revise our spots was probably a sign of dementia, but he was big on the exercise part of the equation. So when we finished the spot on Thursday night, we went for a swim at Barton Springs. When I first came to Austin, Mark had taken me to Barton for a midday training swim and pronounced it the spiritual heart of Austin. At the time I had no idea what he was talking about, but now I was beginning to understand. It was an amazing spring-fed lagoon in a natural depression surrounded by hills of sweeping green grass and rocky enclaves. At night, with a light mist coming up from the water, it was like entering another world. On a bright day, the sun sparkling on the water, the grass a brilliant green, it was like stumbling onto Shangri-la. And it was in the heart of Austin, just a few minutes from both Bush headquarters and the Maverick offices.

Mark and I swam lap after lap and emerged from the water feeling cleansed of New Hampshire, rejuvenated.

"What if McCain doesn't respond?" I asked Mark as we were walking back to the car.

"He has to," he said. "He'll want to."

"You're right," I agreed.

"Doesn't he?" Mark asked, just as we got to our cars.

☆   ☆   ☆

That Sunday in a long meeting we completely redesigned the campaign. I'd never really seen anything like this—it was a basic questioning of just about every aspect of the campaign. Somebody was there from each division—strategy, media, advance, press, finance—and it was one of the first nonfinance meetings that I remember Don Evans attending. It was the beginning of Evans playing an increasingly active role in the race. I thought this was a good thing—he had a laconic, steadying influence and was one of the governor's closest friends.

Meanwhile, the press was convinced that heads were going to roll and rumors were rife about a new team flying in from Washington to rescue the campaign. Reporters were on stakeout in front of 301 Congress, trying to catch a glimpse of the new mystery operatives being smuggled into headquarters. Having a reporter stick a mike in your face and ask how many people have been executed that morning was not the best morale booster. But when you tried to explain that no one was getting fired, the press would look at you in disbelief. "You mean you guys aren't going to do *anything?*" When the Dole campaign had gone through a rough patch in the primary, bodies were sacrificed, not because anybody really thought it would help, but because the volcano was belching and sacrifices were needed. Of course, the end result of this was that most everybody in the campaign started focusing on his or her own survival rather than waking up every morning trying to elect Bob Dole president.

This never happened in Bush world. Inside 301 Congress, it was all nuts and bolts, like taking apart a race car that wasn't delivering the right amount of speed and looking at every part to figure out what wasn't working. It started with the basic format of the day-to-day campaigning. In New Hampshire, our bread-and-butter event had been for Bush to tour a business—insurance company, high-tech plant, bakery—and then meet with workers in a cafeteria or break room, give a little talk and take questions. It rarely seemed to click. The workers seemed bored or embarrassed and the only animated ones were those who had some ax to grind. This was in sharp contrast to McCain's town halls, which exploded with energy and made for fabulous visuals.

Brian Montgomery, head of advance, showed the group various diagrams of how we could revamp the events.

"The key is to get real people behind the governor," Brian said, "and try to get him on the same level as his audience, so it's more intimate." He held up a stage design that had a semi-circle behind Bush's position and a U-shaped audience space, so the governor could walk into the crowd.

There are two kinds of advance pros—those who are hyper and always seem to be in the midst of a crisis and those who have a kind of laid-back *Right Stuff* manner, the voice over the plane intercom saying that, yeah, that engine did look like it was on fire a little, but don't worry, everything will be fine. This was Brian's style and there was something reassuring about hearing him describe various options. Okay, things are broken, let's fix them. For months, in New Hampshire, we were in the middle of events that we couldn't control. Now we were reasserting control.

"What do we want to call this new format?" Karl asked.

Names were thrown around like "George W. Bush Up Close and Personal," "Ask George W. Bush" (his father had used the same thing in 1980, no good) and "Questions and Answers with Governor Bush." Finally we settled on "One on One with George W. Bush."

"It sounds like a sports show," Mindy Tucker said. She

was one of the young press stars in Austin who had worked her way up through Bush's other campaigns.

"Is that good or bad?" Joe Allbaugh asked. Then he answered his own question: "I think it's good."

"It's not grammatically correct," Karl said, knowing that everybody would groan. Which they did. Having spent years in the direct-mail business, Karl had an irresistible urge to correct grammar and spelling. "He's not going to be meeting *one on one.*"

"I can live with that," Joe said dryly, shaking his head. "Anybody got anything better?" he asked. "Fine," he said. "Let's move on." Joe was never one to linger over decisions. " 'One on One' it is."

By the end of the meeting, we had gone over every aspect of the campaign, determined that "Reformer with Results" would be the new slogan, and dispatched Mindy Tucker and another press hotshot, Dan Bartlett, to South Carolina to help coordinate press. In New Hampshire there had developed a disconnect between Austin, the traveling campaign, and the campaign on the ground, which was largely run by New Hampshire staffers. This had to stop. Mindy and Dan would coordinate between Austin and South Carolina. This was going to be hand-to-hand combat for the next twenty days, fighting to win every news cycle.

Karen, who couldn't make the meeting, had come up with the new slogan, Reformer with Results. I've never been big on slogans in campaigns, if only because every campaign wants something brilliant and original and there just aren't that many good ones to be had. A bad slogan can harm you more than a good one can help. But in this case, as part of our need to show that we were actively making changes in the campaign, a new slogan probably was a good idea. I didn't like Reformer with Results, but everybody else seemed to think it worked.

"What worries me," I'd said to Karen, "is that we're play-ing too much on McCain's turf. If reform is the question, isn't McCain the answer?"

"No! We just haven't talked enough about the governor's record on reform. Juvenile justice, education, tort reform," she reeled off a list of Bush's record on reform.

I was convinced the slogan was a mistake but, in retro-spect, South Carolina proved Karen right and me wrong. What I failed to appreciate is how much Bush *wanted* to talk about reform and how essential it was to his political self-image. Us-ing the slogan Reformer with Results we were going head-to-head with McCain on his key issue, which I saw as a mistake. But that's what Bush wanted. He welcomed the contrast and was frustrated that McCain had stolen the Outsider/Reformer label. Karen, who understood Bush as well or better than any-one, realized this on some intuitive level. The slogan gave him a platform to start making the contrast.

Within forty-eight hours of the Sunday meeting, we were on our way to winning South Carolina. It was just a matter of letting events play out. We had finally accomplished what we had needed to do since October—change the campaign dy-namic.

It happened with delicious speed.

At our Monday morning session with Karl, we got word that McCain was going up with a new spot. His media buyers had informed the stations the spot would be called "Desper-ate." We didn't know the text of the ads yet, but we didn't need to. Nobody named a positive ad "Desperate." It was a title I'd used probably a dozen times over the years and it was never to deliver a wet kiss.

By the eleven o'clock message meeting, Warren Thomp-kins had a VHS recording of the spot. "Email it to us, Warren," Karl told him. We were in Karl's office on the speakerphone.

"Email? I don't know how to email video," Warren rasped.

"Gimme a break. I can't program a VCR. Can't I just play the damn thing over the phone?"

We were laughing.

"Play it," Karl said. And he did.

JOHN MCCAIN: I guess it was bound to happen. Governor Bush's campaign is getting desperate with a negative ad about me.

The fact is, I'll use the surplus money to fix Social Security, cut your taxes and pay down the debt. Governor Bush uses all the surplus for tax cuts, but not one new penny for Social Security or the debt.

His ad twists the truth like Clinton—we're all pretty tired of that.

As president, I'll be conservative and always tell you the truth, no matter what.

"He's calling the governor a liar," Warren said. "It's right there. Nobody thinks George W. Bush is like Bill Clinton. McCain's own supporters don't think that."

"I guess we'll just have to respond," I said. "Much as I hate to."

"Such a shame," Mark agreed.

By that evening, we had two new spots on their way to South Carolina. A week earlier, the night before the New Hampshire primary, I'd felt helpless, a mere bystander. Now everything had shifted. Instead of just hoping we would win, we were dictating the flow of the campaign. We had made a spot last Thursday, put it on the air by Friday, everybody in the media had talked about it all weekend and now McCain had responded. So now we would make more spots and within twenty-four hours, everybody in the press campaign echo chamber would be talking about these new spots. And Mc-

Cain would probably respond again. This is how you won races, by seizing the offensive and staying on it.

Our two new spots worked in tandem. One challenged McCain's credentials as an outsider. This was the spot I had been dying to make for weeks.

FEMALE ANNOUNCER [*voice-over*]: John McCain promised a clean campaign . . .
[*On screen: photo of McCain and George W. Bush shaking hands at the January 10, 2000 GOP debate*]
MALE ANNOUNCER [*v/o*]: . . . then attacked Governor Bush with misleading ads.
FEMALE ANNOUNCER: McCain says he's the only candidate who can beat Gore on campaign finance.
MALE ANNOUNCER: But news investigations reveal "McCain solicits money from lobbyists with interests before his committee." . . .
[*On screen:* Source: NBC News, 2/4/2000]
. . . and "pressures agencies on behalf of contributors."
[*On screen:* Source: the *Boston Globe*, 1/25/2000]
FEMALE ANNOUNCER: He attacks special interests, but *The Wall Street Journal* reports . . .
MALE ANNOUNCER: . . . McCain's "campaign is crawling with lobbyists."
[*On screen:* Source: *The Wall Street Journal*, 2/4/2000]
FEMALE ANNOUNCER: His conservative hometown paper warns . . .
MALE ANNOUNCER: . . . "It's time the rest of the nation learns about the (John) McCain we know."
[*On screen:* Source: the *Arizona Republic*, 11/7/1999]

It was filled with third-party validation—NBC News, the *Boston Globe*, *The Wall Street Journal*, the *Arizona Republic*—

so that a viewer wouldn't have to take our word for it, just look at all these sources. How could they all be wrong?

The other spot was intended to drive the Reformer with Results message. When we sat down and wrote it, we asked ourselves why we hadn't made it earlier. It would have been very helpful in October in New Hampshire, when McCain was pushing us into the insider box and claiming the outsider mantle for himself.

> MALE ANNOUNCER [v/o]: As governor, he took on the education establishment and demanded high standards, phonics and charter schools.
> FEMALE ANNOUNCER [v/o]: He fought trial lawyers over lawsuit abuse and beat them.
> MALE ANNOUNCER: While Washington was deadlocked, he passed a patients' bill of rights.
> FEMALE ANNOUNCER: He challenged the status quo and reformed welfare, strengthened juvenile justice laws and cut taxes three billion dollars.
> FEMALE ANNOUNCER: Governor George W. Bush.
> MALE ANNOUNCER: A reformer with results. He will restore integrity and values to the White House.

The McCain campaign responded with a fury, which is exactly what we wanted. We needed confrontation, and they didn't disappoint. "We'll hit back and we'll hit harder than we've been hit," McCain boasted. The word from the McCain bus was that they "seemed gleeful to have this battle with Bush," Fox News reported. And even though the poll numbers were still bleak, the mood at Bush headquarters was much improved. It was *fun* to be fighting back.

"Bush wants to make a spot responding directly to the Clinton thing," Karl told us on Wednesday morning, eight days after New Hampshire and just five days after we had launched our first response spot to McCain. A long time ago, the British politician Sir Harold Wilson once said, "A week is a long time in politics." He was right.

We were having a celebratory breakfast at Las Manitas Avenue Cafe, the Central American cafe right down from the campaign. It was a perennial hangout for Austin's liberal elite—Molly Ivins loved it—and it was amusing to see the stares directed at us, our photo IDs making us conspicuous as Bush staffers. Karl, Mark, Matthew Dowd, Russ and I were crammed into a booth eating *huevos rancheros* and breakfast burritos.

By "Clinton thing," Karl meant McCain's comparing Bush to Clinton in his latest spot. "He wants to do it himself, on camera," Karl said.

"When?" Mark asked.

"Right away. As soon as we can get it shot and up. By the weekend."

By any reasonable standard, this was pretty impossible. First, we had to come up with a script, then find time in the governor's schedule to film him, at a stage in the campaign when he was booked every moment of the day. Then we had to get the film developed, transferred to videotape, edited and distributed by noon on Friday, which would be the cutoff for most stations to air the spot over the weekend. It was crazy.

"We can do that," Russ said.

"Sure," Mark agreed.

Karl looked at us a bit skeptically. "Good," he said, then pulled out some notes. "This is what the governor wants to say."

I was thinking, Great. At least we don't have to worry about script approval.

Russ left immediately for South Carolina to scout locations. Mark was going to fly out at dawn the next morning and go to whatever location Russ found. We had a window of about forty-five minutes Thursday afternoon when Bush might be available. Laura Crawford scrambled to find a local crew but there were no cameramen available. So I called a guy I'd grown up with in Mississippi, Jim Dollarhide, who was a very successful shooter who still worked out of Mississippi. Dollarhide agreed to fly out Thursday morning from Mississippi and meet Mark at the Charlotte airport.

Somehow, Laura talked a film lab and editing facility in Atlanta into staying open all night. The idea was to film Thursday afternoon, after which Mark would rush to catch a flight to Atlanta, get the film to a lab, edit that night and distribute digitally Friday morning. There wasn't much margin for error, but it might work. I was going to stay in Austin and make another "contrast" spot, which we would air over the weekend. We had bought a tremendous amount of air time in South Carolina and were burning through our spots at a ferocious rate. And we wanted to stay on the offense with these new spots.

Russ called that night to say he'd found a perfect place to film. "It's a park about a mile from Rock Hill. He can do it right after he gives his speech at the Catawba fish camp. It'll be perfect."

"He's giving a speech at a fish camp?"

"You're from Mississippi. These are your people. I'm from New York, what do I know about fish camps? Doesn't everybody give speeches at fish camps?"

Russ called the next morning, just before the eleven o'clock message meeting. "This is a disaster," he groaned. "They just canceled the Rock Hill stop. We're screwed! He's driving straight from the fish camp across the state to Columbia."

This was not good. Mark and the cameraman were about to land in Charlotte and we didn't have a location. Not good.

While talking to Russ on the cell phone, I had moved over to the advance section of headquarters where they had detailed maps of South Carolina. Advance specialized in dealing with last-minute changes and chaos. It was a reassuring place to be.

"What's the problem, man?" Patrick Brody, who ran advance from headquarters, asked me. He was in his late twenties and somehow managed to be upbeat despite sleeping about four hours a night and taking the blame for every event that didn't live up to expectations.

"I've got Russ on the phone and they just killed Rock Hill," I moaned. "We don't have a place to shoot."

Patrick immediately understood the life-and-death nature of the emergency. "We can fix this. What do you need to get a good shot?"

"Trees," I said. "An opening with trees. Someplace relatively quiet."

"Trees. Okay," Patrick said, looking relieved, as if he had expected me to request dancing bears and a rainbow. "We can find trees. They have lots of trees in South Carolina."

"Patrick says we can find trees," I reassured Russ.

"I know you can find goddamn trees!" Russ yelled. "Are you crazy? But this has got to be on Interstate Seventy-seven on the way to Columbia."

"Right." To Patrick I said, "We need trees along Interstate Seventy-seven."

"Not a problem. Sounds like a park to me."

We were both poring over a map of South Carolina. Over the phone I could hear Russ honking his horn and tires squealing. He was racing from Rock Hill toward Interstate 77 and our yet-to-be-determined location.

Another call came in on the cell. It was Mark. He had landed and was in the car with Jim Dollarhide. I explained to him that the lunch stop had been canceled. "Well, where the hell are we supposed to go," he asked reasonably, "if we don't know where we are going to shoot?"

"Just head south from the airport toward Interstate Seventy-seven. I'll call you with a location."

"How about a state park?" Patrick asked.

"I like parks. I love parks," I said.

"There's a little state park on Interstate Seventy-seven." Somehow Patrick had produced a book listing all the parks in South Carolina. I loved these advance guys.

I told Russ. "Got it," he said. "Any idea what it looks like?"

"It looks like a park," I said. "How the hell would I know?"

"I think there's a lake," Patrick said.

A half hour later, in the middle of the message meeting, Mark called. Taking cell phone calls in the message meeting was only slightly less acceptable than, say, pulling out a huge joint and lighting up. At the end of the table, Joe Allbaugh scowled. "It's Mark," I whispered to him. Joe nodded. I always suspected that he used his formidable physical presence, along with the flattop and the frequent scowls, to hide what a genuinely nice guy he was. This was the only campaign I'd ever known in which the campaign manager didn't yell at somebody even once. But he was a great scowler. "You know we killed Rock Hill," Joe told me.

I stepped out of the conference room. "Where is this park?" Mark was asking. I had called him with directions, which were simple—go south out of the airport to Interstate 77. "Where are you?" I asked. I could hear him talking to Dollarhide, who was looking at a map.

"We're going north on I-Seventy-seven like you said."

"What?" I screamed. "North? You're heading into North Carolina, not South! You're going in the wrong direction!"

"Crap," Mark mumbled. "We're headed north," he yelled at Dollarhide.

"I was worried about that," I heard Dollarhide say, and I wanted to reach through the phone and strangle him.

"Don't listen to Dollarhide," I yelled. "He's always lost! I've known him all his life!"

"Now you tell me!" Mark shouted. "I'll just turn around here."

"Jesus!" I could hear Dollarhide yelling. "What are you doing?"

"Turning around!"

"We're on an interstate!"

I called Russ and explained what had happened. *"North Carolina!"* Russ yelled. "Does he understand the governor is supposed to be here in forty-five minutes?"

"You're at the park?"

"Yeah."

"What's it look like?"

"A park. There's a lake. It'll work. *If I had a cameraman!*" He sighed. "I'll shoot it on the digital if I have to."

He had one of our little Canon digital cameras with him.

"You don't think the governor will think it's odd that we dragged him into this park to shoot with that tiny thing?" The Canon was a palm-sized camera.

"I think he'll think it's less odd than if we drag his ass out in the middle of nowhere and don't have *any* camera."

He had a point.

Joe came out of the meeting. "How's everything going?" he asked.

"A few little problems but it'll work out," I told him.

"You're not a good liar," he said and laughed.

"Okay. Mark was going to North Carolina by mistake and we don't have a cameraman."

"Anything I can do?"

I thought about it. "Well, Mark's driving about a hundred

miles an hour, I imagine. So if he gets arrested, you might help get him out of jail."

"Never heard of the guy. Keep me posted, okay?" He smiled and walked back into the meeting.

Somehow it all worked out. Mark and Dollarhide arrived moments before the motorcade and were setting up when Bush arrived. He knocked the script off in a few takes and took off. Mark made it to Atlanta, though not before getting in trouble with the authorities for the second time (the first being when he did indeed get stopped for speeding) when he refused to put the film through a metal detector at the airport and made a little scene, finally relenting when large men with guns started arriving. By the next morning, the finished spot was on its way to stations across South Carolina.

It was an ad that ended any chances for McCain's candidacy. We ran it in South Carolina, then changed it slightly and aired it in places where McCain hadn't even run his original attack spot comparing Bush to Clinton. We discovered that it didn't matter whether you had seen the McCain spot or not. The response was self-explanatory.

GEORGE W. BUSH: Politics is tough. But when John McCain compared me to Bill Clinton and said I was untrustworthy, that's over the line. Disagree with me, fine. But do not challenge my integrity. I'm a leader and reformer who gets results. I fought the education establishment for high standards and local control, and won. While Washington politicians deadlocked, I delivered a patients' bill of rights. I challenged the status quo to reform welfare and cut taxes. I fight for what I believe in, and I get results.

Two days after we aired the spot, the McCain campaign realized they had made a huge mistake by responding, and an even bigger mistake by trying to link Bush to Clinton. They announced that they were pulling all negative ads. But it was too late. It simply wasn't credible to go from chest pounding, we're-going-to-beat-their-brains-out rhetoric to unilateral disarmament when it appeared you were getting the worse of the exchange.

We won South Carolina 53 percent to 42 percent. A few days later we were shocked when we lost Michigan 50 percent to 44 percent. We had always assumed, for one reason or another, that whoever won South Carolina would win Michigan. We just forgot to explain this to voters in Michigan. But it was McCain's final hurrah. The candidacy unraveled, stretched too thin for too long.

7 Times Have Never Been Better, Vote for Change

"I DON'T KNOW, GOVERNOR, they just make my butt itch," Jim Ferguson said.

Governor Bush had just asked Fergie what he thought of the Gore campaign commercials.

"Why's that, Fergie?" Governor Bush asked.

"Just the way he looks." Ferguson shrugged. "I get that butt-scratching feeling."

We were in Kennebunkport, Maine, in one of the cottages on the Bush compound. Jim Ferguson had come up from New York with the Young & Rubicam copywriter Janet Kraus. It was the middle of June 2000.

Ferguson had met Bush once before, when Jim had brought his thirteen-year-old daughter to a film shoot at his ranch. They seemed to hit it off from the start, talking about Texas high school football and the joys of ranch life. Jim had explained that he intended at some point to retire from Young & Rubicam and move back to his hometown of Hico, Texas.

When we finished filming, the governor asked Jim if he wanted to stay for lunch.

"I'd love to but my daughter and I are driving back home," Jim said.

"How far is it to Hico?" the governor asked.

"Oh, we're driving to New York," Jim said.

"Right now?" Bush asked, laughing.

"Right now. Just the two of us." Jim put his arm around his daughter.

"In your little convertible?" Bush asked. Jim drove a Mercedes convertible, a style popular with Beverly Hills housewives and upper-echelon drug dealers.

"It's going to be great, ain't it?" Jim asked his daughter. She smiled but seemed a bit unsure. "I'm taking her to Graceland on the way," Fergie promised.

Governor Bush had come to Kennebunkport for his mother's seventy-fifth birthday party and we were using the trip to shoot commercials, talk about the upcoming convention and prep for the debates. We'd had a good spring, an amazing one, actually. At the end of the primary, the conventional wisdom was that we had been beaten up badly and pushed to the right by the process, and that we were headed into the general election as damaged goods. This was in contrast to Gore, who had emerged stronger from the primary, having shown that he was tough enough to beat back a serious opponent. Of course, Gore had also had the luxury of being attacked from the left, a godsend for a Democrat, so that he had won the Democratic nomination *and* established that he was more conservative than Bradley.

But a funny thing happened in the spring. The Gore campaign seemed not to have the remotest idea what to do once they won. It was as though Al Gore had suddenly become Robert Redford in *The Candidate*, who, having triumphed, looks around and asks, "Now what?" It was a syndrome that usually afflicts underdogs who never really expect to win or novice candidates who suddenly find themselves thrust onstage. But Al Gore? This was a guy who had been planning to be president since he was a kid. Now he was the Democratic nominee, the vice president at a time when the economy was booming and the country was at peace, *and he couldn't think of what to do next?*

The press speculated that it was Gore's *style* that was hurting him with voters, but his real weak point was a lack of substance and message, which forced people to focus on his style. Not very likeable people with odd personalities get elected all the time—New York mayor Rudy Giuliani is a perfect example—if they have a compelling message. Both David Dinkins and Ruth Messinger ran and lost to Rudy by spending most of their time trying to prosecute him for being a jerk. The problem was, you could believe Rudy was a flaming asshole and still vote for him because Rudy's message of taking back control of the city was so powerful. Gore had yet to come up with a persuasive message, so people focused on his personality, which seemed to have been manufactured in a laboratory.

We had filled the postprimary period with a series of big and little policy proposals, some new, some recycled and freshened up with new "nuggets" as Josh Bolten, head of the policy team, called them. It was a methodical strategy steered by Karl and Josh. Since the summer of 1999, Karl had been working on a postprimary plan for the campaign. As part of this, he was constantly trying to perfect a single planning calendar that would chart all aspects of the campaign. This had gone from being a simple calendar program printout to an elaborate, multicolored document of legendary complexity. At each meeting, it seemed a new element was added to the calendar.

"Do I get a decoder ring with this thing?" Joe Allbaugh asked one day when the newest version was handed out by Karl's whiz kid, Israel Hernandez of Eagle Pass, Texas. Israel was the keeper of the calendar and there was more than one meeting when the only people who could really interpret its nuances were him and Karl, and probably just him.

"It's simple," Karl would begin, which meant it was going to be incredibly complex. "Everything in black is the governor's schedule. Green is for the governor's speeches and announcements, blue is for holidays and special events and black are events in the House and Senate and miscellaneous themes."

There was a pause as everyone tried to digest this. "I think black is being used for both the governor's schedule and the events in the House and Senate," Josh said. "Or are there different shades of black that I'm just missing?"

"I'm sure there's a reason for this," Karl said solemnly. He looked at Israel, who always sat just behind him at the message meetings. "Israel, what's the answer?"

"The governor's schedule is in *bold-faced black*," Israel explained.

"See!" Karl cried. "Simple."

No one really knew whether the policy proposals would have much of an impact. The odds were that they would simply not register with voters in the postprimary lull, and there was a constant debate as to whether we were doing too much or wasting good policy at the wrong time. But Karl was convinced that it was critical to keep unveiling a steady stream of new details throughout the spring, and the pace he established was fierce. During the last two weeks of March, Bush gave a speech offering new details on his reading initiative; spoke on the need to support teachers; released a plan called "Strong Teachers, Strong Schools"; gave a major environmental speech focusing on the cleanup of brownfields and unveiled a bundle of proposals on taxes, health care and expanding home ownership for low-income families called "A New Prosperity Initiative." On subsequent days he provided more details on these proposals so that there would be a fresh news hook each day.

It worked, which surprised everybody but Karl. Not that

anybody outside of a few journalistic nerds could recite the details of A New Prosperity Initiative, but the overall impression began to soak in that Governor Bush was out there with smart proposals to fix things that were broken. It cast him as an activist, an agent of change who believed government could be part of the solution, not just the problem. It helped that the proposals received consistently high marks for substance, even from those who disagreed with his philosophy.

In the middle of the primary fight, Bush's fav/unfav had been only ten points to the good, 49 to 39, according to ABC News/*Washington Post* poll numbers. By July, it had improved twenty-one points, to 61 percent to 30 percent. Gore, during that same time, had stagnated to 45/35, this despite the fact that Gore, as vice president, had an ability to command attention and make news far greater than a Texas governor who was still waiting to receive his party's nomination.

"But what the hell is this race about?" Fergie asked. He and Janet Kraus, Karl, Mark, Russ and Karen Hughes were sitting outside the inn where we were staying in Kennebunkport. We had planned some filming the following day and were going over different themes and scripts.

"You haven't figured it out?" Mark laughed.

"Hell no. You're the client. You got to tell me why the chicken tastes good and I'll tell you how to sell it. Did I talk to you about Kentucky Fried?" he asked. Kentucky Fried was a big Y&R client.

"I want to know why they dropped rotisserie style," I asked.

"You know the night of the convention," Fergie said, "when the governor goes over the top in delegates and they cut to that shot of him watching television in his room."

We all nodded. This was a classic shot. It always happened.

"I was wondering if maybe he could have a big ole bucket of KFC in his lap. Don't you think that would be great? Really connect with people."

"Or maybe he could wave a Twister at the camera," Janet said. She had been working on Twisters, a new KFC delicacy.

"You want it, Fergie baby," Karl said, "you got it."

"Great. So what the hell is this race about?"

"Reasonable change," Karl said.

"That's a hell of a slogan," Fergie said. "We could do up a logo in gray. Maybe gray on gray."

Karl laughed. "But that's what people *do* want. They aren't looking for revolutionary change like 1994 and they don't think the country is going to hell. But there are things that trouble them."

"What about 'Times Have Never Been Better, Vote for Change,' " I suggested.

"I love that," Janet said. "Bored with peace and prosperity? Vote for change."

"You're right," Karl said, "these guys should be winning this thing in a walk. We shouldn't even be in this race. But we are. People do want change, they just want—"

"Reasonable change," Janet said. She pulled out a few pieces of paper from a thin briefcase.

"Janet worked up some stuff," Fergie said.

"They aren't scripts," Janet explained. "I call them theorems." She shrugged. Then she picked up one of the pieces of paper and began to read. She had been an actress once and was a good reader.

"Now is the time to do the good stuff," Janet read. "Once in a hundred years, a nation has this chance. To be at peace. To be in prosperity. And to have the focus and resources to do something good with it all. We could just lie back and enjoy an easy run. But for George W. Bush, this is the time to tackle the tough stuff. Right here, right now, we can be making our country a better place for everyone's lives. Should we look for new ways to make Social Security as certain and valuable for our grandkids as it will be for us? Should our schools make high achievement a goal for every kid? Isn't this a time—when we have the time—to test new ideas? Fresh approaches? To make life better for everyone, for all time? We have the leadership. We have the ideas. But we may never have another chance in our lives to make it happen."

Janet had several others, each one touching on a different large theme that the campaign might explore. They all had elements that could be turned into ads.

"What does this race have to be about for us to win?" Karl asked.

"Strong leadership," Karen said. "People consistently see the governor as a stronger leader than Gore." She was right. When voters were asked who was a stronger leader, Governor Bush consistently topped the vice president by at least twenty points.

"Strong leadership for what purpose?" Mark asked. "Why do we need a strong leader?"

"To do the tough things," Janet said. "To take on solving the problems that don't get solved."

"Like Social Security," Karen said, "and education, when we keep spending more money and scores get worse. Medicare reform—"

"And prescription drugs," Karl added. "So we establish him as a strong leader who not only has a plan to fix these things but the guts to get it done."

"Guys," Fergie said, "what about 'prosperity with a purpose'? That's a great theme. We can't make the case that the governor is going to improve the economy. We can't fix what ain't broke. So don't we have to talk about using the prosperity for a higher purpose? It's like my kids. They have everything in the world they want, but what does it mean?"

"Write something," Karl said. "Let's try it."

"I was afraid you'd say that," Fergie said.

We talked for a couple of hours, batting around different ideas. It always came down to the dilemma that had existed in the race from the beginning—in a time of peace and record prosperity, how do you get a nation to vote against the status quo and in favor of change, especially when the agent of that change is new to them? There was no one simple message that we could drive home over and over. Somehow we had to piece together elements of different messages and hope it would be enough to get us over the top.

That night after dinner, when we were hanging out in the bar of the little inn, I made a list of what we needed to do to win:

1. Make sure people trust GWB enough to be president. Stop Gore from disqualifying him.
2. Make taxes an issue and win it.
3. Win or tie on education.
4. Not lose on health care/prescription drugs/Medicare.
5. Win or tie on Social Security. Use SS to define leadership.
6. Tie on guns/environment/abortion.
7. Win on character/honor/integrity.

Then I made a list of what Gore needed to do to win:

1. Raise just enough doubts about GWB.
2. Make himself the less risky choice on the economy.
3. Win on prescription drugs/Medicare/health care.
4. Tie on education.

5. Not lose on character/honor/integrity.
6. Win on Social Security.

Then I tried to be honest about who was more likely to accomplish each goal.

Make sure people trust GWB enough to be president. Stop Gore from disqualifying him. We could do this, unless there was some defining moment in the campaign, like a disastrous debate performance. People wouldn't think that Bush was a stronger leader, which they did, if they didn't believe he was up to being president. Gore would always win on experience—he had to if only because he had more of it—but lack of experience is something voters are consistently willing to overlook if they believe the person is up to the job. Experience is a trailing, not a leading indicator. Dukakis didn't lose because he didn't have the experience, he lost because he was judged as smaller than life and too liberal.

Make taxes an issue and win it. This was tough. We would win taxes, that was easy, but it was going to be tough to make taxes a driving issue in the race. People wanted a tax cut, sure, and our base loved it, but it wasn't motivating many swing voters.

Win or tie on education. No Republican in modern history had done this. But we had a shot. People understood that Bush was passionate on the issue. In the primary debates, education questions always brought out the best in him. Still, history wasn't on our side.

Not lose on health care/prescription drugs/Medicare. This was hard. Basically it would be a battle between reforms proposed by Bush and more money promised by Gore. It was hard to bet that reform would come out on top.

Win or tie on Social Security. Use SS to define leadership. They didn't call this issue the third rail of politics for nothing. Yet Bush had proposed what would be the most sweeping reforms in the program's history. It wasn't hard to imagine Gore tearing us apart on this in the fall.

Tie on guns/environment/abortion. This we could do, or even win when you considered that the pro-life and Second Amendment types were incredibly motivated. Gore was already discovering that every time he opened his mouth in public on guns and abortion, he lost conservative Democratic voters in states like Michigan and Pennsylvania. These were battles Gore would probably fight more under the radar screen, through phones and mail. He'd win the environment, but it wouldn't be a major factor in the race.

Win on character/honor/integrity. We could do this. We *had* to do this. The problem was that it was too easy for Gore to limit his downside.

For Gore, each of his goals was either easy or not much tougher than easy.

Raise just enough doubts about GWB. He would not be able to disqualify Governor Bush, but could he raise enough doubts with suburban swing voters to make them stay with the status quo?

Make himself the less risky choice on the economy. The economy was roaring. He was vice president. Easy.

Win on prescription drugs/Medicare/health care. He was a Democrat, for crying out loud. They always won on these issues.

Tie on education. He was a *Democrat*. Easy.

Not lose on character/honor/integrity. This shouldn't be too hard. Monica hadn't been under *his* desk. Sure he had waved the pom-poms around on the front lawn of the White House after Clinton was impeached, but our focus groups tended to discount that and gave him credit for being loyal. Damn focus groups.

Win on Social Security. Right, like this would be tough.

You know what was really depressing? The things that

weren't on the list. No *welfare reform,* no *crime,* no *national defense,* no *save us from the evil empire.* These were the issues, along with taxes, that had been electing Republicans since World War Two. Now, they weren't even on the radar screen as potential wedge issues. National defense was still a huge crowd pleaser and there was no question that we would win overwhelmingly among those who considered it a top issue, but would the fall campaign be a debate on national defense? Not very likely.

It was basically a miserable political environment in which to elect a Republican president. No national security crisis, people weren't up in arms over taxes, crime had all but disappeared, welfare reform was yesterday's news. Instead, all the big issues were of the classic Democratic safety net variety: Medicare, prescription drugs, Social Security. Realistically, there wasn't a reason in the world that Gore shouldn't win this thing in a walk.

This was why in August at the annual meeting of the American Political Science Association, every academic analyst predicted Gore would win the race. The *Washington Post* did a major story headlined "Academics Say It's Elementary: Gore Wins." The political scientists used models to predict the race that "have proven highly accurate in the past. Several of the formulas have repeatedly been more accurate than even election eve public opinion polls."

"It's not even going to be close," said one of the academic teams with a superb record of forecasting the results.

☆   ☆   ☆

"He's not going to do that," Bush laughed. "No way."

"Governor, that's what he does," Karen said. "It's his style."

Bush shook his head. "Interrupt like that?"

"Worse," Senator Gregg said.

This was the second of two debate prep sessions we were having at Kennebunkport. Senator Gregg had snuck into the Bush compound, ducking low to avoid reporters, since we didn't want to advertise that debate preparations were underway. They had actually begun in May under Karen's direction. She had outlined a format that was working well—we'd do twenty minutes to a half hour on one subject with Senator Gregg playing Al Gore, then break, analyze the responses and move on to another subject.

It was interesting to see how eager Bush was to dive into the prep sessions. He seemed to really enjoy the encounters with Senator Gregg and liked it when Gregg took Gore-like nasty shots at him and the Texas record. I'd wondered whether Senator Gregg, who in real life is a quiet, extremely pleasant guy with a wry sense of humor, could match Gore's level of bombastic self-promotion and cutting barbs. But he was great. Before each session he would listen to tapes of Gore on his Walkman, and he'd mastered Gore's patterns and tendencies to an eerie degree.

We had a serious advantage over the Gore team given the amount of material to study on Gore. We simply had more game film on the other team. A group at the Republican National Committee put together a five-hundred-plus-page tome analyzing Gore's performance over the years. They studied his debates in 1988, 1992, 1996, 2000, plus twenty-two appearances on *Meet the Press,* nineteen appearances on *This Week,* sixteen appearances on *Face the Nation,* a showdown with John McCain on *MacNeil-Lehrer NewsHour* in 1988, three *Nightlines* and a bunch of other shows.

Gore had earned a rep as a successful debater based largely on his trouncing of Ross Perot on *Larry King Live.* And in the primary he had decimated Bradley in the Iowa debate when he lied—as he often did—about Bradley's opposition to flood relief for Iowa.

But these were only the most notorious examples of Gore's alleged prowess as a debater. I had watched every one of his debates going back to 1987 and had come away convinced the guy was way overrated. Let's face it, how much credit should you get for beating a nutcase like Perot or an amiable but hapless politician like Bradley? Everyone who ran against Bradley looked good—that's how Christie Whitman had gotten started, when she came out of nowhere and almost beat him in 1990. When you looked at Gore's debates with his Democratic opponents in the '88 race, Gore never won a single one, though he did manage to inflict pain, which seemed to be his primary objective. He was like some steroid-crazed football player running around dying to put a lick on anything that moved, not caring whether or not it helped him win. Against Dan Quayle and Jack Kemp, Gore certainly hadn't lost, but he hadn't scored resounding victories either and nobody was drafting Quayle or Kemp into the debating Hall of Fame.

It was fascinating to see how Gore's debating tactics repeated themselves. He relied on well-rehearsed themes that he returned to again and again. When he was on his game, it gave a consistency to his constant attacks. But often it sounded robotic and disingenuous. He attacked relentlessly, often with snide, personal digs intended to fluster and embarrass his opponents. In his opening statement against Quayle, he managed to bring up both Bentsen's "You're no Jack Kennedy" jab and a "deer caught in the headlights" reference. He accused Bradley of racism, attacked Dick Gephardt in 1988 for flipping on abortion just as he himself had earlier done, made fun of Jesse Jackson for being a preacher and was the first to use the Willie Horton pardon against Dukakis, when he,

Dukakis and Jackson were running in the New York primary and it had particular resonance.

He lied in debates, knowing it would more often than not flabbergast his opponents. And he had a very accomplished manner of lying. The classic example was when he scolded Quayle for voting for legislation that he himself had voted for, which left Quayle all but sputtering. He accused Bradley of supporting raising the retirement age on Social Security when Gore himself had voted for legislation that did exactly that. He was consistently mendacious about his record on abortion, something that had driven his debating opponents crazy since 1988. When trapped in a lie, Gore's technique was to simply deny it, understanding that there was not a referee who would correct him. And he appreciated how much it frustrated his opponents, giving him an advantage.

Gore loved to badger and interrupt his opponents. He used annoying tricks like rustling paper in front of a microphone when the other guy was speaking, but his favorite was to end his responses with a question for his opponent. If his opponent ignored the question, Gore often interrupted, asking why he was refusing to answer the question. And if an opponent took the bait and actually answered the question, Gore would interrupt to correct the opponent.

It was this last technique of Gore's—the badgering, the interrupting—that we were practicing in Kennebunkport that morning. Senator Gregg had mastered Gore's technique of ending his response with a question, and now was following up his question with a constant refrain.

"Why don't you answer the question, Governor?" Pause. To the audience, "We haven't heard the answer, have we? Governor, are you going to answer the question? Governor?"

Bush finally started laughing. "Won't the moderator stop him?"

"Maybe," Robert Zoellick said, "but you can't count on it." Zoellick was a foreign policy and trade expert who had been brought in to help. He was focused, no-nonsense and wicked smart.

"You can't look to the moderator to help," I said. All of us on the prep team had talked about this and agreed. It was a natural instinct for Bush to play by the rules and expect the same from his opponent. Bradley had been the same way, as had Quayle and Dukakis and Gephardt. But when Gore ignored the rules of the debate, as he frequently did, and an opponent turned to the moderator for relief, it invariably looked weak, as though he was looking to be bailed out.

"You can't run up and down the court signaling to the ref," Condi Rice added. She was a very serious sports fan.

The governor held up his hand. "Got it. Let's try it again."

I was playing the moderator and I asked another question, directed at Senator Gregg. "Mr. Vice President, as a result of investigations into the Clinton–Gore fund-raising, twenty-one people have fled the country, eighty-three people have pled the Fifth Amendment under oath, twenty-four have been indicted and fourteen convicted. Given this record, how can the American people trust you on campaign finance reform?"

I loved asking Gore tough questions—even a fake Gore. It was deeply gratifying.

"There are two candidates on this stage and unfortunately, only one of us supports McCain–Feingold campaign reform . . ."

Gregg had Gore *nailed*. That was exactly how Gore would answer—he'd ignore the question and just launch into an attack on Bush. At the end of his answer, Gregg turned to the governor and said, "Will you join me tonight in pledging that you will make McCain–Feingold your number one priority?"

The governor started in on his answer and Gregg interrupted. "Why can't you answer this simple question? Why can't—"

"Mr. Moderator," Bush pleaded, "tell him to quit bullying me. Please?"

We all cracked up. Over the next twenty minutes, the governor tried different responses to Gregg/Gore's interruptions. He tried pausing and smiling, as though dealing with a child who was being rude. That didn't work because Gregg/Gore would jump on the silence and fill it with his own answers. He tried turning to Gregg/Gore and admonishing him not to interrupt. But that was ceding control to Gore, letting him dictate the flow of the debate. What seemed to work best was for Bush to continue to talk over Gore, ignoring him while raising his voice just enough to be assertive.

"When you do that," Karen said, "Gore looks petulant. It frustrates him."

"I *am* petulant," Senator Gregg insisted. "I *am* frustrated."

Bush practiced it several times. It was like watching a pitcher learning a new pitch, getting more comfortable with the motion until finally he had it mastered.

Logan Walters, the governor's assistant, interrupted to say that Dick Cheney was on the phone. Bush left to take the call at the main house. These kinds of interruptions by Cheney had become more and more frequent as the vice presidential selection process accelerated. We sat around in the little cottage and talked about everything but why the governor was taking the call. It was always that way. There seemed to be an unstated rule that *no one* discussed the vice presidential pick, not even in the idlest, most gossipy way. I think everybody thought that it was like getting married—if he wanted our opinion, he would ask. Otherwise it was just bad form to speculate.

When Bush returned, he was very upbeat. "This is great," he said. "Finally."

We glanced around the room at one another. Had he made a decision? Was he going to tell us?

He played out the moment. "Great news, just great." He looked around at us, knowing what we were wondering. "I talked to the guys at the ranch. Got a lot of rain. The pond is filling up." He laughed. "Let's do some more. You ready, Mr. Vice President?"

☆   ☆   ☆

Janet and Fergie both came up with scripts while we were in Kennebunkport. Janet had written three spots taken from her "now's the time to do the hard things" theorem, one on education, one on Social Security and one that she called an "anthem" for the campaign.

"An anthem?" I asked her. "Really?"

We were having breakfast before the shoot at the terribly cute inn in Kennebunkport where we were staying. Janet was smoking and looking a lot more chic than anyone else in Kennebunkport.

"Yeah, you know. Anthem." She shrugged. "Do you think I'm not supposed to smoke in here?" she asked.

I loved these guys. They knew how to package everything. We would have called it just another spot, but when you styled an ad as an "anthem," it automatically sounded grander, more powerful.

"Don't you call big theme spots anthems?" she asked.

"I will now," I promised.

Janet's scripts were neatly printed out; somewhere she had found a printer to hook up to her computer. She handed them to me.

GOVERNOR BUSH *on Camera;* TV 30;
"Hard Things—Education."

How come the hard things don't get done?

Because they're hard.

If we really want to make sure no child gets left behind in America, we need the courage to do some tough things.

We need to raise standards in our schools.

We need more accountability, more discipline.

And we need to stop promoting failing kids to the next grade because we've given up on them.

It's easy to spend more.

Let's start by expecting more.

GOVERNOR BUSH *on Camera;* TV 30;
"Not Afraid."

Social Security.

For too long, too many politicians have been afraid to touch it.

I'm not.

Because we need to strengthen it, right now.

We need to give people more choices in how they build their nest eggs.

I have a plan.

Protect the benefits of retirees and near-retirees.

You earned it. You get it. No change. Period.

And if you're part of the next generation, you should have the choice to put some of your Social Security in a personal retirement account *you* control.

It's time to make Social Security more secure.

GOVERNOR BUSH *on Camera;* TV 60;
"Moment in History"

There aren't many moments in history when you have the chance to focus on the tough problems.

We're in a moment like that now.

But to make schools better for all children—it takes fresh ideas.

To strengthen Social Security—it takes the courage to try something different.

It's not always popular to say, "Our kids can't read."

"Social Security isn't doing all it could."

"We have a budget surplus and a deficit in values."

But those are the right things to say.

And the right way to make America better for everyone is to be bold and decisive, to unite instead of divide.

Now is the time to do the hard things.

While I was reading, Fergie came down to join us at breakfast, dressed in his usual cowboy boots, jeans and linen shirts. "You gotta have a look in New York, Stevens," he had told me, "and this is my look." He downed an orange juice in one gulp and then started writing on a paper place mat. Janet and I looked at each other and shrugged.

"So great to see you too, Fergie," she said.

A few moments later Fergie handed us his place mat.

"Here's mine," he said. At the top, he'd scribbled "Something's Missing." It went like this:

Something's missing in America.
    Something's just not quite right.

It's hard to say exactly what. But Americans know it . . . deep down.

Our wallets are full but our hearts are empty.

It's a time of peace but we're not at peace.

Our national symbols are no longer symbols of pride.

It's time we put the heart back into America.

Time to take accountability in our actions.

Time to make Social Security secure again.

Time to educate our children.

Time to be proud again.

Now's the time to elect George W. Bush President of the United States.

I read it over. I loved it. "Is the governor talking?" I asked.

"Are you nuts? It's an announcer, for Chrissake. Can I get sausage here?"

"Fergie, you can have whatever you want."

"I'm on a diet but what the hell. I have to go to the Cannes Advertising Festival and be a judge next week. That's a big deal, you know."

Karen joined us and I passed her the scripts.

"When you wear those thongs on the beach," Fergie asked Karen, "do you put that little triangle thingie in the front or back?"

☆　　　☆　　　☆

We spent the afternoon filming former President and Mrs. Bush. The goal was to get material for the convention film about the senior Bush—we'd decided to make a film about the three living Republican presidents, Ford, Reagan and Bush— as well as the centerpiece film on Governor Bush, which would run just before he gave his acceptance speech.

We were working from outlines rather than scripts, and

the idea was to get everything we needed in interviews with the former president and Mrs. Bush. The location we'd picked was one of the cottages on the Bush compound. By moving around the camera, we could create the impression of more than one setting. We could film Governor Bush in a warm and informal setting, with books behind him (which was important because we didn't want the shot to scream Maine), and former President and Mrs. Bush with a large plate glass window that overlooked the sea behind them.

While waiting for the lighting to be adjusted, George Sr. was relaxed and funny.

"Ready for the A team to show 'em how it's done," he cracked, loud enough to make sure his son overheard.

Though former President Bush couldn't have been more informal and cordial, there was something about having a *president* in the room that affected everyone. We were all going about our business but it was like being at a small party with a famous actor—it just changes how everyone acts, if only because you are concentrating on not letting anything change. We all believed that there was a very good chance that Governor Bush would be president but President Bush *had been* a president. It was different and I wondered how we would all react if a few months from now, George W. Bush became president. It would change everything, even for those who were closest to him, like Karen and Karl.

Of course, he understood that better than most candidates, having seen it up close. I think he had a bittersweet feeling about how his life would change if he won. In New Hampshire, he had talked a lot about the sacrifices it took to run and the press had jumped all over him, saying he sounded homesick, questioning if he had what it took to win. He quit trying to talk about it in public, but it was easy to understand what he was feeling. He *enjoyed* his life, wanted to protect his family and knew that his life and his family would change in ways that were impossible to imagine. Ten years ago, he never would have predicted his life would take the turn that it had. For anyone who wasn't completely defined by their ambition—the Clintons being the perfect example—becoming president must, on some level, be terribly daunting and disconcerting.

Russ interviewed President Bush—they had known each other since Russ worked for him in 1988. When Russ asked him about the White House and the role of the president, his jaw tensed a bit and he looked off camera for just a beat. He talked about how the presidency was bigger than any one man and how even in the thick of Watergate when people said respect for the White House would never return, it did. Russ prompted him a little on the Clinton years and he just raised a hand, as if batting the question away. He wasn't going to touch it.

"What's it like to know that your son might be president of the United States?" Russ asked.

The former president started to answer then turned away, his eyes full of tears. He smiled apologetically. "Sorry," he murmured.

Several of the crew, a bunch of battle-hardened pros Laura Crawford had brought up from Texas, looked down or away, their eyes watering.

Later, when we were about to film Mrs. Bush and everyone had commented on how nice she looked, which she did, Mark asked her with a smile, "Does anyone ever tell you that you don't look great, Mrs. Bush?"

"Oh, yes," she said, smiling, "but they don't last long."

8

Start Me Up

THEY WERE OVERDRESSED. I knew this would happen. It always did.

We were doing a live remote shot of Governor Bush beamed in from a school near Columbus, Ohio, on opening night of the Republican National Convention. The idea was to have the governor say a few words about education, then introduce Laura Bush, who would also speak on education. Every night of the convention had a theme, and Monday's opening night was, you guessed it, education.

The remote had seemed like a great idea back in Kennebunkport when we were thinking of ways of making sure the governor appeared in prime time every night, while maintaining the tradition of not appearing at the convention site until the day before his acceptance speech. We had made a real effort to analyze every aspect of the convention with one motive—what would most help George W. Bush get elected? That may seem simple, but conventions are like the ultimate wedding from hell, when every member of the family has a different idea of what you should wear and some want to quote from the original mass in Latin while others are insisting on Kahlil Gibran.

Andy Card, who was running the convention, had begun with the goal of making Governor Bush the only elected official who would speak at the convention. "It'll never happen," Andy had cheerfully admitted, "but it's a good starting point." From the very beginning, Andy had insisted that every night of the convention needed to reveal personal information about George W. Bush, reveal some aspect of his background, his personality, his values. Andy was one of those guys who was easy to underestimate. He never came on with a lot of pyrotechnics and never was one to pull an Al Haig. But when the day was done, he had invariably gotten what he wanted, usually with a minimum of heartache and bloodshed. He had a perfect operating style for the Bush world—effective, low-key, informal and low-maintenance. He wasn't a guy who needed or wanted a lot of attention.

I'd worked with Andy in the last gubernatorial race in Massachusetts when he had come in to help, much as Don Evans had in the current Bush campaign. He was a close personal friend of Paul Cellucci, the former lieutenant governor who had become governor when Bill Weld resigned to become, he thought, ambassador to Mexico. The Cellucci race had been a nasty, complicated one which we had every reason to think we would lose. Sometimes in a race you are absolutely certain of the right course of action, and it all comes down to execution. I love races like that, even if you lose. At least you know you lost *trying* to do the right things. The Cellucci race was more of a curveball: all over the place, hard to define, difficult to understand. But Andy was rock solid and always backed us up, even when we didn't have a clue whether what we were doing was smart or dumb—usually it was a little of both.

The whole concept of doing a live remote from the school was odd—broadcasting from a high school *at night?* The obvious question was, What the hell were those kids doing in a classroom at 8 P.M. when they ought to be home studying? But we liked the idea, so we decided not to care.

"They have classes at night for kids, don't they?" I'd said to Karl.

"You mean like night school for high school students?" Karl asked skeptically.

"I'm sure it happens all the time."

"What do you know? You don't have kids." Karl laughed.

"People will get the joke," I said, trying to convince myself. "Nobody is going to be so literal, right?"

"You tell me," Karl said.

But right now the question of what we were doing in a high school at night wasn't my biggest concern. What had me worried was that the kids who had volunteered to be in the scene had shown up dressed like they had escaped from a fashion spread. And there was another small catch: a few of them looked to be in their early twenties.

"These *are* all students, aren't they?" I asked one of the teachers.

"Well, all of them went to school here, yes."

Went? Like five *years ago?*

"Oh," I said. "And they kind of dressed up a little."

The teacher looked at me. "Of course they did! They're going to be on national television, aren't they?"

Some of them will, I was thinking. The ones who look old enough to be on *Friends,* I'll stick off in a corner or right behind the governor.

People love to dress up for television, it's just a fact of life. In the 1996 presidential, we had planned a big event to film Bob Dole at a college gym in Iowa and the crowd, despite being told to dress casual, showed up mostly in coat and tie. Of course. It was Iowa, this was a presidential race, they were going to be on television. We didn't have time to send everybody home, so I went to a Target down the street and bought two thousand dollars' worth of sweaters and shirts. The manager came out and shook my hand. It was their largest single sale ever. Then we lined everybody up like some kind of Red Cross relief program and handed out the stuff. The sensible Iowans were happy to oblige and only wanted to know one thing: Could they keep the clothes?

I thought about trying to do the same thing for our high school kids, but we didn't really have the time. Anyway, with a little luck, nobody would notice. Or they'd be so busy trying to figure out what the hell twenty-two year olds were doing in a high school classroom in the middle of the night that they wouldn't be worried about the fact that they looked like they were auditioning for a fashion show.

The great horror of remote uplinks is that there is no room for error. Everything is live and if any one of about a dozen things go wrong, even a momentary glitch, it's a disaster. If there is a delay in transmission of even thirty seconds, that leaves the whole world watching a blank screen, waiting for the soon-to-be nominee of the Republican party to materialize out of cyberspace. If the audio is delayed and the video is fine, that's even worse—he looks like an idiot. Or there could be a power blackout or . . .

We were two minutes from the broadcast and we were still having problems. Ostensibly, I was in charge of this for the campaign, but in truth I was useless. If the entire transmission setup suddenly burst into flames, I might have been able to throw some water on it, but anything more technical than that and I was utter dead wood.

"Everything okay?" Governor Bush asked. He could tell the mood was tense. The head of the satellite uplink crew was whispering furiously into his microphone, talking to his counterpart in Philadelphia. It was also getting very hot in the room and everybody except the governor was starting to sweat. A lot. We had fans going but mostly all they did was make a lot of noise. I was kicking myself for not bringing in portable AC units.

"It'll work," I told him.

He laughed. "Who are you trying to convince?" He was perched on a stool and he looked restless but not particularly annoyed or troubled. He always seemed restless when he had to sit or stand in one position for very long. He had a kinetic sort of energy that needed to be released through activity.

"Look," I tried to joke, "only forty or fifty million people are watching. No big deal."

He shrugged and then turned around and started talking to the kids behind him. We had arranged the shot so that he was in front of the kids who were sitting at desks. The desks, for some reason, seemed exceptionally small, so that some of the larger guys looked as though they had been jammed into kiddie desks. Originally the plan had been for Bush to sit, so that he would be on the same level as the kids, but he had rejected that notion, preferring to stand. That meant he would be on a different level than the kids, which might be good, since he would block more of them, but also might look odd, like some kind of foreshortened Diane Arbus photograph. I was hating that we had ever considered doing this uplink. There was a reason nominees never appeared on opening nights. The gods of history were angry with us.

"Who's working this summer?" the governor asked the kids, trying to get them to talk.

A couple of 'em are probably registered stock brokers, I was thinking.

"Tell me everything is going to be okay," I whispered to the director of the satellite operation.

He looked at me, sweat pouring off his face. "I've never screwed one of these up yet," he said.

"That means the law of averages is against us," I told him.

Then suddenly he smiled. "We're up."

The two minute broadcast went well enough and afterward, standing in the classroom with the kids, we watched Laura Bush give her speech. The governor was beaming. He pointed out how she was using all three TelePrompTers—left, right, center—with ease, though later we learned that the left one was partially obscured by some of the confetti that had been dumped as part of her introduction. He phoned her as soon as she stepped offstage. "You did great!" he told her, then held up the phone. "Wasn't she great?" he asked the kids who had watched it with us and they cheered and clapped. "You're a hit in Ohio," he assured her. He stayed for an hour or so talking with the kids and their teachers about everything from baseball to vouchers for private school.

I went outside and started to fall asleep, slumped against the school. There was a faint breeze and it felt wonderful to be out of that hot, crowded classroom. Someone from the neighborhood wandered over to see what was going on. "Why are these kids here at night?" he asked sharply, as though he had stumbled onto the set of some kiddie porn film. I tried to explain what we were doing. He looked to be in his late seventies and was wearing a battered Ohio State baseball hat. "You're telling me George Bush is in there?" he said accusingly.

"Yes."

"But what are the kids doing here *at night?*"

I gave up.

In seventy-two hours, George W. Bush would be giving his acceptance speech.

☆   ☆   ☆

Political conventions are strange subcultures that exist for a few days and then, thankfully, evaporate. It's the badges and credentials that are the worst part. The proper tags hanging around your neck bestow inordinate prestige and access and then suddenly they are as worthless as last year's Mardi Gras beads.

Everybody wants the right credentials. People you haven't seen in years are suddenly your best friends, and obscure relatives emerge from hiding, demanding passes to the convention. Why? To take part in an event that is interesting only for an hour or so, and even then is probably best watched on television. It's all about proving that you have access, like getting invited to the right party even if you don't want to go. In that way, it's like Hollywood culture at its worst, only with far less attractive people.

For over a year, our Austin crowd had seen one another every day, on the road, in Austin, in scores of message meetings, in early morning spin sessions and now, suddenly, it was as though the whole world was crashing our party. Who are all these people, I kept thinking, watching the endless scrum that snaked through the sky boxes, everybody eager to seem like a real insider.

The Bush plane arrived on Wednesday morning, after another remote uplink on Tuesday evening, this one from Dwight Eisenhower's former office in Gettysburg. As the plane taxied to a stop in front of the mandatory arrival ceremony, Bush looked out at the crowd through the plane windows. "Who we got here?" he asked. "Who's greeting us?"

"Well, there's George Washington, James Madison, Ben Franklin . . ." Gordon Johndroe, one of the press aides, said. He pointed to the period figures who were part of the arrival ceremony.

The governor laughed. "Excellent, Gordo."

We were all in a good mood and why not? The poll numbers were outrageously good, 43 to 39 percent in our favor and sure to get better over the next week. They always did during your convention, unless you mixed in a major riot or two with your nominating speeches, like the Dems in Chicago 1968. There are maybe three to five defining moments in a campaign. Some you can't choose—when Ed Muskie started crying in the snow, it was hardly on that day's schedule. Or when Ronald Reagan grabbed the microphone and declared, "I paid for this microphone, Mr. Green!" it was as close to open field running as you get in politics. They gave him the ball, he headed for daylight.

The convention speech would be one of those moments.

Mike Gerson had hidden himself away at the Bush Library at Texas A & M to write the speech, returning with a wild look in his eyes and a first draft. Then the inevitable revision process started, and by the time I first heard it, at the governor's mansion on an incredibly hot July day, Mike was into something like draft sixteen. I had just returned from New York where I was editing the convention film. Having been away for a couple of weeks, there was something reassuring about finding everything more or less as I had left it. The governor was impatient, Karl was running late, Gerson was nervous, chewing on a pencil and incessantly doodling, Karen was dealing with some reporter who was about to write a lousy story, Mark had been on the road and looked exhausted, Josh was carrying three massive notebooks and looked even more tired than Mark. The governor had just returned from a Southern swing, the last stop being in Lafayette, Louisiana, and everybody was talking about how hot it had been. I was incredulous.

"Hotter than Austin?" I asked.

"It was like *The Bridge Over the River Kwai*," Mark said. "The airport hangar was like where they put prisoners to punish them."

Karl and Karen were both talking on cell phones, dealing with the crisis of the moment, when the governor finally announced, "I'm just going to give this speech and if anybody wants to listen, that's fine." He was standing up and eating a peanut butter and jelly sandwich.

Josh, who looked like he was about to fall asleep, spoke up. "I'll listen, Governor."

"Thank you, Josh. I hope it won't bore you."

"If I look like I'm dozing off in the middle, I'm really just concentrating extra hard," Josh assured him.

I was the only one who hadn't heard or even read the speech, except for sections that Gerson used to read me when I'd run across him at the hip coffee shop around the corner from the campaign. He'd sit in the back near the Free Tibet posters, chewing on his pen and scribbling madly, and no one seemed aware that there was an actual Republican in their midst.

A podium with two TelePrompTer screens had been set up in the small parlor where we usually met. Finally, when the fires of the moment had been extinguished, the governor did a full run-through. It's not an easy thing for the person practicing to take rehearsals of this sort seriously. It's a bit like putting on a play in your own living room. You needed a crowd, some tension, a stage, but Bush was focused and surprisingly intense for a hot afternoon when he'd already given a couple of speeches.

"So?" Karen asked, looking at me when the governor had finished.

"It's terrific," I said. It really was.

"Really?" Karen laughed. "I was watching you, you didn't show much emotion."

"I was concentrating. Guys, it's a great speech. I'd tell you if I didn't like it."

"He's a glass-half-empty guy," Mark reminded them.

"You really like it?" the governor asked.

I did.

Mike wanted to change the order of some of the passages and we went back and forth on that, but it was all minor stuff. I mostly stayed out of it; there was nothing worse than someone coming into a writing process at the very end with a different vision. And they were just playing around the edges, tweaking things. The speech worked.

Probably because he had been around the big leagues of politics and has good instincts, Bush was graced with the two qualities that help good pro quarterbacks—he could see a lot of the field at once and he understood the natural rhythm of the season. He knew when to lay back—despite the pressure always to do more—and when to pour it on. Now Bush was preparing for the acceptance speech with an intensity that matched his debate prep focus. This was classic Bush management style. Unlike a lot of candidates who are consumed with the moment-to-moment ebb and flow of a race, he understood that much of what seemed important at any given moment in a campaign probably didn't matter in the least. But there would be a few big moments, and when the spotlight was on there would be no excuses for failure. If the acceptance speech or the debates went badly, that could cost him the election.

The Gore people loved to make fun of Bush as a slacker, but in truth, I bet Gore's hyperkinetic, meddlesome nature drove them nuts. Here was a guy who woke his staff up at 4 A.M. to insist they make the spot he just wrote on a nuclear arms treaty *right now*. This is a quality that is amusing in poets but downright dangerous in a president. *Hey guys, wake up, I've got a great idea! Let's bomb some country!* (In the final endgame of Florida, when Gore seemed determined to transform himself into the ultimate precinct boss of America, his dual inability to grasp the big picture and to let professionals do their jobs probably cost him any chance he had.)

I suggested renting a hall in Austin and practicing the speech with taped crowd sounds to prepare for the reality of giving a speech in front of thousands of screaming, crazed supporters. It was the sort of thing I half expected him to reject as contrived. But he was willing to do it, if we could keep it private, no press, no gawkers. "I don't want an audience for this thing," he said.

"We can keep it quiet, Governor," Karen assured him. "Like the debate preps."

"The press knows about that," he shot back with that familiar teasing look.

"We told them!" Karen laughed.

"Likely story. Okay, fine, let's do it."

We used a large ballroom on the ground floor of the Erwin Center at the University of Texas, the same hall that had been used for the Cheney V.P. announcement. Austin was crawling with reporters, and I was terrified that at least one enterprising sort might be tracking the governor's movements and appear, notebook in hand, to inquire what the hell we were doing. But amazingly, even in a small place like Austin, we seemed able to move around without attracting attention, though the Secret Service was careful to use just a couple of cars, no motorcade.

The hall was outfitted with a booming sound system that was deafening at full volume. Mark and Karen and Gerson sat on folding chairs in the big, empty space and I stood in the rear with a sound technician, cuing him when to hit the crowd sounds. We used a sound effects CD that had everything from wild applause to taunting jeers. Logan Walters, the governor's assistant, introduced him. "Ladies and gentlemen, the next president of the United States!" As Bush walked onstage, he was greeted by an avalanche of boos.

"Jesus Christ," I mumbled, frantically trying to find the right track on the sound effects CD.

"They hate it, Gerson!" Bush yelled.

"Sorry," I yelled, as the hall filled with wild cheers. Bush took a step back and motioned for louder cheers.

"More, more!" McKinnon yelled.

He went through the whole speech nonstop as we alternated applause and cheers at points we were confident the crowd would respond. We had talked about the speech being a duet between himself and the crowd and told him that it was critical to gauge when to pause for the crowd and when to continue, raising his voice to surf over the noise. There was one section in particular toward the end where we fully expected the convention hall to be going absolutely wild. It was when he started a refrain of "but it won't be long now." Here's how it went:

The wait has been long, but it won't be long now.

A prosperous nation is ready to renew its purpose and unite behind great goals. And it won't be long now.

Our nation must renew the hopes of that boy I talked with in jail, and so many like him. And it won't be long now.

Our country is ready for high standards and new leaders. And it won't be long now.

An era of tarnished ideals is giving way to a responsibility era. And it won't be long now.

I know how serious the task is before me.

I know the presidency is an office that turns pride into prayer.

But I am eager to start on the work ahead.

And I believe America is ready for a new
beginning.

He practiced this section a couple of times, as the crowd
noise swelled under him. Even though we were in this empty
hall with a canned crowd, my heart started racing as though it
was a pregame pep rally. It suddenly hit me—this is for *real*.
He's going to step out there and give this speech and the
whole world will be watching and *he's going to knock 'em
dead*.

☆   ☆   ☆

"As songs about vibrators go," Russ Schriefer was saying,
"I think it's probably one of the better ones, don't get me
wrong."

It was a couple of hours before Bush's acceptance speech
and we were in the bowels of the Philadelphia Convention
Hall going over the final details of the program, from fireworks to music. Russ had just noticed that on the minute-to-
minute countdown for the evening, the Rolling Stones's "Start
Me Up" was scheduled to play immediately after Bush's acceptance speech.

"Do you think anybody really knows that?" David Nash
asked. David was the pro who had been on-site in Philadelphia before we won the nomination and had helped put together every Republican National Convention over the last
twenty years.

"Well," Russ said and laughed, "maybe not. But who's
going to defend it if the *Times* writes tomorrow, 'Governor
Bush's acceptance speech, in which he spoke of the era of
personal responsibility, was followed by a Rolling Stones song
generally assumed to be an ode to a vibrator.' "

One of the women in the meeting—there were all these

people running the convention and those of us from Austin never could figure out who half of them were—said, "Maybe that would help us."

Everybody around the table looked like those soldiers in war photos, the ones who have been on the front line too long. There is really nothing in live television production like a political convention except, perhaps, the Olympics. Even though the networks had cut back on their air time, cable channels were covering it from gavel to gavel. It was like putting on a four-day play on national television cast only with amateurs, most of whom had never done anything like this before and never would again.

Russ had been in Philadelphia for weeks as the Austin message guy. This meant that he was the point person squeezed between all the nutty ideas we came up with in Austin and the nutty ideas proposed by the rest of the world. There is something about conventions that make normally sane people lose all contact with reality. Million-dollar-a-year lobbyists suddenly decide that George W. Bush will be the next president of the United States only if Elton John performs "Philadelphia Fever" at the convention. Or a governor of a major state is convinced the way to win the Irish Catholic vote is for U2 to make an appearance. Many urgent conference calls are convened on these topics.

I'd be in New York deep into editing the convention film and I'd get a call from Austin or Philadelphia saying that there was a very important conference call in fifteen minutes. Once on the call, I'd discover that the topic was whether or not it would be better to have Arnold Schwarzenegger or Bruce Willis open the convention dressed as Benjamin Franklin reading from the Declaration of Independence. This would be discussed for an hour or so and only at the end would somebody mention that, of course, as with Elton John or U2, *no-*

body had actually contacted these people. Nobody had asked Arnold how keen he was to appear in a powdered wig on national television. Nobody had actually asked Elton John (who probably hated Republicans more than he hated growing old) or U2 (who, despite the fact they come from a country that can't even govern itself, seemed to have quite a few opinions on how to perfect the world) whether they would love nothing more than to perform in front of a few thousand Republican yahoos in Philadelphia for free. These conference calls were like talking to people on hallucinogenic drugs, only they *didn't realize* they were on drugs.

Democrats have it so much easier. They have tons of legitimate film and rock stars just dying to show off at their conventions. Not Republicans. I was complaining about this on one of the interminable conference calls when someone excitedly announced that Ted Nugent wanted to play at the convention.

I groaned. "Don't we have anyone who maybe has been on the cover of *Rolling Stone* more than *Guns and Ammo?*"

"Will he bring large-caliber weapons with him onstage?" Russ asked. "That could be impressive. We could do a balloon drop and he could try to shoot them all."

"I thought U2 was playing," somebody said.

"What about Elton John?"

"Is Michael Jackson singing on education night or national defense night?" (Yes, there was actually a movement to get him to perform at the convention. Great idea, huh?)

Russ had been dealing with all this in his calm way for weeks.

"If we don't go with 'Start Me Up,' " David Nash said, "we could use 'Cup of Life.' That's the World Cup song," he explained patiently when our stares made it clear we had no idea what he was talking about. "It's uptempo, a little Hispanic feel. Good stuff."

"I don't understand how this is going to work after the governor finishes speaking. Is he offstage before Chaka Khan starts singing?"

For some reason, Chaka Khan was closing out the convention. Which was fine by me; better than Ted Nugent.

"We'll have movement issues," Nash said, "if she's going up the stairs and the governor and his family are coming down the stairs."

"Stairs?" one of the talent coordinators said. "Chaka doesn't do stairs. She's coming up in the elevator or she isn't coming. This has been made very clear by her people."

There were both stairs and an elevator servicing the stage area.

"I'm more worried about the podium going down," Nash said.

The podium was designed to rise from underneath the stage.

"After the governor finishes speaking, we drop the podium, to get it out of the shot. But he has to step back far enough or he goes down with the podium."

This was a *truly* terrifying image.

We pointed this out to the governor during the final walkthrough late that afternoon.

"Don't worry," he said, "I won't fall through." You could tell he thought our concern was crazy. "It drops, there's a big hole, I won't step in it."

"But there's going to be a lot of confetti," Mark said.

"And the mother of all balloon drops," I added.

He looked at us and suddenly I felt like a doddering, overprotective parent suggesting that a grown son wear *two* overcoats in case one is stolen. "I'm *not* going to fall," he said. "And if I do, it's your job to say we planned it that way."

We walked through all the details. The plan was to show the film just before the speech. Then toward the end of the film, the governor would enter from stage left, unannounced and, hopefully, unnoticed. As the film ended, he would suddenly appear, backlit, revealed for the first time to the crowd. If it all went as planned, it had the makings of an incredibly dramatic moment.

"The other option," I said, "is for you to rise up *with* the podium as it is raised from down below. We could pump smoke and play the theme from *2001: A Space Odyssey.*"

"Let's do it." He laughed. Then he looked out at the convention floor where delegates were milling about, surprised to find the nominee in their midst. "This is going to be great," he murmured.

☆   ☆   ☆

From my position in the lighting booth, I had a perfect view of the screen as the last moments of the film played. "I want to remind Americans how fortunate we are to be Americans," the governor said, bouncing around in an old Ford Bronco on his ranch. The film looked fabulous.

At past conventions, multiple-panel screens had been used as the big projection screens at conventions. These were basically scores of television monitors linked together to form one giant screen. By playing different images on each monitor, past campaigns had achieved stunning mosaic effects, but when the convention films had been shown, the lines separating the monitors became clearly visible, creating a checkerboard effect. This looked terrible. Which didn't matter to anyone in the convention hall, since they were so in love with the candidate they would have cheered if the film had been shown on a single thirteen-inch television screen. The problem was with the networks and how they covered the convention film. Ideally, we wanted them to take a direct video feed of the film, which would guarantee that the audience at home saw the highest quality version of it. But in recent years they had started refusing to accept the feed and instead would cover the convention film as if it were another convention speaker. This meant that they used cameras at the rear of the convention hall and simply shot the screen on which the film was being broadcast. When the screens were of the checkerboard design, the film looked terrible.

We hated the way the checkerboard screens looked and had gone to great lengths to seek an alternative. David Nash had contacted Phillips, which had developed a new plasma screen that was, in essence, a giant LCD. He and Russ had flown to San Francisco for a test and came back absolutely raving about the clarity.

"The only potential hitch," Nash had warned, "is that no one has ever really used them and they might not work. The whole thing could be a disaster."

But we had taken the chance and now, watching the film, it was clear they'd made the right call. The screen was huge and the clarity was astounding, almost like watching HDTV. The core of the film was a long interview filmed as Bush drove a 1970 Bronco around his ranch. Wayne Forster, the cameraman, had sat in the passenger's seat and I'd crouched in the rear of the bouncing SUV and asked Bush questions. There was something about being in motion that made the whole interview process less stilted and more like a normal conversation between two people as they drove around in the country. Bush had been relaxed and expansive, playful and eager to talk. Wayne had kept the camera very tight and you could see him sweating and the wrinkles around his eyes as he squinted in the July sun. It was intimate, a side of George W. Bush that most people never saw.

Watching the film, I thought that maybe we might have finally come close to capturing the real Bush, or at least a part of him that would ring true to those who knew him well. The sound track of the film swelled over a final montage of great moments in twentieth-century American history, from Kitty Hawk to the moon landings. All during the primary, we had struggled unsuccessfully to find a piece of music to use as a theme for the campaign. For the film, I'd contacted a composer named David Horowitz in New York, who had scored many of the most successful commercials in ad history.

"Why don't you send over some footage and a script and I'll noodle around a little," David had said.

"Well, there really isn't a script. But I'll send you some footage."

"What kind of feel do you want?" he asked.

"American," I said. "Very American and big but intimate. A touch of the West." I thought I was babbling but he was used to people who can't really talk about music describing music. It happens all the time in the ad business.

A few days later, Horowitz called and said he had "a little something to listen to." I stepped off the elevator in his office at Broadway and Twenty-eighth Street and heard a melody playing. It reminded me of Aaron Copland, simple but strong.

"Is that our stuff?" I asked. David was chain-smoking as usual, sitting behind his desk with a keyboard linked to a synthesizer. He was a huge Yankees fan and his office was filled with a combination of music awards and baseball memorabilia.

He motioned for me to sit. On the television screen above his keyboard, scenes we had sent him of the governor at his ranch began to roll. David played along on his keyboard. It was exactly what I had hoped for but couldn't articulate—very American, powerful but not grandiose.

He played a couple of minutes then stopped, waving his cigarette. "Like that, got it? Whatcha think?"

It was perfect. Later, for the final score, David wanted to

bring in a small horn section to give more texture to the syn-thesized score. "Is it worth the money?" I'd asked.

"When you hear it with the big speakers and see it on the screen, it'll be worth it."

And now it was. I was so involved in the last frames of the film that I almost missed seeing Bush walk out onstage. It went perfectly—the crowd didn't notice him until the film ended and the back lights came up, highlighting him, just as we had planned. The hall exploded.

In the theater, there's a phrase directors use called "hold-ing the moment." It means knowing how to work with the au-dience's attention, not hurrying it, playing off the crowd but not overplaying your hand. Not many untrained actors do it well, and often Bush seemed a touch embarrassed by the adu-lation of large crowds and either hurried through the moment or sort of hammed it up in some fashion, laughing and joking around.

But that night he held the moment. He looked happy but serious, without the boyish "aw shucks" quality that was part of his charm. If I had been a Gore guy, hoping that Bush would boot the speech, I would have given up any hope right then. He was going to give the best speech of his life—you could just smell it. Jim Ferguson and Janet Kraus were up in the lighting booth with me and Fergie leaned down and yelled over the applause, "He's gonna goddamn slay 'em." The light-ing engineers kept looking nervously at Fergie, not a small guy, who due to some eye infection was wearing a patch over one eye. Clearly they had visions of Fergie stumbling over one of the massive cables snaking over the floor, plunging the stage into darkness. I could sympathize. They had worked on this thing for months and the last thing they needed was some guy who looked like a hip pirate literally pulling the plug on their show.

We had decided to keep the convention hall dark during

Bush's speech. The idea was to increase the drama of the moment and to make it difficult for the network cameras to focus on anything but the guy who was standing on the stage. Normally the convention hall remains well lit and it enables the cameras to roam at will, looking for the best reaction shot. Or what the *networks* think is the best reaction shot—it could be someone crying, but it could just as easily be someone looking bored or distracted. That was the problem with staging a convention—you couldn't cast the damn thing. If we could have filled the hall with actors, I wouldn't have been so worried. But real people, well, they were unpredictable and this was not a moment to leave anything to chance.

Bill Klages was the convention lighting designer, the winner of seven Emmys. I was standing next to him with a text of the speech, trying to cue him when to expect the crowd to react so that he could trigger a starburst light effect that would sweep the convention hall with flashing, staccato lights, which invariably made the crowd roar even louder. It's the sort of thing they do at rock concerts all the time and was borderline inappropriate for this kind of speech, a bit like using a disco ball at church and spinning it during the really good parts of the sermon. But the speech was going to be an hour long and it was better to use every trick in the book to keep the level of excitement high than to run the risk of having reporters sense that the crowd's interest had lagged.

We were five minutes into the speech when the networks started phoning, raising hell about the hall being too dark for their reaction shots.

"What do you think we should tell them?" Klages asked me, covering the phone with his hand.

"I think it looks great," I said.

"So do I," he nodded, then, into the phone, "We thought about it and we've decided you can go screw yourself. Okay?" He hung up the phone. "What's our next cue?" he asked.

When the speech was over and the first balloon drop was coming down and the fireworks were starting to go off inside the hall—that was one of David Nash's little tricks, using fireworks *inside* the hall, which had not pleased the Secret Service—Bush stepped back and the podium dropped down. From our vantage point high in the lighting booth, we had a clear view of it going down, leaving, for a moment, a gaping hole in the floor.

"What if he falls through?" Janet Kraus yelled, laughing.

"He's not going to fall through," Russ and I said together but we were both holding our breath until the floor closed up.

Curiously, there was a strong breeze sweeping across the lighting platform. Probably they had cranked the ventilation fans to the max to clear out the smoke from the fireworks that had made the Secret Service so nervous. (When one of the technicians had protested that they were harmless, an agent had suggested that he volunteer to sit on top of a box of them while the agent lit the fuses.) "Cup of Life" was blasting through the speakers and the stage was crowded with Cheney and Bush family members. I had the chart detailing the sequence of postspeech balloon drops, confetti and what the sheet called "PYRO." In bold letters under the section for the confetti cannons and the pyro was written SHOOT NOTHING TOWARDS STAGE. God help some poor confetti cannon operator who got a little confused and pointed his confetti in the wrong direction. They would probably be taken out by one of the Secret Service snipers perched in the rafters. The last note on the cue sheet was SHOOT WHAT'S LEFT.

It was an apt enough metaphor for the stage of the campaign we were now entering: Shoot what's left. We were in the endgame. There was nothing worth holding back now.

Back at the campaign hotel late that night when Karl walked in, looking exhausted, the bar crowd, all Bush campaign people and Republican foot soldiers of one type or another, started applauding. It startled Karl and he looked around to see who had walked in. Then it hit him that *they were applauding him*. McKinnon, Matthew Dowd, Russ, Laura, the whole Maverick crowd, started chanting "Rove, Rove, Rove!" and laughing. Karl looked our way and shook his head with a look that said "you guys will pay." But out of our four days in Philadelphia, where everything had been scripted and planned and designed, that little eruption of gratitude, respect, camaraderie—call it what you will—was one of the most spontaneous and genuine moments of the whole affair.

Fourteen months earlier, Karl had diagrammed it all on a napkin and now at least part of it had come true. George W. Bush was the Republican nominee and we were ahead of the incumbent vice president.

Rats, Moles and Bad Polls 9

W HEN ARE YOU GUYS GOING TO ATTACK?" Jay Carney of
Time asked.

It was the day after the Republican National Convention,
and we were on a train from Pittsburgh to Akron, Ohio. It was
an odd scene—we'd all slept only a few hours the night before
and it was like the aftermath of a wild Mardi Gras party that
had gone on for days, with people sprawled all over the train.
The idea was to go from Pennsylvania to Michigan and stop
along the way for a few "spontaneous" small rallies and a couple of major ones. The train was equipped with tons of satellite gear and in between stops, Bush and Cheney, who both
looked surprisingly chipper would be giving interviews both
to the nets and to media in key markets in swing states.

Everybody was wondering when we would hit back at
the Democrats. Even before the Republican Convention was
over, the Dems had started running some very nasty ads. They
had two lines of attack—trying to paint Dick Cheney as a rabid
right-winger and going after Bush's Texas record.

The Cheney attacks, we were convinced, were a total
waste. The notion that somehow they were going to turn the
low-key, amiable Dick Cheney into a hated figure was pre-
posterous. It wasn't going to work. The guy you saw on television on *Meet the Press* came across as eminently reasonable; 191

plus, the press *liked* Cheney. They weren't going to participate in some feeding frenzy to demonize him. The attacks were based on votes Cheney had cast years earlier as a congressman and as attacks go, they were awfully weak stuff. First, nobody outside of Wyoming even *knew* that Dick Cheney had been a congressman. To the extent he had a public profile, it was as defense secretary during the Gulf War. So first the Dems had to educate people that he had been a congressman, then convince people he had done terrible things as a congressman, then try to establish why this mattered fifteen years later and, by the way, forget about the Dick Cheney you came to respect and admire during the Gulf War.

"You know the great thing about these attacks against Cheney?" I said to Carney.

"Tell me how much you like them. I want to hear this, Stevens."

"They completely legitimize going after Gore's congressional record. Those votes he cast that the NRA loved so much, the votes against abortion, the pro-tobacco stuff, now we can go after all that stuff if we want and they can't say, 'Hey, that's ancient history. What's it have to do with anything?' If long-ago congressional votes count for Cheney, they sure as hell count for Gore."

"What about the Texas record attacks?" Carney asked. "You can't tell me that won't work."

Gore was attacking the Texas record on every front imaginable. His health care attack was typical:

ANNOUNCER: The issue: health care. Al Gore is for a real patients' bill of rights and a prescription drug benefit under Medicare.

George W. Bush says no.

He sides with the big drug companies, the HMOs and the insurance industry.

In Texas, Bush even opposed health coverage for
two hundred thousand more children.

Texas now ranks second to last in America for
children with health insurance . . .

And last for people with health coverage.

George Bush—his plan protects special interests
instead of working families.

The truth was that we didn't know whether this line of
anti-Texas attacks would work. My gut feeling was that it
would be very hard to convince people that Texas was a negative. The model for these attacks was the 1988 Bush campaign against Dukakis, but Texas wasn't Massachusetts. There
was just too much positive mythology embodied in Texas.
People *liked* the idea of Texas. It was the Alamo, *Lonesome
Dove,* independence, cowboys, the Dixie Chicks and Lyle
Lovett, Tex-Mex. People understood that Texas was different
and, sure, rich, arrogant Texans were hated, but Texas wasn't
a national joke or some primeval swamp. It was one of the
fastest-growing states in America, a leader in high-tech jobs.
And if things in Texas were so bad, how come so many people
were moving there? Thirty-five thousand people had moved to
Austin alone in 1998. The state was *booming.*

"Don't you think it's a little odd that Gore is attacking the
second-largest state in America? Let's get this straight—the
country is doing great except the second-largest state, which is
a virtual hellhole. This make sense to you?"

"It's going to be a slaughterhouse." Carney grinned, clearly
relishing the thought. "Trained killers."

He was spouting Donna Brazile's line of the past week
about Gore campaign headquarters: "I call this the slaughterhouse. They may look like gentle people. But they are killers."

"We don't have a chance," I said. "We're gonna get killed."

Karl walked by on his way back to the railroad car that we

had discovered had the most comfortable seats. This had quickly been dubbed the "nap car."

"You guys scared?" Jay asked. "Stevens says you're going to get killed."

"Don't have a chance," Karl agreed. "But I'm going to take a nap first, okay?"

"I'm coming with you," I said.

"Carney, you look terrible, go to sleep," Karl teased.

"How can I sleep, this is too exciting." He leaned back and closed his eyes.

☆　　　☆　　　☆

It's customary for each party's nominee to keep a low profile during the opposing party's convention. For the governor, this was easy—he spent the convention at his ranch outside of Crawford, which is so low a profile that you have to drive twenty miles to get cable television. The first two days of the Democratic National Convention we spent in debate prep sessions at the ranch. Senator Gregg flew in to play Gore and the usual debate crew—Condi, Josh Bolten, Karl, Karen, Mark, Robert Zoellick, Don Evans, Larry Lindsey, Gary Edson—assembled. The heat was stunning. It seemed to drain every bit of moisture out of your body and made it hard to focus on anything else. Josh rode one of his motorcycles out from Austin and had to stop along a shady section of the road. "I thought I was going to die," he marveled. "I've never been so hot in my life. It was like riding a heater through an oven."

Our focus was preparing for a debate with Tim Russert or at least for a Russert-style, *Meet the Press* format, with the candidates sitting around a table with a moderator. It was a totally different experience than a podium debate and one the governor was convinced he preferred. In almost any situation, he'd choose a more casual setting over a formal one, from debates to dinner. The consensus seemed to be to push for one debate with Russert, one podium-style debate as proposed by the Presidential Commission on Debates and one debate with Larry King.

The commission was insisting on three debates and appeared unwilling to negotiate on anything, from the locations to the format. All of us resisted the idea of having these terms dictated by an organization that had no formal authority and that seemed to be acting with a certain imperious arrogance. In 1996, Clinton agreed to only two debates, and we were prepared to go to three plus two vice-presidential debates. It was also hard to see how anyone could think that proposing a Tim Russert debate was a cop-out. Nobody had a rep for being tougher than Russert. As for the Larry King option, the Gore people had bragged for years about how Gore destroyed Ross Perot on *Larry King Live,* so they were certainly invested in the legitimacy of King as a moderator.

I was all for not accepting the terms of debates as mandated by the commission but was against the Russert debate for two reasons—it was wildly unpredictable and Russert, while he may not have liked Gore, was a former Democratic political operative and still saw the world through a Democratic prism. He intuitively thought a big tax cut was bad policy and was suspicious of education reforms like school vouchers. It wasn't even conscious, it was just part of his DNA. The format was potentially lethal—it had no time limits or restrictions on follow-up questions and allowed Russert the freedom to grill either candidate on any subject for as long as he liked. Plus, Gore had debated Bradley with Russert and had done shows like *Meet the Press* a million times through the years. To me, we were asking to play an away game with very high risk.

But everyone else was convinced that the format would be an advantage for the governor. "And most important,"

Karen pointed out, "the governor thinks that. He wants to go toe-to-toe with Gore in a loose setting. If that's what he thinks will be the best format, he'll be the most comfortable."

Who could say? It was one of those situations where you had to follow your best hunch. There was something terribly passive about just accepting the commission's proposals that ran counter to every political instinct to mold a situation to one's best advantage. Gore had been clamoring for debates ever since he clinched the nomination, at one point proposing that he and Bush square off twice weekly, which would have made for no fewer than sixty debates. This was typical of the silly, disingenuous stuff Gore threw out like schoolboy taunts. He had said on Russert that he would love to debate Bush on the show. So now we would call his bluff.

The mocks at the ranch were held in a cramped cabin stuck out in a field that the governor was converting to a gym. There was always something slightly comical about assembling in this little house in the middle of nowhere. It had a tiny kitchen, a full weight set and two uncomfortable single beds. We brought in three chairs and a table to replicate the set of a Russert show and everybody else either piled onto one of the beds or sat on the floor.

We tried to replicate as closely as possible exactly how Russert ran his show, including using video clips of particularly embarrassing statements or quotes. We set up a little combo television/VCR on the small table, and playing the Russert role, I'd open up a line of questioning by running a piece of the tape. Sometimes it would be just a quote, other times a clip from one of the primary debates or a news conference or a piece from a speech.

After the Monday afternoon session, we went back to the small house where the governor and Mrs. Bush were staying while their house was being built. We had hamburgers—Karl cooked on the grill—outside on the patio behind the house. A breeze had picked up as it usually did in the early evening and in the shade of the porch with the sun setting, it was suddenly very pleasant. I was starting to understand how you could fall in love with this landscape. There was something very appealing and distinctly western about its extremes and rough edges. It was utterly without pretense, barely domesticated and once it got under your skin, I could imagine that there would be something unsatisfying about more processed environments.

Inside the house, the telephone kept ringing with friends calling to joke about the things the Democrats were saying at their convention. Senator Gregg asked the governor if he was planning to watch any of Clinton's speech that night and he laughed. Friends were coming over from Midland and the Bushes planned to watch a movie.

He seemed completely at ease, not in the least anxious about the grueling stage that the campaign was about to enter. I believe that he thought he probably would win, but if he didn't, he still had a life he loved and a piece of the world carved out for himself near Crawford that he found deeply enjoyable and satisfying. I could understand why he wanted to come back to this place as much as possible—it was everything the outside world wasn't. Peaceful, strangely beautiful, predictable, dominated by nature. It was a perfect haven.

☆   ☆   ☆

That night I watched Clinton's speech from the hotel gym in Waco, the closest town to Crawford that had hotels. It was all so delicious—an interminable speech in which Clinton barely mentioned Gore, followed the next night by Jesse Jackson and Ted Kennedy. What more could you ask for? The Dems were in the same position Republicans had been in back in '96 and '92, needing to use their convention to solidify and energize their base. It was a terrible predicament for any party to be in and was a sign of fundamental, near desperate weakness.

We knew Gore would get a bounce out of his convention. Monday night with Clinton and Tuesday night with Kennedy and Jackson weren't going to help the Democrats much, but once they moved on to Lieberman, whom we all agreed was a very smart choice, and Gore, their numbers would start to pick up. If Gore had a good night on Thursday, we figured they could move ahead of us by four or five points from the three to six points they were behind at the moment, depending on which polls you believed. Then, as their bounce faded, we hoped they would slip a point or three, possibly more, behind us by the Labor Day polls.

Internally, we were practically obsessed with the Gallup post–Labor Day poll. For months when we were ahead, we had touted to reporters—and one another—the historical fact that whichever candidate was ahead in the Gallup post–Labor Day ended up winning the race. It had been true in every presidential election since Gallup started polling, with the exception of Reagan versus Carter in 1980, when Reagan was a point behind, still within the margin of error. Lately, watching the polls narrow, we had gotten nervous enough to drop the subject publicly, but it was something we still were anxiously watching. It wasn't as though we figured we would lose if we were four or five down in the poll—it just would make us all feel a hell of a lot better to be ahead and would save us from having to concoct some elegant spin to explain why we had been wrong all year in pointing to the Gallup numbers as a significant historical indicator. I was confident we could come up with a spin—you could spin anything if you did it with enough confidence—but it would be one of the more tortured spins.

It was partly to boost the Labor Day polls that we had decided to go up with a heavy ad buy the week of August 21. Our thought was to let the Dem convention bounce settle down for a week, then go up with our stuff. We were opening with two education spots, one with Bush on camera, one a voice-over. It was important to go out with education first, if only to draw attention to the emphasis we were giving the issue. We still felt that if on Election Day we were tied or close with Gore on who could do more for education, there was no way we would lose. It wasn't really that the issue was that powerful, it was more like a key vital sign indicating whether or not we were healthy. Gore was going to try and paint Bush as a right-winger who couldn't be trusted on social issues from education to Social Security. If we were holding up on the education front, it was a sure sign we were strong.

But the positive ads wouldn't work on their own. There had to be negative information about Gore in the political bloodstream, something to remind people of what they didn't like about the guy and keep him from surfing the positive national mood. We were really running not against Al Gore but against that mood. Consistently, we were getting no more than 25 to 30 percent of voters who thought that the country was on the right track, but Gore was only getting about 17 percent of people who believed the country was going in the wrong direction. The math was easy—if on Election Day voters were split fifty-fifty between those who thought the country was going in the right direction and those who thought it was going in the wrong direction, we would win in a landslide. But every time positive indicators like consumer confidence rose and the number of right-track voters increased, our share of the voter pie decreased. It was like swimming upstream, and you could only go so fast against a wicked current.

Mondale had the same problem in 1984 when he ran in a very positive environment. His solution had been to try to convince everyone that things weren't as good as they seemed. That, plus *promising* to raise taxes, made for a disaster. We knew we'd fail if we were the pessimistic candidate, and besides, Bush was a natural raving optimist. Our hope lay in talking about how things could be *better*—like education, Social Security, Medicare, defense—and in forcing Gore into a position of defending the status quo in areas that people knew needed improvement. People may have thought that the country was on the right track, but they damn sure didn't believe education couldn't be improved, or Medicare was perfect, or Social Security was in peachy shape or that the country's military had never seen better days.

Gore should have been winning in a landslide, that was obvious. Something was blocking him from benefiting from a political environment that was ideal for an incumbent party. His problem seemed to be an indeterminable mix of Clinton's baggage and his own personality and lack of message. There was something about the guy that bothered people, and for some strange reason he had been unable to articulate why he should be president in a consistent, compelling manner.

We couldn't control whether or not Gore might suddenly wake up and latch onto a powerful, coherent message. But we could remind people why they didn't like Gore.

Alex Castellanos was working with the Republican National Committee to make the ads for the RNC's independent expenditure campaign. The DNC was doing the same thing, only they were using the same guys—Bob Schrum's firm—to make both Gore's ads and the DNC's ads. Federal law required some separation between the campaign and the independent expenditure, a law whose spirit, if not letter, had been blatantly disregarded by Clinton, who had actually written DNC spots in 1996. The Gore people never really explained how Schrum could make an ad for Gore one minute and an ad for the DNC in support of Gore the next and remain independent from himself. They just shrugged and said, in essence, "so what, sue us." And since the FEC had proven during the Clinton-Dole campaign to be about as serious about enforcing the law as a bouncer at spring break checking IDs, they knew they could get away with doing whatever the hell they wanted.

Meanwhile Gore kept saying that campaign finance reform was his number one priority, which highlighted his basic problem: He really *would* say anything to get elected. Here was a guy who had passed the hat at a Buddhist temple—which he still denied, even though his aides admitted it, the Secret Service admitted it, the Buddhists admitted it—and who was still trying to say with a straight face that he was taking the high road on campaign finance reform.

Alex, who never needed a road map to the jugular, had made two very effective spots that nailed Gore's hypocrisy and mendacity. One used footage of Gore running for president in 1988 in which he appealed to tobacco farmers to vote for him since he was one of them. Clips of this famous speech had been shown before on the news, but the RNC had gotten ahold of the original footage and it was just spectacular. Here was Al Gore *begging* these tobacco farmers to vote for him, telling them how he had raised tobacco all his life, and even how he had *sold* tobacco. Alex had cut this footage together with shots of Gore at the 1996 convention trying to hold back tears after describing his sister's death from smoking, pledging that he would fight tobacco with his dying breath. But it had been four years *after* his sister died of lung cancer that Gore gave his "I'm one of you" pro-tobacco pitch to the tobacco farmers.

I loved the spot.

The other was taken from an interview Gore had done with NBC correspondent Lisa Myers, in which she asked Gore whether he or Clinton had ever told a lie as a politician. What Gore said wasn't as important as *how* he said it and how he *looked*. He hemmed and hawed and couldn't give a straight answer. In thirty seconds, it was everything you didn't like about Al Gore. The interview, we understood, was from 1998.

The rough plan was for the RNC to run these ads shortly after the Democratic convention, the idea being that they would help squash any bounce from the convention. They would run in more or less the same states as our positive education ads. It was a good plan.

☆   ☆   ☆

"The RNC doesn't want to go with the Gore tobacco spot," Matthew said.

This was a few days after the Democratic National Convention and Gore was enjoying a big bounce. *Very* big.

"Why?" We were at headquarters in Matthew's office.

"It didn't test well in the last focus group. And people were nervous."

I hated this. Of course a focus group didn't like it. Negative spots always tested terribly. Who was going to sit there with a group of strangers and yell, "Yeah, I love that spot where you rip the guy's heart out and eat it on camera! Can we see that one again?" But the spot would work, I just knew it would.

"But the Lisa Myers spot, that's okay?"

"People *love* that spot," Matthew said. "It tested better than anything."

Of course, I quickly seized on this as proof the spot worked. "I knew it would work," I said.

Matthew laughed. "It's being shipped today."

All day I felt better knowing that this little love note was in the mail. We needed it. In the CNN/*USA Today* polls, Gore's fav/unfav had gone from 52/42 on August 5, the day right after the Republican National Convention, to 64/30 after their convention, compared to Bush at 60/34. This was a total shift of *twenty-four points* in two weeks. We couldn't let him float around in this kind of cotton candy world. It was time to start putting him in the pain locker.

The next morning at the usual 7:30 A.M. spin meeting, there wasn't a lot of great news in the clips. The governor had said that he "needed to do a better job of explaining his tax plan," and this had been seized on by everybody from the nets to the Gore folks to beat us up. At other times, a remark like this might not have drawn much attention, but now it was being used as a symbol of our stumbles, which was clearly the post–Democratic convention story line. It was obvious we were entering a down press cycle. You can sense this in a campaign like a weather front moving in, and there just isn't a lot you can do to stop it. The question was, How long would it last and how bad would it be? For almost two months, the story line had been Gore floundering and Bush doing well. That was bound to change. Gore simply had too much going for him not to rebound. The biggest worry was the fact that we were entering a down cycle this close to the Labor Day polls.

The debate story was not breaking well either. It was beginning to look like we had underestimated the ferocity with which the press would defend the presidential debate format. It struck me as a knee-jerk reaction, since there was good reason to believe that the alternative we were proposing would do a much better job of letting people really see the two men engage. Instead of rigid time limits and rules, which helped the candidates avoid answering questions, why not use the same format that journalists used to grill candidates? If the approaches we were suggesting were so flawed, why did Russert and King use them?

We might just as well have gone to church and refused to stand up when everyone else did. Somehow the press had decided that podium debates were sacrosanct and that we were violating an age-old ritual. And even though we had agreed to do one, that wasn't enough. A whole generation of journalists had grown up with the Kennedy–Nixon debates and had a pack mentality about this element of the race. I've always thought the skills needed to perform well in a debate, or what we call debates, have almost nothing to do with the skills needed to be a great president. Under an English system of Parliamentary debate, perhaps the skills were transferable, but in America, once elected, no president ever debates again, at least not until four years roll by and everybody gets in a lather all over again. The notion that somehow you get to see candidates think on their feet in debates is ludicrous—candidates *perform* in a rigid, podium-styled debate. It's an acquired skill, and there are terrible debaters who might make great presidents and some debaters who can slay dragons but who don't possess a single one of the real qualities being president requires.

The Gore camp's reaction to our debate proposal was, like their attack on Dick Cheney, basically glandular. We had offered them two formats at which Gore had excelled and which played to the advantage of the more aggressive candidate. The odds of them landing some kind of serious blow were much greater in a Russert and King format. Both could have drawn huge audiences, particularly the Russert format, which could have been moved to network prime time instead of the usual Sunday morning slot. And if there was some defining moment, even if the debate were held at midnight on

Alaskan cable access, that moment would be replayed countless times on every television station in America.

My sense was that the Gore people were determined to
be against anything we were for, which was understandable
if not terribly useful for their candidate. And they realized—
correctly—that ultimately we wouldn't be able to fight off the
pressure to do the presidential debates on their terms. But in
retrospect, there's every reason to think that a combination
of one podium debate, a Russert debate and a King debate
would have better served Gore. Particularly since we were
proposing that the Russert debate be the leadoff debate and
we were pushing to have it in mid-September which, had
Gore turned in a great performance, might have fatally damaged our chances.

The key element to getting out of a negative press cycle is
changing the dynamic of the race, or at least producing the appearance of change. We stood a good chance of doing this
with the RNC spot, which the press would consume with great
relish. The Gore people would invariably spin that we were
desperate, but at least we would be on offense, rather than just
wallowing through a bad stretch. And once people started seeing the spot in the key battleground states, it would help us.

"There's a problem with the RNC spot," Mark said to me
right after the press meeting.

"What kind of problem? Isn't it already at the stations?"

"That's part of the problem."

We convened in Don Evans's office. Karen was there, and
Don and Karl and Mark, and nobody looked happy.

"The Lisa Myers interview is from 1994, not 1998," Karl
said.

"Awww, man," I groaned. "How'd this happen?"

"Doesn't matter," Don said, "but it happened. At least we
caught it before it aired."

"If that spot is at the stations, the press will find out about it," Karen said matter-of-factly.

Nobody disagreed.

"Why can't they put a date on the spot and run it?" I asked. "Isn't it just as good? Maybe better. So what if it's from 1994? That makes it pre-Lewinsky. It's better."

"The context is troubling," Karl said. He handed me a transcript of the entire Lisa Myers interview. "She's asking questions that had to do with Gore criticizing Ollie North for not telling the truth."

"The governor just won't be comfortable with running this thing now, I can promise you," Karen said.

One of Don's assistants stuck his head in the door to say that Ron Fournier of AP was calling, asking questions about the spot at the station.

"I bet he is," Don quipped. "How many stations did this go to?"

"A lot. Fifty or sixty at least," Karl said.

Don just shook his head.

Matthew Dowd came in, having just heard the news. He also argued that Alex should just put a date on the spot and we could still run it. He had seen how well it had played in the focus groups.

But the issue was dead. The worst thing was that it had been presented to the governor as one thing when in fact it was another. We might have had a chance of selling the idea of using a 1994 interview, but not after it had been sold as a 1998 interview in an entirely different context.

It was a classic case of the left hand not knowing what the right hand was doing—a situation in which the Gore people would never find themselves, if only because they had the same guys making both ads for the DNC and the Gore campaign. There was something to be said for not taking those pesky FEC regulations too seriously.

"Can't we just go with the tobacco spot?" I asked. I had to make one last pitch.

Nobody was for that, except me. Even Matthew, who generally liked the tougher approach, had become convinced that the spot wouldn't work.

Don hated the idea anyway. "We can't run something like that, with him talking about his sister." He all but shuddered at the idea. "If the governor has a problem with an old interview, why in the world would he like this?"

That was it. Both spots were dead. Even though I would have loved to have run them in rotation—that would have been a wonderful one-two punch—I'd learned with dead certainty that if a campaign wasn't ready to defend a spot, it would be a disaster. There had to be the collective will to support an attack or it would be like the Bay of Pigs, the troops dying on the beach.

"So what's the RNC going to put up?" Mark asked.

The question just hung there. Finally Karl got up to deal with Fournier.

For the first time in a long time, I had a really bad feeling.

☆   ☆   ☆

We were waiting for it all day. Matthew Dowd usually got the numbers first. By noon, after explaining a dozen times or so that the numbers wouldn't be released until later in the afternoon, he finally left and went for a run just to get away from everybody.

It was the Gallup post-Labor Day poll that we were salivating over. We'd been in a down cycle for three weeks, long enough that it was starting to be hard to remember when it hadn't been this way. It was like we were caught in a storm that just wouldn't move on.

Like every other time when the campaign had hit a bad patch, the press was filled with rumors of staff shake-ups.

The sources for these stories were invariably "Bush advisers" in Washington, which could mean anybody from an intern on the Republican National Committee to a United States senator.

"Some Republicans are openly complaining that the Bush campaign is fumbling," Candy Crowley reported. One RNC official was quoted in a *New York Times* story saying that "they [the Austin campaign] acted like they were the smartest people in the world—and that no one in Washington had anything to contribute. Their view was: 'We really understand the American people. You people in Washington don't.' " That was true enough.

It was everywhere. Bill Kristol, still trying to get over the fact that John McCain wasn't in the race, gleefully bubbled that Washington Republicans were "worried, verging on panic. . . . It's been a big deterioration pretty fast." The thought that there was widespread panic in D.C. was one of the few consoling factors during this whole period. It almost made waking up every morning and getting the crap kicked out of you worthwhile. These were the same people who would have their tongues out ready to lick Karl or Joe or Don's boots if Bush won. *We always believed in you. Brilliant campaign.*

"Margin of error," Karl said, looking relieved. He held the Gallup press release in his hand. "Three points down among likely voters." Gallup had Gore at 46 and Bush at 43 with likely voters.

"Spinnable," I said. We were all crowded into Karl's office, reading the numbers.

"Major league spinnable," Karl said. Everybody laughed.

We were in a slump and anything short of a death sentence was welcome news. The campaign was starting to feel like one of those dreams where you're trapped and there's a way to get out but you just can't quite get there. Everybody knew that we had to get back on offense but everything we tried just wasn't working.

After the Lisa Myers and tobacco spots flamed out, Alex had come up with two new ads. One was a contrast/attack on prescription drugs, an issue the Gore campaign had been using to beat our brains out since the Republican convention. It had helped them open up a huge gender gap, and we were starting to slide with seniors. Alex's spot was a straightforward, off-tackle approach:

> ANNOUNCER: Under Clinton–Gore, prescription drug prices have skyrocketed, and nothing's been done. George Bush has a plan: Add a prescription drug benefit to Medicare.
> GEORGE W. BUSH [on *Camera*]: Every senior will have access to prescription drug benefits.
> ANNOUNCER: And Al Gore? Gore opposed bipartisan reform. He's pushing a big government plan that lets Washington bureaucrats interfere with what your doctors prescribe.
> The Gore prescription plan: Bureaucrats decide.
> The Bush prescription plan: Seniors choose.

This was the kind of spot you hated to run but sometimes had to. It was pure defense couched as offense. We weren't going to win on prescription drugs—no Republican would—but we damn sure could lose if we didn't fight back.

The other spot used footage from Gore's Buddhist temple visit.

> ANNOUNCER: There's Al Gore, reinventing himself on television. Like I'm not going to notice. Who's he going to be today?

> The Al Gore who raises campaign money at a Buddhist temple? Or the one who promises campaign finance reform? . . . Al Gore, claiming credit for things he didn't do.
> AL GORE [*from CNN interview*]: "I took the initiative in creating the Internet."

We knew we'd take heat for the spot—from Republicans for appearing desperate, from the press for going negative (though they would quietly love it) and of course from the Gore campaign, which would squeal like Ned Beatty in *Deliverance*. This would be a good sign. The worst thing that can happen is for nobody to complain when you put up a spot that you believe is powerful. Gore's reaction could easily be predicted. He'd feign disappointment and sorrow—this from the guy who boasted that the way to win was "rip the other guy's lungs out."

The key here was credibility. We weren't going to win this race just by making the case that Al Gore was saying the wrong things and had the wrong plans. Sure, that was part of it, but we had to raise doubts so that when voters heard stuff from Gore they liked, they still would pause before accepting it. You could do it with large-scale failed promises, like his vow to fix health care in 1992, a debacle people still remembered, or with the little stuff that drove people nuts about Gore—the "I invented the Internet, I was the model for *Love Story,* I discovered the Love Canal" stuff.

He really will say anything to get elected. That had to be out there in the mainstream consciousness or we probably didn't stand a chance. That wasn't enough to win, but it might give us a *chance* to win. It was like taking on the death star—there was one narrow, treacherous path to get inside, but if you made it, fun could be had.

☆   ☆   ☆

"Did Berke call you?" Mark was calling from his cell phone. I was at our production office, in a low-slung limestone building that had once been a jail. It was called 501 Studios and it serviced everything from rock videos for Austin's latest bands to the nightly drawing of the lottery. It was dark and cool inside, a relief from the suffocating heat of September in Austin.

"Yeah, I haven't called him back. I've been avoiding it. Nothing good happens when I talk to him."

Berke was Rick Berke, the lead national political reporter for *The New York Times*. I'd known him and liked him for years, but he wasn't the type who would be calling just to check in before he wrote that wet kiss of a story. When Berke called it almost always meant trouble of some kind or another. I was in a bad news blackout and had tuned all my receptors to only receive good news. Rick Berke was the last person I wanted to talk to.

"He got me on the cell. He says there's something weird about Alex's spot. It has rats in it or something."

I started laughing. "Rats? Like crawling around?"

"I don't know what the hell he's talking about," Mark said. "He says it comes up on the screen subliminally." I was really laughing now. "He's on high gain about it. Can you check it out?"

There was a copy of the spot around the office. I put it in the VCR and played it. There were no rats crawling around, nor did I feel like there was a subliminally delivered message now lodged in my brain.

I called Mark back. "This is crazy. This spot has been on the air for over a week. Everybody and his brother has written about it, including *The New York Times,* which reviewed it. What the hell is Berke talking about?"

Mark had talked to him again. "He says it comes up when the word 'bureaucrats' is on the screen."

"Mark, I just looked at the thing. There's nothing there."

"Try again."

"How long is it supposed to be on the screen?"

"I don't know! Christ, I haven't seen it. Run it through the Avid and let's meet over at the campaign."

Laura Crawford, the Maverick production wizard, and I ran the spot through a $100,000 Avid editing machine. When the word "bureaucrats" came on the screen, we went through it frame by frame. For one frame, the letters *rats* were on the screen, separated from *bureauc. One frame.* There are nine hundred frames in a thirty-second spot. The human eye can't perceive a single frame of video or film, which is what creates the illusion of moving images. It's why we call films "movies" and not "stillies."

I went back over to the campaign and found Mark in Matthew's office. "I can't believe Berke is going to write about this," I said to Mark. "One frame?"

Mark looked incredibly depressed. It had been a lousy month, it was 102 degrees outside, and now Rick Berke was excited about one frame in a spot.

"What does Alex say?" I asked Mark.

Mark shrugged. "He says he didn't have any idea it was there until Berke called him."

I put in another tape. It was part of a commercial for Bob Dole. "Why are you showing this?" Mark asked.

I slowed the tape down. In the spot was a swirl of color we'd used to divide two scenes, a "swish" of color is what editors would call it. I had shot the tiny piece of colored film we'd used—all thirty frames of it—the weekend the Berlin Wall came down. It was footage of the wall itself with brightly colored graffiti. When it flashed by for thirty frames, all you

saw was an interesting texture and bright colors. But if you ex-
amined the film frame by frame, you could actually read the
graffiti, all of it in German. "Look," I said, "this probably says
'Gorbachev is an asshole' in German. This thing played thousands of times. Rick Berke's seen it. Nobody analyzed it frame
by frame. This is crazy."

"Tell me about it." Mark looked miserable.

"Berke's really serious about this?"

"Call him!"

"If he's big on this, he'll get it on page one, just watch
him," I said.

I started to get a real sick feeling. If Berke wanted to push
a story onto page one, he could do it. And once a story was on
page one of the *Times,* there would be an ungodly feeding
frenzy. Nothing drove television coverage like a *New York
Times* story. The *Times* went online every night between 11
P.M. and midnight EST and it wasn't unusual for there to be
a buzz going about what was in the *Times* within a half
hour. This seemed to most affect the television correspondents covering the campaign; day after day, it seemed their
show producers were taking their cues straight from the *Times*
coverage, as were the bookers on an infinite number of cable
shows.

By midnight, I had over a dozen messages from reporters
asking about the Berke story. Sure enough, it was on page
one, above the fold.

The only amusing thing about the whole affair was listening to the Gore people—and Gore—express shock and dis-
may at one frame in a spot. Here was the campaign that had
bragged they were a "slaughterhouse" full of "killers" and they
were acting outraged over one frame? "I find it a very disap-
pointing development," lamented Gore. "I've never seen anything like it." This from a guy who mocked Jesse Jackson for

being a *preacher* in a 1988 debate? The *Times* had frozen the one frame and put it on its front page, as if it were actually visible when the spot played in real time. The article failed to mention that the one frame was so subliminal that the *Times* reporters who reviewed the ad had failed to see it, as had ABC, NBC, CNN, Fox—not a single station who had originally broadcast the spot as part of their news shows had ever noticed that one frame featured this evil message.

It turned out that Chris Lehane of the Gore campaign had tipped Berke to the single frame, even taking him down to an editing studio in Washington and showing it to him. Of course, it made me want to go through every Gore spot and see what I could find in each frame. If every thirty-second spot had nine hundred frames, and there were forty or fifty spots that had been aired, that meant we'd have to look at . . .

The whole thing was monumentally stupid. Stupid on our part, I suppose, not to catch the single frame earlier, though I promise you, I have never gone through a spot frame by frame in my life. Stupid in the way the whole presidential circus gets distracted by whatever is sexy at the moment. The only thing that wasn't stupid was the way Chris Lehane had planted the story with Berke. That was clever. But then again, Lehane was a trained killer, so what chance did we have?

The rats story was big news for days. Then just as it was clearing up, I got another phone call from Mark. "You know where your debate book is?" he asked. He meant the big notebooks we used for debate prep sessions with the governor. "And your copy of the debate tape?"

I had a moment of panic. I was driving back to the campaign after running myself into a stupor around Town Lake, Austin's great downtown running trail. It was the only way I knew to block out the campaign for an hour or so.

"I keep all that stuff at the house. In that big file box I take to debate prep sessions."

"You sure it's there?" Mark asked.

I made a U-turn and headed back to my house, which was only minutes from the campaign.

"Why?" I asked. I had that bad adrenaline-rush feeling.

"Supposedly somebody sent a copy of the stuff to Tom Downey."

"What? That's impossible!"

"Call me when you're at the house."

Oh, Jesus, I was thinking, what if I left that stuff somewhere. Where? It was in the car. Did somebody steal it out of the car? Or take it from the house? But it was all there, sitting in the big plastic file box I'd bought to keep the debate materials in one place.

Back at Karl's office, the news was coming in. That morning Tom Downey had supposedly received a copy of "debate materials," including a tape of one of the mock debates.

My first instinct was that the whole thing was some kind of mistake. We didn't really know what he had received, and it was impossible to imagine that he had been sent the real goods. A log had been kept of every debate book and of the tapes we'd made of the debate practices. Nobody was missing anything.

What did Downey get? That was the key question. If he really had a copy of a debate tape, that meant somebody would have needed to copy one of our tapes, either a copy of a copy or from the master tape, since none of our copies were missing. The tapes were either at headquarters, at the Maverick office or at my house. How would somebody get access to copy a tape and then replace it?

"I don't believe it," I kept saying. "He doesn't have one of the debate tapes."

"So what was it?" Karl wondered.

"Remember when we were at the moot court room of the law center? Maybe there was some kind of surveillance camera, a security camera and it recorded a tape and somebody got that."

Karl and Mark stared at me. "I like the 'aliens landed and grabbed it' scenario better," Karl said.

"I'm open to that," I admitted.

Downey's story was that he had been in a debate prep session in his law office with three associates when his secretary had brought in a package. He opened it and discovered the tape and some kind of debate materials. Downey claimed to have looked at the materials "briefly," viewed the tape "briefly" and then turned it over to the FBI.

There were some odd things about Downey's account. First, what was he doing opening his mail in the middle of a debate prep session? We had a lot of debate prep meetings and nobody wandered in and said, "Hey, here's some mail you might want to open while you're working." It was, well, curious. And while Downey had recused himself from any further debate prep, they were refusing to release the names of the three associates who were with him or to say whether or not they would still be involved in debate prep.

My gut was that while there were some odd things about Downey's story, it was probably just that—odd, and that he was telling the truth. Every reporter in America appeared to be feeding on the story, and why not? It was ridiculously juicy, with elements of a bad spy thriller mixed with Watergate.

Mark Halperin of ABC News, who always seemed to know more than anyone else, called, trying to figure out more. I told him that I didn't think it was a real debate tape, but before I could go further, he cut me off. "I don't think that'll fly. It's a tape of Bush and Gregg and you're in the middle with a television set. So how'd they get it?"

Jesus Christ. This was incredible. What Halperin had described was the ranch tape, on which was a mock Russert session. "What about the involvement of aliens?" I asked.

"Produce one or some close facsimile and we will do a live shot. Come on, what kind of security do you guys have there? Can somebody just walk in? Is this stuff lying around?"

"Don't blame the victim! We don't know a damn thing."

First rats, now this.

The FBI descended two days later. By then, we had a good idea that the tape and briefing book had come from the Maverick office based on information that identified the book as Mark's (each book was coded). The Maverick offices were attached to a video editing house, connected by a fire door that didn't lock. This had always bothered us, since it meant that if you had access to the editing facility, you could access Maverick. Apparently the fire code prohibited the door from being locked.

The troubling thing was that the editing facility was used by political consultants of both parties, which meant that Democratic consultants were sometimes in the facility for late-night editing after everyone had left the Maverick offices. The staff at the editing facility was first rate and completely trustworthy, but it would be impossible for them always to keep track of every person who might come into an editing session. God knows that in late-night editing sessions, I'd wandered all over editing houses from New York to the Philippines, bored and trying to stay awake.

Of course, we had no reason to believe that a Democratic consultant was involved. We didn't have a reason to believe anything—we were totally clueless, literally and figuratively.

I was over at our production office working on a spot when the FBI came to the Maverick office. "You're not going to believe this," Scott Morris told me. Scott helped run the Maverick offices and had come down from Washington when Russ Schriefer and I first signed onto the campaign. If Scott had been in the military—and he looked like he was—he would have ended up in the Delta Force. "They think Yvette did it."

"That's insane," I said. It seemed to be an opinion I was expressing a lot these days about the state of the world.

Yvette was Yvette Lozano. She was from Austin and had been close to Mark's family for years, baby-sitting for his kids. They had first met during the Ann Richards campaign in 1990 when Yvette was the official baby-sitter for the campaign (having a campaign baby-sitter was a very Ann Richards thing).

I loved Yvette. She was funny and wicked smart and was always a calming presence, which is invaluable in a campaign world where it's easy to believe that death and destruction lurk around every corner. She had stayed in our apartment in New York on a weekend trip to see the Yankees—she was a fanatical baseball fan—and stayed in our house in Austin to take care of our cats whenever we went out of town.

"Did they fingerprint in the office or do anything else?"

Scott shook his head. "I don't think so."

Soon Yvette's name was leaked to the press and she was hurled into that peculiarly American volcano of press scandal treatment. She seemed dazed by it all. After a lengthy interview session with the FBI, she came back to the Maverick office with two FBI agents in tow. I was the only one at the office, and when she told me that they were going to her house so they could search it, I took her aside in our conference room.

"Yvette, you've got to get a lawyer involved," I whispered urgently. "You can't let these guys go into your house without talking to a lawyer."

"I don't mind," she said and shrugged. "I don't have anything to hide."

"It doesn't matter! You just can't do it."

"But won't they think I'm guilty if I get a lawyer?"

"Listen, they will think you're crazy if you don't." We could see the two agents pacing in the office. "They *expect* you to get a lawyer."

She finally relented, and I went out to tell the agents what was happening. They said they understood and would be glad to wait until a lawyer had been retained. Mark arrived looking stunned. Yvette was like a member of his family. Now there were FBI agents in the office wanting to search her home. How did this all happen?

We worked the phones and found a lawyer. He started immediately talking to the FBI agents, who in turn were talking to Washington.

That was really all we could do. Now Yvette had a lawyer, and there would be all sorts of restrictions on what she could say and how we could communicate. It was utterly unimaginable to me that she had done anything wrong.

☆   ☆   ☆

September was a black hole. By the middle of the month, *Newsweek* had us down by twelve points with registered voters and, strangely, down by fourteen points with "likely voters." It was a crazy number, like looking up at halftime at the Super Bowl and being down by forty-five points.

"Just remember," I said, sitting in Karl's office, "they had us by nine in their last New Hampshire poll."

"That's a great spin." Karl laughed. "Don't forget that the only bit of good news we had before New Hampshire was way off."

"You don't think that works?"

Fortunately, not every poll showed us down by double-digit numbers or we would have faded from the scene like Michael Dukakis or Walter Mondale, guys who were so plainly out of the race by October that all but their core supporters threw in the towel. That was always our greatest fear, what Mark and I took to calling "the horror show." That Gore would suddenly pop and the race would be over. It could have happened so easily. All Gore needed to do was to find a way to articulate why it was silly to think about taking a chance on an unknown when things were going along just fine. It would have taken two or three weeks of a steady, consistent, clear message and we probably would have been toast.

But just when it looked like he might be near to closing the deal, Gore would go too far and make a mistake that would bite him in the ass. It happened just days after *Newsweek* had us down by fourteen, after we'd been pretty well bombed with rats and the debate tape story, just when we felt like we were holding on by our fingertips—Gore started handing us gifts. Not big gifts, but enough to keep us alive.

The gifts were his strange, irrepressible need to exaggerate or simply make things up for no apparent reason. He told a Teamsters meeting that his baby-sitter used to sing "Look for the Union Label" as a lullaby. In fact, the song wasn't written until he was in high school. Then he started telling senior citizens in Florida that his mother-in-law took the same arthritis medicine as his dog and that it cost more for his mother-in-law. Only it turned out that there was a generic version available for half the cost of the dog's medicine, and for God's sake, why did he need to say any of this in the first place? He was a Democrat, people intuitively believed him when he said prescription drugs cost too much, at least anybody who might remotely vote for him, and by the way, *didn't he and Clinton promise they were going to fix this health care mess?* (As a Mississippian, I was mildly amused that the dog's name was Shiloh; what kind of Southerner named his dog after a battle which turned into a Southern slaughter? It would be like a German naming a dog Stalingrad. Maybe a focus group had liked it.)

Gore was like a comic book character who keeps dropping marbles out of his pocket in the middle of a foot race. He'd been doing great then, wham, he was flailing around, slipping on the marbles, trying to regain his balance. He never actually fell flat on his face, but he sure as hell lost his momentum.

A strange realization began to sink into the Bush world as September wore on. The conventional wisdom had always been that our best-case scenario for the debates was to emerge unscathed, *not to lose* the race in the debates. But now we were in a situation where it looked like we needed *to win* the debates to have a shot at coming out on top in November.

We had retreated from our initial debate offer and basically accepted the commission proposals of three prime-time, hour-and-a-half debates. There would be one podium debate, one roundtable debate and one town meeting debate, in that order. Jim Lehrer would be the single moderator. These basics were all worked out by Don Evans, Joe Allbaugh and Andy Card for the Bush campaign and Bill Daley, Alexis Herman and Jim Johnson on the other side. Everybody shook hands, declared victory and then the real fun began—working out the details.

I've always loved debate negotiations because they offer a sterling excuse to be unrelentingly petty. No detail is too small to be ignored, no advantage too insignificant to battle over. And why not? Presidential scholars tell us—and they might even be right—that Nixon lost to Kennedy because he had lousy makeup and sweated too much.

No doubt that's what the Gore campaign was thinking when they insisted that each of the debate halls be sixty-five degrees.

"Sixty-five degrees?" Don laughed. "You're going to get up there and see your breath."

It was part of a whole bundle of details that had to be worked out. Our first goal was to get the other guys to agree to all the details that the governor wanted, which were pretty few in number. One of our major requests was for microphones attached to the podiums, rather than lapel mikes, so that each candidate would be more or less tethered to the podiums. We were trying to discourage Gore's ability to pull some stunt, like walking over to the governor with a pledge to end global warming by that weekend or some such nonsense. But we were also trying to figure out which of the various demands Gore was making were actually important to him and, if denied, might throw him off his game. Like a seemingly innocuous item in the draft debate agreement that read:

> (ix) Each candidate shall be entitled to placement of a television monitor in a location that is visible to that candidate from his position on the stage, which location shall be approved by a representative of that candidate.

"What's this all about?" Don asked.

We were in his office going over the draft agreement with Joe Allbaugh; Ben Ginsburg, the campaign attorney; and Scott Sforza, who handled the campaign's in-house television production and coordination with networks. Scott had set up a little studio in the campaign headquarters that allowed us to do interviews on-site without going out to another studio. He was there for the first morning show interview anybody might be doing, usually around 5:30 A.M. Texas time, until the last late-night cable show wrapped. This meant he basically lived at the campaign and went home on occasion to change clothes.

"He wants a monitor to see himself," Scott said.

"Is that usual?" Don asked.

"Most people hate that," I said. "It's distracting."

"The governor always wants us to turn off any monitors in the room when he does live interviews," Scott said.

"Why's he want it?" Don asked. Around headquarters, Don was a jovial, upbeat presence, quick to break any tension with a quip delivered in the West Texas accent that made him sound like Don Meredith. At the height of the rats feeding frenzy, when Gore had suggested that Republicans should be ashamed of themselves, Don had drawled, "That's it. I'm telling the governor he oughta withdraw. Al's right." At a 7:30 press meeting, when you can't remember the last good clip you read and everybody is starting to look like anxious relatives who have been keeping all-night vigils at the hospital for weeks, this kind of humor is most appreciated.

But while working out the details of the debate, Don was all focus and intensity and you could see in a heartbeat why he had done well in the tough West Texas oil world.

"I think we ought to let him have it and hope he uses it," I said.

Don shook his head. "He wants it for a reason. Why?"

I shrugged. "Maybe he just wants to see how he looks on camera."

"See if his bald spot is showing," Scott said, not joking. "Newscasters use them but they are used to it."

"Maybe he's asking for it because he wants both podiums to have monitors and he thinks it will be distracting for the governor."

"It's voluntary for each candidate," Don said, reading over the agreement. "We don't have to use it, we just can. I don't think we let him have it. No way."

We went through each line of the thirty-one-page agreement like this, trying to play every angle. One item the Gore camp had inserted jumped out at Scott and me:

(vi) The camera located at the rear of the stage shall be
used only to take shots of the moderator.

"It's so his bald spot won't show," I said.

"Has to be," Scott agreed. "Why else would he care?"

"He ought to just cut his hair like me," Joe Allbaugh said,
running his head over his flattop.

Don laughed. "Let him have that one," he said, meaning
the request for no rearview camera shots. "Come on guys,
show a little compassion." He paused. "Compassionate Conservatism."

I Invented Debates 10

"LAMBS TO THE SLAUGHTER," Mark said, looking out the dark window as we drove through Crawford. At 11 P.M., even on a Friday night, Crawford wasn't a hotbed of activity.

"It wasn't that bad," I said.

"Are you kidding me?" Mark seemed to shudder.

It *had* been a strange evening, the last formal debate prep before the first debate, which would be held on October 3 in Boston. To try to make the debate as realistic as possible, we had abandoned the small gym cabin and moved to the nearest place large enough to set up two podiums in a quasi-realistic setting—a small Methodist church in a pasture a few miles from the governor's ranch. We'd dragged two large podiums from Austin into the church's fellowship hall, a big, empty space that reminded me of thousands of church dinners from my Mississippi youth. It had metal folding tables and chairs and a concrete slab floor.

To make it more like the real thing, the prep was scheduled to begin at the same time as the real debate—9 P.M. Central time. We met for dinner at the ranch—Don Evans brought a trunkload of barbeque from County Line Barbeque in Austin—and talked general strategy. The governor looked as tired as I'd ever seen him, a deep kind of exhaustion that made you ache just looking at him. Several people commented on it

225

and he brushed it off. "I'll be fine, quit worrying about me." He hated being fussed over.

The plan was to have debate prep Friday night and Saturday, then for Bush to rest and study on Sunday, fly to West Virginia to overnight on Monday and then head to Boston for the Tuesday debate.

After dinner, we drove in a makeshift caravan to the nearby church. There had been concern that reporters might follow us, but nobody had made the trip from Austin. The entire press crew was as worn-out as the governor after months on the road. It felt surreptitious and vaguely mysterious to be meeting at this dark church in the middle of nowhere, armed men with radios in their ears standing guard.

"Where's Karl?" the governor asked as we assembled at the church.

He had been the first to leave and should have been waiting for us when we arrived. "How could he get lost?" Bush sighed. This was the last thing he wanted to deal with.

Two or three people tried calling his cell phone with no response. We moved inside the stark fellowship hall. "Tell you what," the governor said to Senator Gregg, "I'll be Gore, you be Bush."

Gregg shook his head. "No way. It's more fun to be nasty."

Larry Lindsey was the official timekeeper. As he was creating cue cards by writing "fifteen seconds" and "thirty seconds" on torn pages from a yellow legal pad, Karl came in, looking sheepish. He had gone to the wrong church and had been waiting for everybody else to show up.

It had been over a month since we had practiced a formal debate and weeks since a practice of any sort. Our focus at first had been on the Russert format, and then we had been distracted by the debate on debates. Six weeks earlier, we had been ahead of the curve in our prep. Now we were playing catch-up.

Amazingly, we had never done a ninety-minute debate straight through. Our custom had been either to concentrate on one subject for twenty to thirty minutes, touching on every possible angle of a question on Social Security or taxes or education, or to stage more realistic sessions with questions on various topics, but limited to forty-five minutes or so, followed by a critique and then another session.

"We have to 'run' the debate," Condi Rice had said. "Like when you practice for a concert." Along with her five languages, impressive knowledge of pro football and world-class figure skating, Condi had a background as a concert pianist. "You run the whole concert and if you make a mistake, you keep going, just like when you're onstage."

This would be our one formal "run." And it was hardly a formal dress rehearsal: We had podiums but no stage lights and no timing lights, just Larry Lindsey sitting in a chair holding up torn pieces of yellow notepaper.

There was something about this approach that terrified me and something about it that was very endearing.

Al Gore had immersed himself in a formal debate "camp" with so many consultants that news accounts said that some had to sit in another room and watch it on a remote. He'd recruited various demographically correct citizens to advise him on debate strategy, in essence concocting his own focus group to critique the debates. Gore was famous for insisting on realistic settings, down to the exact temperature of the room. It was all very Gore, sort of stiff, a bit mannered, but possibly very effective.

George W. Bush, on the other hand, had gathered a few advisers together in an old church after a big dinner of County Line's best barbeque. Tomorrow we'd have another session, this one in the gym cabin, and then talk about it over hamburgers he'd cook at the house. No focus groups, no battery of consultants, no insistence that he couldn't practice unless the room was exactly the right temperature. You had to admire his lack of pretense, his refusal to play the prima donna, the confidence that he understood best how he should prepare.

Senator Gregg was careful to break almost every rule of the debate agreement, which we fully expected of Gore. He brought with him a pledge on campaign finance and demanded that the governor sign it (breaking two rules—one against issuing any challenges or pledges, the other against bringing props); he interrupted in a most annoying and prohibited fashion; he left his podium and walked over to the governor and offered his hand in a pledge on Social Security. He was high energy and biting and very good. The governor looked like what he was, exhausted, and whereas in previous debate preps he had seemed to enjoy the sparring with Gregg, tonight he had been flat and allowed many of the Gregg/Gore attacks to go unanswered.

"Lambs to the slaughter," Mark said and sighed afterward. There was no question that Gregg/Gore had dominated the debate, but it was hardly a fair fight. He was rested, primed for battle and he didn't have to worry about being *too* aggressive or obnoxious. It didn't matter if Gregg came across as a complete jerk—that was his job.

"He'll be ready," I said.

"I can't believe you're the optimist," Mark said anxiously. "That proves we're in trouble."

☆   ☆   ☆

The next afternoon, Gary Edson and I flew from Waco to Jackson Hole, Wyoming, for the final Cheney debate preps. Gary was one of the propeller heads in charge of preparing the debate prep books. The propeller heads all seemed to be brilliant and loved to argue about such sexy subjects as the socio-economic impact of school vouchers improving reading skills in the third grade of low-income schools. Gary looked about twenty-five but was in fact in his early forties, and though he hung out at headquarters and worked the usual nineteen-hour days and ate cold pizza at midnight like everybody else, I discovered quite by accident that he had actually started and sold a couple of businesses and had made serious money along the way. But he was still a propeller head at heart. "I love public policy," he said with an almost embarrassed shrug. "I find this stuff incredibly interesting."

Gary and his comrades generated more written material than the Renaissance. Every few minutes they were churning out a new briefing book or position paper, most of which turned up in one form or another in debate prep materials. At an earlier practice session in Jackson Hole, Gary had handed Elizabeth Cheney, who was running the debate prep for her father, a stack of notebooks.

"Which do you want him to read first, Gary?" Liz had asked.

"What?" Gary asked.

"Gary," Liz said, "he will read it all. What do you want him to read first?"

I thought Gary was going to start crying. *Someone was actually reading this stuff?*

Almost every weekend in September, we had been having debate preps with the secretary, either in D.C. or Jackson Hole. Gary and I came up from Austin to play the moderators and help out as best we could. Paul Wolfowitz was there with Scooter Libby and Stephen Hadley, all high-level guys in the previous Bush administration. The Cheney campaign was the first national campaign run entirely by women. Kathleen

Shanahan was the campaign manager and Juleanna Glover was the press secretary. And both daughters had formal roles in the campaign: Elizabeth was in charge of debate prep and Mary served as a traveling aide for her father. Dirk Vande Beck, who also handled press, was one of the few males in the traveling road show.

Elizabeth had organized the final sessions with a precision that Condi would have loved. Each session began at the same time the actual debate would begin and ran uninterrupted for an hour and a half. Then Secretary Cheney would leave and everybody would sit around and hash out a critique. This avoided the problem of everyone offering different advice while he was around. The next morning, a small group of us led by Ohio Congressman Rob Portman, who was playing Lieberman in the mock debates, would go over the points with the secretary. Then he would study his briefing books in the afternoon and have another mock debate at night.

When Gary and I arrived Saturday night from Crawford, they had already started the evening session, which was being held at a Jackson Hole theater. Elizabeth's husband Phil was playing the moderator. The theater felt like a cross between a frontier opera house and a bordello, complete with overstuffed red velvet seats. There were top hats lying around backstage, and after the mock debate, Phil and Rob Portman clowned around onstage, posing for *Newsweek* photographer David Kennerly against a florid painted landscape. It was a long way from the stark church in Crawford.

If Republicans are lucky, some day Liz Cheney will run for president. I loved watching her direct her father's advisers, not a shy and retiring crowd. She did it with a deft hand and a lot of humor. Everybody had his say, and, as usual, there were wildly contradictory suggestions of all sorts. The advisers were heavy on foreign policy experience and had this natural tendency to try to inject some aspect of foreign affairs into every response. It was left to Liz to say, "No, guys, I really don't think the best way to explain the need for tax cuts is to use the Hong Kong analogy. Not that it doesn't make sense."

Rob Portman had Lieberman down perfectly, capturing his funny but biting style, which could be more deadly than Gore's sledgehammer technique. Over the years, Lieberman had mastered a way of attacking with grace and good humor, a powerful combination which he had used to great effect in his acceptance speech. As a debate opponent, if you let yourself respond with even a hint of anger, Lieberman had you in his kill zone and would just rip you apart, with the audience laughing all the time. The only guaranteed way to trump him was using pointed humor in return, which was impossible to script. How do you prepare a counterpunch to a joke that you haven't heard? All you could do was practice the *kind* of exchanges you were likely to have, rather than trying to write responses.

The format was similar to that of *Meet the Press,* which was a natural for Cheney, who had been on shows like that scores of times. He knew and liked Bernie Shaw, who was the designated moderator. The debate was going to be held in Danville, Kentucky—the Thriller in the Ville, they were calling it—which was the sort of small town that would naturally support Bush–Cheney. Short of holding the debate in Wyoming, it was as close to having a home field advantage as we could imagine.

Even spending just forty-eight hours in Jackson Hole was transforming. You could walk around outside without immediately sweating, go for a run at noon and not feel your brain cooking. It didn't have the claustrophobic feel that had settled over Austin, where it seemed impossible to go anywhere without running into reporters or network producers. The mood at

301 Congress had been so tense for so long that it was easy to forget that there was a different world out there, a world that didn't live or die by the morning tracking reports or the voracious news cycles that demanded to be fed on the half hour.

The Cheneys were still able to lead a relatively normal life here, and being with them was like joining a large, very welcoming extended family. He liked to cook and still went shopping at the town's one large grocery store; when the one Starbucks in town was late opening, the morning debate review was delayed while we waited for the caffeine crisis to pass. We talked about skiing and what flies worked best in the local streams.

The press had been in love with Lieberman since the day Gore announced him and brought him down to Tennessee, where he tried to explain how Lieberman was really a Southerner because his son was married to one or something like that. (If he had known he was going to lose his home state, maybe Gore would have spent more time trying to explain how *he* was from Tennessee.) The consensus was that Cheney would probably do okay in the debate—everybody knew he was smart and knowledgeable—but that Lieberman would steal the show.

Leaving Jackson Hole for Boston and the first debate, I thought there was a good chance that Bush would win the first debate. There was also a chance that things might go terribly wrong. But I was absolutely convinced that Cheney would win decisively on Thursday.

☆   ☆   ☆

We got left on the tarmac.

Mark, Karl and I were waiting at the airport when the Bush campaign plane arrived from West Virginia. It had been Karl's idea for Bush to overnight in West Virginia on the way to the debate. For months he had been fixated on the idea that we could win West Virginia, a state that hadn't gone for a nonincumbent Republican presidential candidate in eighty years. The polls were tight, but we were all convinced—except Karl—that in the end, gravity would set in and the Dems would come home for Gore.

"We can pick his pocket," Karl would say whenever he was making the case for either Bush or Cheney to do an event in West Virginia. "Just steal it from 'em before they know it."

We humored him the way you do, say, a Chicago Cubs fan who is convinced this year the Cubs are going to win it all. *Sure, Karl. Of course we're going to win West Virginia.*

"How was the hotel?" I asked Jack Oliver, the campaign finance director who had made the trip from Austin with the Bush entourage. There had been a lot of concern about the hotel. Everybody remembered horror stories of candidates who couldn't sleep the night before a debate.

"Next to a railroad track, beds were awful, room service sucked," Jack said, fumbling for a cigarette. He hated that there was no smoking on the campaign plane.

"How's the big guy feel?"

Jack shrugged. "I feel like crap myself. I don't know about him."

Great, I thought. There's only the presidency riding on this thing.

When the reporters spilled out of the plane, they immediately surrounded Karl, Mark and me, mostly focusing on Mark. There had been fresh rumors in the stolen debate tapes story, including rumors that Mark was a suspect and that a split had developed between Karl and Mark. Both were absurd, but the story was out there and the beast had to be fed. Not to answer questions would only make everything worse.

We were standing there in the usual gaggle of mikes

and cameras when we saw the car carrying Bush take off in a small motorcade. The plan was for him to go straight to the debate site for the walk-through, while the press went to the hotel.

"We just got left," I said to Karl. We were supposed to be in one of the vans following Bush's car. But the rules of the road were clear—the motorcade (or the plane) waited on nobody. Except the candidate. Once after filming Bush and President Vicente Fox Quesada, we had left a tardy film crew member in Mexico to find his own way back to Austin.

We begged a campaign volunteer to drive us and made it to the location just as Bush was starting the walk-through. The debate was being held at the University of Massachusetts and I remembered it well from an earlier Bill Weld–John Silber debate. It was not the best of memories. I'd sat in the holding room helplessly as Silber baited Weld into defending the legalization of some automatic weapons, not the most popular position in Massachusetts.

Protesters were already lining up along the entrance to the U Mass at Boston campus. It underscored what we already knew: The debate was not on the friendliest of turf. To avoid driving through this scene before the debate, Bush advance chief Brian Montgomery and his staff had come up with a novel scheme—Bush would arrive by boat. The plan, which had miraculously remained a secret, was for the governor to cross Boston Harbor by boat, from the hotel to the U Mass campus. It was worth doing, if only to annoy the protesters who would have spent hours just waiting for a chance to yell when Bush drove by.

"It's cold in here," Bush said, slapping his arms around. He was joking, but it *was* cold. I had a sudden vision of the United Air Conditioner Workers conspiring behind the scenes to drop the room down to the morguelike temperature Gore had requested. We were all hanging out on the stage, trying to be useful but mostly feeling tense. But Bush seemed perfectly relaxed, even jovial.

"You guys holding a press conference at the airport?" he joked to Mark and me.

"Don't worry," Mark said, "we've already declared victory."

We were standing on the stage looking out at the audience. "Where will Laura be sitting?" he asked.

"She'll be off to your right," Mark said, "so that when you are looking at your main camera, you should be able to see her."

"I'll make lots of silly faces, I promise," Mrs. Bush said.

Looking at the two podiums under the stage lights, there was something vaguely odd about the lighting. I borrowed a light meter from one of the photographers and took quick readings by each podium. The Gore podium was a full stop brighter than the Bush one. I started to complain—it was always good to complain about something at these walk-throughs, if only to feel important—but in truth, the slightly softer light for the Bush podium was more flattering. It was not a dramatic enough difference to make him look dark or underlit, it was more that the Gore side looked too hot. I kept my mouth shut and wondered if the Gore people had wanted it that way. Maybe it was a quirk of Gore's, like the deep-freeze air-conditioning.

The director asked Karen Hughes to stand behind the Gore podium for a sound check.

"Go on," Bush teased, "take your best shot. Let me have it."

☆　　　☆　　　☆

Presidential debates have become the opera of politics—overblown, blustery spectacles with predictable plotlines, excuses for the spectators to parade around, gaudy in their self-importance. In the giant spin room before the debate, the Gore crowd reeked of arrogant condescension. This would be their moment, when it would all come together and they would expose the Emperor Bush as having no clothes.

This really was the belly of the beast, one of the last places on earth where the Eastern Intellectual Establishment could pretend they still mattered, where being a Kennedy still meant something more than just having some interesting personal items to auction after you died, where the *Boston Globe* editorial page was a moral touchstone, not notes from a dead era. For years I had watched this world with bemused appreciation, taking delicious pleasure in helping Weld and Cellucci win in a state that had fewer than 14 percent registered Republicans. My only regret was that Joe Kennedy had chickened out of challenging Paul Cellucci for governor in 1998. It would have been so sweet for the first-generation Italian American to defeat the self-important peacock.

Bush and Gore were both southerners who had migrated north to be educated at Yale and Harvard. But their reaction to the experience had been mirror opposites. Gore had made himself into a northeastern moderate with intellectual pretensions. Bush did everything he could to assert not only his Texas roots but his *West Texas* identity. There's a classic photo of Bush at Harvard Business School sitting in a lecture wearing his Texas Air National Guard flight jacket, jeans and cowboy boots. That said it all. He wore his Texas identity like a 1968 dashiki: *This is who I am. Don't expect me to change.*

Standing there in the spin room before the debate, I thought, God, if only we could beat this guy Gore. Here. Tonight. At their homecoming game. It would be so great.

As soon as Gore stepped out onstage, I knew we had won at least a partial victory. He looked utterly bizarre, painted up like a clumsy transvestite, red cheeks, bright lips. *What were they thinking? How did they let this happen?* Even if people watching television in their living rooms weren't consciously aware of the strange makeup, it would still hurt Gore. *There's just something about him. I don't know . . . can't put my finger on it.*

Both seemed nervous at the start, Bush more than Gore. After all, what did Al Gore have to worry about? He was going to kill this dummy Bush, right? Tie him up in knots, do a full Perot on his know-nothing head.

"He's lying!" Dan Bartlett yelled.

We were in the rapid-response room on the debate site. There were a half dozen computers and open phone lines to Austin, where the oppo dudes, Tim Morrison and Bill Clark, were standing by to catch every Gore misstatement. They had even set up a special website called debatefacts.com and were updating it moment by moment during the debate.

Dan Bartlett, one of the communication wizards who had worked his way up after the 1994 gubernatorial campaign, was coordinating between Austin and Boston. It was Gore's answer to the very first question that had gotten him excited.

Lehrer's first question was, "Vice President Gore, you have questioned whether Governor Bush has the experience to be president of the United States. What exactly do you mean?"

Instead of hitting it out of the park like the softball it was, Gore took it as an accusation and *denied it.* "I have actually not questioned Governor Bush's experience; I have questioned his proposals."

Which was simply not true and quickly provable as such. Within two minutes of the question, the guys in Austin had come up with a juicy quote from an article by Katherine Seelye in the April 13 edition of *The New York Times:* "In any case, Mr. Gore continued his theme from the morning speech, saying that Mr. Bush's call for a huge tax cut 'raises the question, Does he have the experience to be president?' " There were other similar quotes bouncing around as well. The question was, Why did Gore deny it? It was a wet kiss of a question, inviting Gore to compare his experience in government with Bush, which would hardly have been considered a cheap shot. But Gore seemed to click into some recurrent pathological need to lie even when it wasn't necessary. Probably his denial was also a result of his overstrenuous preparation. He wanted to get out his first statement, which he had memorized, and couldn't allow *answering* the question to throw him offtrack. So he just denied the premise of the question and moved on. The only problem was, he was lying and Lehrer knew it.

Lehrer came right back at Gore. "So I take it by your answer then, Mr. Vice President, that in your—an interview recently with *The New York Times,* when you said that you question whether vice president—or Governor Bush was experienced enough to be president, you were talking about strictly policy differences?" This was as close as mild-mannered Jim Lehrer got to telling somebody they were full of crap.

The debate soon settled into a predictable pattern—Gore attacked along the same fault lines he had since the convention, which was the right approach. A debate was a terrible time to suddenly shift tactics. The governor parried and focused on making a few key points:

- He was the outsider, Gore was the insider.
- He was the successful governor of the nation's second-largest state. He had the experience.
- The tax cut was affordable with the projected surplus.
- Gore was a big-spending liberal.
- It was time to change the tone in Washington.
- Times are good, yes, but key problems are being

avoided—fixing Social Security, Medicare reform,
education reform.

After ten minutes or so, we knew the night wouldn't be a
disaster and suspected that it had the chance to be a solid win.
Despite some initial nervousness, Bush was finding a groove
and, most important, he was starting to look like he was enjoying himself, mixing it up with Gore. We had worried for
months about Gore's ability to dominate a debate with his
standard tricks—ending every answer with a question, interrupting, refusing to yield time. Tonight he was using them all
but they weren't really working. Gore was visibly trying too
hard, like a fastball pitcher who was overthrowing.

"Am I wrong," I said to no one in particular in the response room, "or is this guy acting like an even bigger asshole
than usual?"

Gore was coming across as a petulant know-it-all, the
kind of kid you draw straws with your buddies in high school
for the right to beat up this week.

"Why does he keep sighing?" Karen asked. "Doesn't he
know the camera's on him?"

Actually, he might not have, since the debate agreement
called for no reaction shots of the candidate who wasn't talking. And in the negotiations Don Evans had blocked Gore
from having the monitor he had requested, so Gore had no
way of knowing whether he was on camera or not. Still, he had
to have been coached always to assume he was on camera.

We were feeling good about the night and then, toward
the end, Gore made two critical mistakes. The first involved
one of the little stories he was so fond of.

"I'd like to tell you a quick story," he began. We all
groaned as soon as we heard that opening. It was like your
grandparents bringing out the slide projector. "I got a letter to-

day, as I left Sarasota, Florida. I'm here with a group of thirteen people from around the country who helped me prepare and we had a great time. But two days ago we ate lunch at a restaurant and the guy who served us lunch sent—got me a letter today. His name is Randy Ellis, he has a fifteen-year-old daughter named Kailey, who's in Sarasota High School. Her science class was supposed to be for twenty-four students. She is the thirty-sixth student in that classroom, sent me a picture of her in the classroom. They can't squeeze another desk in for her, so she has to stand during class."

"I bet that's a lie," Dan Bartlett said.

"He doesn't lie *all* the time, Bartlett," Mark kidded him.

Dan shook his head. "It's just phony. You watch."

The second mistake came when Lehrer asked one of the more interesting questions of the evening: "We've been talking about a lot of specific issues. It's often said that, in the final analysis, about ninety percent of being the president of the United States is dealing with the unexpected, not with issues that came up in the campaign. Can you point to a decision, an action you have taken, that illustrates your ability to handle the unexpected, the crisis under fire, et cetera?"

Bush talked about responding to natural disasters in Texas, particularly a series of fires and floods that had devastated part of southern Texas, which he had toured with the head of the Federal Emergency Management Agency, James Lee Witt. Gore countered by saying, "Yes, first, I want to compliment the governor on his response to those fires and floods in Texas. I accompanied James Lee Witt down to Texas when those fires broke out."

Karen bolted out of her metal folding chair. "He did not! I was there! Gore never toured with James Lee Witt. Check it, but I'm sure he didn't."

So there it was. Gore was ending the debate the way he

began it, with an unforced foul that went directly to his greatest vulnerability—credibility. He had started and ended with lies. And sighed and generally made an ass out of himself in between.

We'd won. We knew we'd won. The only problem was convincing the rest of the world that this was the case. We huddled quickly to go over talking points: Bush won by going toe to toe with Gore, was in command of the issues, laid out his vision and agenda, stressed less government. The usual points. But the key offense against Gore was to hit him on the distortions and on his inability to tell the truth.

On the spin room floor, the Gore people could not have been more smug. They were convinced that their guy had exposed Bush as a provincial dummy. Of course, win or lose, they *had* to spin that Gore had won—just as we did for our team—but the confidence they radiated in the postdebate spin battles wasn't feigned. It was the genuine, aren't-we-smart, didn't-we-kick-ass kind of glow.

The problem was, they had a lot of people agreeing with them. Russert was saying, "It was the most positive I've seen Al Gore in any debate setting." Jacob Weisberg of *Slate* was claiming that "Bush got his clock cleaned." And, shockingly, George Stephanopoulos had looked deep into his heart and come to the conclusion that "Gore dominated the debate."

"It was a draw," Jonathan Alter said when we were standing around after the first frantic rush of spinning had waned and people were actually starting to talk to each other like humans instead of combatants. "You should be happy, your guy did better than most people thought he would."

"We're going to ram this debate right up his ass," I said. "Just you watch. The sighing, the interruptions, the exaggerations."

"Gimme a break," Al Franken said. "Your guy has a tax

plan that will bankrupt the country and you're saying Gore maybe sighed too much?"

Franken was just part of the collection of celebrity types who would turn up at the debates, adding to a carnival feel. The Democrats were always better at this than Republicans. We'd get some obscure attorney general to help us spin the importance of tort reform and they'd get Erin Brockovich.

"The old Al Gore was back tonight and he's going to pay," I said. It sounded an awful lot like a schoolboy taunt. This whole spin game was starting to feel like life imitating high school:

"We won!"

"No, we won!"

"Kick your ass!"

"Do you really think we can push this credibility thing?" I asked Dan Bartlett and Ed Gillespie back at the bar. Now that we were out of spin frenzy, we were trying to honestly assess what had happened.

"We got a good shot," Gillespie said. Ed had been drafted down to Austin to help out in the communications shop after the Republican convention. A top Republican operative in Washington, he was Irish, smart and had a great feel for how far we could push a story with the press. Those of us who had been in Austin for over a year were so deep into the campaign that we had lost any semblance of judgment. We were in that state of mind that I imagine happens to you in the front lines of war: The other side is evil, they must be destroyed at all costs. Ed still had his sanity.

"The thing is," Ed said, "the press needs a new plot. If we can get them to buy 'Gore's back to his old ways,' that's a hell of a good story."

"They want to write something different, you can feel it," Dan Bartlett said.

"Of course, there's always a chance they'll write the debates were our last hope and we didn't turn it around," Ed said and shrugged.

Bartlett and I looked at each other. "My official opinion on that happening is that it would really suck if it did."

"But I think the Candy Gram Committee," Ed continued, "can have some serious fun this week. You really think he made up that thing about the girl standing up?" Ed had started a daily meeting down in Austin that picked the best hit on Gore to push with the press. He called it the Candy Gram Committee.

"Something's not right," Bartlett said. He had been heading the Austin rapid-response effort for months.

"So this race is going to come down to whether or not some sixth-grade girl is still standing up or not?" I said.

"We can spin it without that," Ed said, smiling. "But it sure would be fun with it."

11

Tennessee?

A WEEK LATER, THE WORLD HAD CHANGED.

Or at least it felt that way. The Gore campaign was on the defensive for the first time in what seemed like months. Cheney had aced the vice-presidential debate, effectively ending the press's love affair with Lieberman and all but taking Lieberman out of the race. And now, on the day before the second presidential debate, Al Gore was actually on national television apologizing for his performance in the first one.

"I'll do my best to get the details right. And I'll also be sighing a little bit less in this debate," Gore said on CNN. On ABC, Gore said, "I will try to do better in getting all the details right and not giving people reason to think that I have stretched a story to make a point."

So sweet. The classroom story had proven to be a simple mistake rather than an exaggeration. Yes, the girl had not had a desk—but only for a day or so. Still, everywhere you turned, the story had become Gore's exaggerations, his sighing, his makeup. CNN's Jonathan Karl said, "Aides say Gore's heavy makeup was also a distraction in the first debate, taking away from what they say was his clear victory on substance."

The governor and Mrs. Bush took our little debate team out to dinner the night before the second debate in North Carolina. It was like a vacation. He was as relaxed as I'd seen him since the preconvention love fest. Gone was the deep exhaustion that made you feel like you were watching a friend hit the wall in a marathon. He seemed rejuvenated, eager, and we spent the dinner talking about everything in the world except the race and what might or might not happen the next night. When we were leaving, people in the restaurant suddenly recognized him and some stood up to applaud—this kind of thing happened frequently in places like North Carolina, but it was still startling. *Oh, yeah, there's a presidential race.*

Even the weather seemed to be in a good mood. In Kentucky, the day of the Cheney–Lieberman debate had been a glorious warm fall day. We'd arrived around noon at the debate site, done a quick walk-through and then gone back to an old redbrick inn that had been taken over by the Cheney advance team. It was a wonderfully luxurious feeling not to have anything to do except hang out and be on call in case anything came up, which of course it wouldn't. It was too late for any more debate preps; everything was on auto-pilot now.

We used an old stable next to the inn that had been converted into an office as the staff headquarters. Several televisions had been set up—the advance team always arranged for lots of televisions—and the Cheney foreign policy debate team—Paul Wolfowitz, Scooter Libby, Stephen Hadley—were closely monitoring what was happening in the former Yugoslavia, as Milosevic's hold was crumbling. I went for a run, came back and fell asleep in the sun while Wolfie and Scooter talked through the implications of Milosevic's ouster. I woke up and listened for a while, came to the conclusion that the world would get along just fine if I didn't have an opinion on this subject and went back to sleep.

It was the same kind of weather in North Carolina the day of the second Bush–Gore debate—sunny with just a hint of coolness. Mark and I went for a run—that's what you did on debate day, you worked out because you had the time and because you needed to do something to burn off the nervousness and because it was a good way to get away from reporters. We talked about the ads we would run for the rest of the campaign. By luck, as much as anything, the ad we were currently running had made us look very good. It was a sixty-second spot called "Trust," and we had it in the can ready to go after the first debate, completely unaware, of course, that Gore's performance in the debate would send the issue of credibility into hyperdrive:

> GOVERNOR BUSH: I believe we need to encourage personal responsibility so people are accountable for their actions. And I believe in government that is responsible to the people. That's the difference in philosophy between my opponent and me. He trusts government. I trust you. I trust you to invest some of your own Social Security money for higher returns. I trust local people to run their own schools. In return for federal money, I will insist on performance. And if schools continue to fail, we'll give parents different options. I trust you with some of the budget surplus. I believe one-fourth of the surplus should go back to the people who pay the bills. My opponent proposes targeted tax cuts only for those he calls the right people. And that means half of all income taxpayers get nothing at all. We should help people live their lives but not run them.
>
> Because when we trust individuals, when we respect local control of schools, when we empower communities, together we can ignite America's spirit and renew our purpose.

The spot had taken shape during the dark days of September, when we were frustrated at our inability to cut through the campaign clutter with a "big-picture" message. Ever since the Democratic National Convention, we had been off-stride, had allowed Gore to set the agenda. It had started with the stutter step of the RNC Lisa Myers spot, and we had never regained our footing. We had been sucked into a running tactical fight on issues that were more favorable to Gore, like prescription drugs, and forced to defend the tax cut proposal and Social Security reform. In all the back and forth, we weren't really reminding people of the big reasons to vote for George W. Bush.

Now that "Trust" was on the air, our hope was that undecided and swing voters would see George W. Bush looking relaxed and likable, laying out a vision of the role of government with which they would instinctively agree. It wasn't a fire-and-brimstone, to-the-barricades kind of message, but we weren't working in an environment in which people were seeking drastic change.

We also hoped that the second debate would continue the credentialing process that had begun when we first rolled out the "Successful Leader" commercial in the fall of '99; the goal was to get people comfortable with the idea of George W. Bush as president. It had been a long, gradual process that was at times factual (here's what Bush did in Texas, here's what he wants to do for America) and at times an almost mystical combination of personality and values.

Without a single driving issue or great desire for change, picking a president is a lot like choosing a spouse. You want to know some of the facts—what is their background, what choices have they made in their lives—but you also want somebody whom you would feel good about waking up next to, somebody you would trust to raise the kids. A good and decent person who seems genuine, someone you can respect and who you know would respect you as well.

Gore still had it much easier. All he had to do was be reasonably likable, a reassuring presence who could be trusted to give people what they wanted from the Clinton agenda while erasing the tawdry stains. At the Democratic National Convention, Gore had succeeded in creating just such an impression and his candidacy had taken off.

Now, largely because of self-inflicted wounds—we hadn't really laid a glove on the guy—Gore was faltering.

At every big, defining moment, Bush had stepped up to the plate like one of his beloved baseball heroes and done what he had to do. He'd made mistakes, of course—nobody runs for president who doesn't. But had Gore performed on Bush's level, the race would have been over.

The dynamic of the race was clear: When Gore made mistakes, we moved ahead. But what would happen if during the last week of the campaign he hit a good stretch and didn't make mistakes? Whenever I thought about this, I came to one not very original conclusion: We needed to attack more. We couldn't risk heading into the election without doing everything we could to remind voters of what they didn't like about Al Gore. I was convinced that in key markets like Miami and Philadelphia, we should be running a mix of media that would be 80 percent negative/contrast, 20 percent positive.

Matthew Dowd and I actually had a heated argument over this, one where we were close to yelling at each other—unusual in the Bush campaign, which is in itself unusual. Matthew was convinced that we needed to keep more of a positive message in the mix. I thought in markets like Miami, which we were losing, our positives were doing nothing for us, and we might as well go to full contrast. "It's like the last scene in the *Alien* movies when they start coming out of the air vents. It's time to go to full flame-throwers."

"Miami's not the problem, it's Orlando," Matthew shot back.

"Go seventy-thirty negative to positive in Orlando, then. It's our best shot."

Matthew and I went at it for a while, of course coming to no resolution. But I think we both felt better.

The point Matthew was making was an excellent one—that if we didn't keep enough positive information about our candidate in the flow of daily information, the comfort level that people were beginning to feel with Bush would slip away, allowing the Gore campaign to define us negatively with their endless barrage of negative commercials. This was a huge, potentially lethal danger. But I thought the greater danger was not keeping enough pressure on Gore and allowing the positive mood of the country to lift him up over the finish line.

The wonderful and horrible thing about being in the middle of a political campaign is that both of us were probably half-right, and neither of us could prove his point with empirical evidence. But I doubted my opinion would carry the day. Every campaign has its own culture, and the Bush campaign culture had a decided tilt toward the positive. The Gore campaign—with its "slaughterhouse" of "killers," all those smart Harvard lawyers—had a much more sardonic, slashing style. Gore was intuitively a slash-and-burn kind of candidate. Which didn't mean that he was a bad person or couldn't be a great president, it was just his style, and that style permeated his campaign. It was reinforced by the Gore campaign's deep belief that Bush, as Paul Begala kept saying, was a lightweight. They adopted a bullying attitude toward Bush, heavily laced with a kind of cultural elitism. Bush was from Texas, and, except for a few good Texas liberals, Texas was guns and people who didn't understand the need for proper zoning, a state that still depended upon the oil business *(how retro was that?)*, a state that still executed people. The notion that America might elect a *Texan* president—*a conservative Texan*—was simply unimaginable, especially when a sensible Alan Alda type like Gore was a viable option.

☆　　　☆　　　☆

The second debate went so well, I actually started to feel sorry for Gore at one point. He spoke like someone recovering from a stroke and had the demeanor of a severely scolded child. The governor was relaxed, funny, on top of his game. Sitting side by side with Gore, he did what no one had ever done before in a debate with Gore—he dominated the guy. It was as close to a slam dunk as you get in a presidential debate with two well-prepared, relatively well-matched candidates.

Afterward the Gore forces seemed shell-shocked by their candidate's performance. Now they were reduced to arguing that the debates really weren't that important, that they weren't likely to alter the outcome of the race. This from the crowd that had been crowing for a year and a half that Al Gore would decimate George W. Bush in debates.

What had seemed at one point to be an unimaginable long shot was actually now taking place: Bush was winning the presidential race largely based on his performance in the debates. Afterward, he seemed nonplussed about it all. "I thought we did okay," he conceded. But on some level, he had to be deeply gratified. Regardless of the outcome of the presidential race, he had taken on the man considered to be the most formidable debater in modern American politics and beaten him.

☆　　　☆　　　☆

George W. Bush had been running for president for a year and a half. From the very beginning, one of the forces propelling his candidacy was the perception that he was a different kind of Republican. But in the afterglow of the Democratic convention, too often we'd lost that message, which hurt us the most with moderate suburban voters. These were people comfortable voting for either party, and many of them hadn't voted for a Republican presidential candidate since 1988. Education had always been the best way to reach these voters. It worked because they cared about education, and they could sense that George W. Bush was passionate about it as well. Here was where the status quo was failing, so at last our message of change would really resonate. And it helped that—unlike crime, welfare, taxes or foreign policy—education wasn't a typical Republican issue.

On the campaign trail, education became our default. If the governor was going into a town where we weren't sure what to do, we would always try to put together an education event. Why not? It gave him a chance to talk about an issue he loved, and the pictures were great. In making education spots—and we made a ton of them—we had always believed that Bush was his own best messenger and tried to build the spot around him talking on camera. But this late in the campaign, we were sensitive to the possibility that people were tuning out both Bush and Gore. It was just a case of overexposure—*I don't want to hear from these guys, I've seen them too much, when is this thing going to be over?*

"Why not go with Phyllis Hunter?" Russ suggested. Phyllis Hunter was an African American Texan who had been involved with reading programs supported by Bush. She had appeared in the convention film, talking about what Bush had done to help education in Texas, and she played to rave reviews. "We could cut a thirty out of the convention film," Russ said.

It was appealing to use Hunter because she would not

only help deliver a message about education, she would also serve as a credible witness to put on the stand to testify that Texas wasn't the hell that Gore was trying to portray. If this bright, compelling African American woman said that George W. Bush had done great things for education in Texas, maybe Gore was exaggerating. *You know how that Gore exaggerates.*

The DNC seemed to have an endless stream of attacks on Texas ready to air. In one day they released three new ones: They all were similar to this one:

> ANNOUNCER: There's nothing wrong with your screen. What you're seeing is the worst smog in America.
>
> The city? Houston, Texas.
>
> As governor, George W. Bush made key air pollution rules in Texas voluntary . . . even for some plants near schools. Last year, Houston overtook Los Angeles as America's smoggiest city.
>
> Now take a deep breath and imagine Seattle with Bush's Texas-style environmental regulation.
>
> George Bush.
>
> Before he talks about cleaning up Washington, maybe he should clean up Texas.

Russ cut the Phyllis Hunter footage into a spot, and we started airing it in markets like Philadelphia, Detroit, St. Louis, Pittsburgh, Portland, Seattle, all places where we felt that the outcome depended on suburban voters.

> PHYLLIS HUNTER: I have seen a big difference since he has been governor of the state of Texas.
>
> GOVERNOR BUSH: I want every child to be able to access the greatness of America and we'll start by teaching every child to read.

HUNTER: He said, "You need it, we'll get it for you." We have websites, we have grant programs and we have George leading the way. People ask me why have I followed him so intently in education and reading. I've followed him because he's been a leader.

GOVERNOR BUSH: Reading is the new civil right. Because if you can't read, you can't access the American dream.

Alex Castellanos was also working on a spot that would challenge Gore on his credibility. The fact that Al Gore embellished the truth was becoming an established fact in the campaign. Now we needed to communicate to voters that the same guy who exaggerates his own record would surely do the same when it came to his opponent's. If we could help voters make that connection, it would go a long way toward "blowing up the aircraft carrier instead of shooting down the planes," as it was known in political circles. The planes were the constant attacks on Texas. Gore's credibility was the aircraft carrier. We knew that if we responded to any specific charge, they would just launch another. It made for a classic battle of agendas: Gore was trying to turn the race into a referendum on the negative portrait he was painting of Texas over the last four years. We were trying to focus attention on what was wrong in America over the last eight years, like failures in education, the need for Medicare, Social Security reform and, of course, restoring honor and dignity to the White House.

☆   ☆   ☆

"You see these numbers on the debate?" Karl asked the day after the North Carolina debate. We had flown back to Austin late that night and gotten home around 3 A.M. We were drinking coffee in Karl's office the next morning around

8:30, tired, but feeling better about life than we had in a long time. The numbers Karl had were an early release of a CNN/ *USA Today* postdebate poll. Any way you cut it, Bush had won big.

On a straight-up, "Who did the better job in the debate?" question, Bush won by thirteen points, which was pretty amazing considering the tendency of the debates to reinforce partisanship. Everybody liked to believe their guy won. But even Gore voters were shaken by his performance. Only 46 percent said they were more certain they would vote for Gore after the debate, versus 60 percent for Bush. On "likability" based on debate performance, Bush won by fourteen points. On "believability," Bush also won by thirteen points. And when asked "who agreed with you on issues you cared about," Bush beat Gore by nine points.

The postdebate spin out of the Gore camp was an effort to counterattack on the credibility front, trying to make the case that Bush had exaggerated just like Gore. Their main evidence was a statement by Bush that the three men convicted of murdering James Byrd in the horrible dragging case had all been sentenced to death. This wasn't accurate—only two had received the death penalty and one had been given life without parole. When this had come up in the debate, we talked about it in the rapid-response room. There wasn't any point in defending it; it was just wrong, a mistake. But rather than wait until the Gore camp brought it up, Karen had the communication shop issue a press release noting that the governor had misspoken and setting the record straight.

That the Gore people were trying to attack us on credibility was a sign of just how badly they thought the debate had gone. This was a classic "your mama too" kind of spin. They weren't trying to deny that Gore had a problem with the truth, they were just saying that Bush did too.

"If they want to make this race about personal credibility," Karl said, "let's have it."

At 301 Congress Street, the mood was more upbeat than it had been since before the conventions. Partly it was just a relief to have survived September and to not have to wake up every day to a constant barrage of bad stories and pundits spouting off about the blunders and stupidity of the Bush campaign. That was one of the curious things about a presidential campaign in the era of the twenty-four-hour news cycle. All of your missteps were chronicled for the world, debated endlessly, ridiculed openly. To survive, you had to accept the reality of public humiliation on a grand scale. Just imagine what it's like to work in an office in which televisions are constantly on and constantly talking about *you, what you were doing that very moment.* It was like the worst of *The Truman Show.*

For weeks we had been getting our brains beaten out by the pundits, and now the Gore campaign was getting the same treatment. *Gore was wooden, apologizing, doesn't have a message. Losing the debates.* It was time for us to take control of the campaign and move into the lead. Everything was going our way.

But it didn't happen. We couldn't break out.

Every day scores of poll numbers were released, analyzed, debated. Of the public polls, we liked to focus on the Voter.com/Battleground poll, a joint effort by the Republican Tarrance Group and the Democratic Lake Snell Perry firm. We liked it because both firms involved were staffed with professionals who made their living from political work; it wasn't something they did every two years when commissioned by a newspaper or network. In 1996, they had proven to be the most accurate pollsters, predicting that the race would tighten in the final four or five days (which meant that Dole *only* lost by nine points). But we also liked the Battleground poll because it consistently had the best numbers for us.

Hey, it's only human. You're looking at reports from ten or fifteen different doctors and all of them conclude that you are probably going to die in a very short time and there's one—from a credible, big-deal doctor—that says, no, there is a very good chance you might not only live for a while longer but actually beat the disease. Now don't tell me you're not going to listen to that doctor very carefully.

Battleground showed us with a three-point lead. Normally, if you're a challenger, that means you're going to win comfortably, by five or more points. How so? One of the rules of political polling is that the incumbent picks up very little of the undecided vote at the end of a race. This is how challengers like Christie Whitman of New Jersey or Chuck Hagel of Nebraska go from being behind in the last polls of the race to shocking victories. The undecided voters either stay home or vote for the challenger. It makes sense. If someone has been a governor or senator or president for four or eight years and a voter still hasn't decided whether they deserve rehiring on Election Day, odds are that voter is either going to sit the election out or give somebody else a chance. It's as though you've been married for ten years and a pollster wakes you up in the middle of the night and asks whether you want to stay married. If you say you're undecided, it's not a good sign for the marriage.

Gore, of course, wasn't the incumbent, but he was a hell of a lot more of one than Bush. None of us talked about it much, as if afraid we'd jinx it, but our deepest hope was that this tightest of races would suddenly break our way as the undecideds moved. We kept waiting, watching, hoping.

As close as the race was in the national polls, it got even tighter when you started working the Electoral College numbers. We did this constantly, trying to evaluate where to spend money and, even more critically, to decide where Bush should travel. Back in August and September, there had been a period when it seemed a visit by Bush generated little or no movement in tight states. It was maddening. He would come in, do a great event and a day or two later, it was like it never happened.

Now that had changed. The numbers went up—a point or two or three or sometimes five—but then Gore would drop into the same market and the bounce would flatten. It was why both candidates kept chasing each other around the same key markets—Philadelphia, Detroit, St. Louis, Tampa.

Every pollster had a similar list of toss-up states. The remarkable thing was just how long the list was this late in the game: Arizona, Florida, Iowa, Maine, Michigan, Missouri, Nevada, New Hampshire, New Mexico, Oregon, Tennessee, Washington, West Virginia and Wisconsin.

States that we had no business winning—West Virginia, Oregon—were still up for grabs, while a state like Florida, which five months earlier we all assumed we'd win, was definitely in play for Gore. Not that we thought Gore *would* win Florida. In the end, we believed it would come our way, if only by a few points. Then there was the critical lineup of Michigan, Pennsylvania, Ohio, Illinois. We figured we'd win Ohio, lose Illinois and split Michigan and Pennsylvania, but we couldn't see losing both.

"With Florida, we don't have to win Pennsylvania and Michigan," Matthew Dowd would always remind me when I was obsessing over our consistently lousy numbers in the Philadelphia media market. "Look at Tennessee—we're going to win his home state! Ohio is over. Arkansas is going down. We got a shot in Oregon and Washington State. New Mexico we ought to win.

"Look what Gore has to do," Matthew continued. "He's gotta run the table. Win Pennsylvania, Michigan, probably Florida. He can't lose anything on the West Coast. He has to win everything in New England, and Maine is looking like it could go our way. What we have to do is easier than what he has to do."

We'd kick around different combinations of getting to 270 electoral votes, the magic number. Then the next day, when there were new polling numbers, we'd do it all over again. "If we win New Mexico, Oregon and Iowa, we can even lose Florida . . ."

☆   ☆   ☆

When we landed in St. Louis for the final debate, a TWA jet was sitting in the mud where it had skidded off the tarmac. It was a nasty, cold day, spitting rain. We sat on the runway in the gray light of late afternoon, watching them work to free the stuck plane. Before the first debate, the mood had been expectant, bristling, eager. In North Carolina a week later, the feeling had been extreme confidence verging on cockiness. *We can win this thing.*

Now it was simply matter-of-fact—*Let's get this over with and move on.* Short of Gore declaring that he was an agent of Satan, it was hard to imagine how the debates could have turned out better. (Knowing Gore, though, he'd have claimed that he had invented satanism.) There had been a period in September when Gore had been close to knocking us out of contention. The first two debates had reestablished the equilibrium of the race and moved us slightly ahead of Gore. That was as good as we could hope for and now it was time to move on to the endgame.

"We get the debates behind us and then we just get out the vote," Bush said in our final debate practice.

As usual, he seemed very matter-of-fact and strikingly unanxious about the final stretch of the campaign. Everybody always compares a presidential race to a marathon, but really it resembles a long baseball season, with its cycle of daily games, some more meaningful than others, intense series against key rivals followed by lulls, all building to one climactic moment, the final out of a World Series. Bush understood this rhythm and viewed the daily tumult of the campaign with a certain bemused detachment. There had been a great panic among the Republican political class that Al Gore would destroy George W. Bush in the debates. He'd shrugged that off, just as he had the talk that he had won the race after the second debate. "Told you not to write us off," he'd tweak reporters who had been writing the Bush obituary in September.

The final debate was a town meeting with audience questions, held before a supposedly impartial group of swing voters selected by the Gallup organization. We held one practice, a typically informal affair at the governor's mansion, with the usual debate prep crew—Josh Bolten, Condi Rice, Karen Hughes, Karl Rove, Larry Lindsey, Mark McKinnon, Gary Edson—playing the role of swing voters. Rob Portman, the congressman from Ohio who had played Lieberman in the Cheney mock debates, took on the Gore role in the final practice.

As the governor was answering the first question, Portman got off his stool and walked over to stand threateningly close to him. Portman just stood there, staring, until finally the governor threw his arm around him and kissed him on the head, laughing.

"He's going to do that," Portman warned.

"What, try to get in my face like that?" Bush asked.

"You bet he will," Portman said. "He's going to try and intimidate you. Clinton did it to Dole."

"Good luck," the governor said.

"I have a question for the governor," Karl Rove said. "I'm eighty-six and on Social Security," Karl said, "and now you want to force me to put my money in the stock market. Even Larry Lindsey won't put his money in the stock market." Larry's aversion to the stock market was a running joke in the campaign.

"First let me say, that you don't look a day over sixty-five," the governor answered. "That Rogaine seems to be working. And don't listen to Larry Lindsey. Nobody else does."

"I invented Rogaine," Rob Portman interjected, "and I'm glad to see that it's helping America's working families."

☆   ☆   ☆

We were at the bar when the cell phones started ringing with the rumor: A small private plane had crashed and there was a chance Governor of Missouri Mel Carnahan had been onboard.

We all believed it was true as soon as we heard. The report was too specific to be coincidence. Governor Carnahan had been flying in the area, from one event to another. He was overdue at the second event. It was a nasty night, and we'd seen that jet off the runway at the airport. It just felt bad.

The bar was full of reporters and Bush people. Quickly the news got worse—Carnahan's son was believed to have been piloting the plane. His top aide was with him too. A few people started crying. The local stations had the news now and were in full crisis-reporting mode. Most of the Bush traveling press left the bar to call their editors and work the story from the press filing center across the lobby. Everybody was wondering whether the debate would be canceled. From a purely political point of view, none of us liked that idea. Our guy was ready to debate now, and dragging it out for another week would only stall the campaign. Gore was in a slump. We wanted it now.

But of course there was nothing we could do about it. We couldn't take a position one way or the other; it had to be up to the Commission on Presidential Debates. Word came they were having a conference call about it. No one seemed to know what would happen.

"One thing for sure," Ed Gillespie said, "this has to change the mood of the debate for everybody. Gore can't come out and attack full throttle, not in front of a crowd of Carnahan's constituents."

I agreed. "The whole thing would have to be subdued," I said. "You can't open a debate with a moment of silence and a memorial to a governor who just died and then turn around and try to rip somebody's face off. Not even Gore."

Carnahan's death was soon confirmed but the debate wasn't canceled. And Gore came after Bush on the first question. He even used the obligatory praise of Carnahan as a pivot to attack. Which had to be a first—combining a tribute to a politician who had just died with an attack on another. "He was a fantastic governor of Missouri," Gore said of Carnahan. "This state became one of the top five in the nation for health care coverage for children under his leadership." The subtext, of course, being that Carnahan had done a better job in Missouri than Bush had done in Texas, a point quickly rammed home.

I loved watching Gore in this debate. Gone was the timid, apologetic nice guy of the previous week, replaced by the rip-your-lungs-out Al, snide, sarcastic, so pushy that Lehrer had to remind him of the rules of the debate within the first few minutes. The week before, you had to almost feel sorry for the man, as though he were some kind of abused child. Feeling sympathy for Gore was a disturbing, not very pleasant experience. The Al Gore of St. Louis was a hectoring, sanctimonious, pompous ass. This was much better. I didn't want to feel sorry for this creepy bully, I wanted to teach him a little humility.

Just as Portman predicted, Gore stalked Bush, moving right over to him like a drunken frat boy trying to pick a fight in a bar.

"Look at this guy!" somebody shouted in the rapid-response room.

Bush looked over at Gore with a bemused half-grin, nodded at him and continued to answer the question. The audience in the debate chuckled. Gore just stood there and eventually returned to his stool.

"He put the move on me," the governor laughed afterward. Ed Gillespie and I had run into him as he was getting into his car. "I thought he was going to do an Austin Powers jujitsu move," Bush said, shaking his head. "How'd we do, Eddie?"

"I don't think they are planning on winning this thing through the debates anymore," Ed said.

"Now we just have to get our people out," Bush said, sitting down in the car. He suddenly looked very tired, like an athlete after a tough game. The motorcade backed out of the covered entrance—the Secret Service tried to make sure every entrance and exit was "covered," obscured from view by anything from a tent to a parking garage—and slowly drove away. Ed and I got in one of the staff vans and headed back to the hotel. The endgame had begun.

Once More, with Feeling 12

I T'S OFTEN SAID THAT THE OLDER WE GET, the more we become like ourselves. We don't really change, we just become more exaggerated. That's how the end of this campaign felt.

We started the race trying to articulate the need for change despite peace and prosperity, and so it was ending. It had never been an easy case to make and the closer we got to the election, the more we feared that the allure of continuity would overcome the desire for change, that voters who had flirted with us would end up going home with the status quo.

Al Gore had started a general election campaign in the spring of 2000 with slashing attacks. For a brief time at the convention, his campaign had focused on trying to get people to like Al Gore. But after the debates, they wisely gave up on that tack. Gore just wasn't very likable. Few had liked him in the U.S. Senate, and while he may have had a private side that was funny, profane and sensitive—everybody said he did—it was proving impossible (as it had been for Bob Dole and Lyndon Johnson before him) to convey this personal side to the public.

So in the final two weeks of the campaign, he went back on the attack with one goal: to disqualify George Bush. This was smart. He didn't have to persuade people that times were good; they already felt that. Nor did he need to make much of a case that he would improve things. All he had to do was convince people that things might get a little bit worse if they went out on a limb and voted for this guy that nobody outside of Texas knew very well.

The Gore campaign started hammering us on Social Security and it scared me to death. It was the attack that was most likely to work. Over the last eight months, they had tried to convince people that Texas was an environmental disaster and that if Bush was elected president, they wouldn't be able to leave their houses without a gas mask. They'd tried to convince parents that their sick children would die in crowded emergency rooms as America was transformed into another Calcutta under George W. Bush. They'd argued that Bush's tax cut would bankrupt the country. All these attacks were troubling but none had really caught fire and captured the attention of key swing voters.

But the Social Security attack might be different. First, there was the not-insignificant point that Gore's attack had some basis in reality. When he accused George W. Bush of supporting the most sweeping changes in the Social Security system since its creation, that was arguably true. Proposing true reform of Social Security had helped define Bush as a strong leader, willing to challenge the status quo. And poll numbers indicated support for Bush's program by as much as a twenty-point margin. The problem was intensity. The people who cared most about Social Security were the people *on* Social Security. And the only promise we were making to them was that things wouldn't get worse. The reform angle, especially being allowed to invest some of your Social Security funds in the stock market, only appealed to younger voters, most of whom didn't believe Social Security would be around when they retired anyway. So while they supported the reforms, they didn't really care.

Gore had done the politically smart thing and handled Social Security reform with a wink and a nod. He had some scheme that no one really understood involving IOUs. This sounded nonthreatening but still gave him something to say when asked how he intended to save the system. And when it started looking like voters were responding to Bush's stock market investment approach, Gore came up with a plan that he called Social Security Plus that allowed him to claim he was giving people a chance to invest in the stock market as well. But his major message to voters was *Bush wants to change Social Security and I want to keep it the same.* This was basically true—it just overlooked the awkward fact that Gore had no real plan to save the system. But never mind, Gore could legitimately claim to be the defender of the Social Security status quo and could legitimately attack Bush as an agent of change.

What Gore was doing was no worse than what politicians have been doing for the last twenty years—hiding the truth about Social Security's precarious state and attacking his opponent for trying to fix it. I had done it myself in a score or more of races. The scary thing was, it usually worked. No one had ever been elected to office espousing the kind of reforms that George W. Bush supported in Social Security.

Gore had attacked sporadically on Social Security since before the convention, but he had attacked on everything. Now, like a fastball pitcher who kept trying to throw curves, Gore finally listened to his catcher screaming advice: "You do one thing well, throw heat! George W. Bush wants to change Social Security! Florida is in play! Older voters in Pennsylvania are in play! Older voters in Michigan are in play! What the hell are you doing talking about global warming in Florida? People in Florida don't think it can get any hotter! They have air-conditioning. But they do care about Social Security!"

We had talked about responding to Gore's Social Security

attacks as soon as they started. It wasn't like we didn't realize that we were doing more than just touching "the third rail of politics," as everybody called Social Security, we were close to *having sex with it.* But with Gore attacking on everything, nothing much was sticking. So in the aftermath of the third debate, when Gore started attacking on Social Security, we waited to see if he would sustain the attack or move onto something else, like the Secret Bush Plan to Invade Canada.

The problem with the wait-and-see approach is that once you realize the attack is for real, odds are you're already bleeding. I was for responding right away with a strong counterpunch, though I had been in favor of more attacks for so long that I was close to being relegated to the lunatic fringe, the Unabomber of Austin. Still, I gave it one more try.

"Look, guys," I started, "I know everybody thinks that I have some personal vendetta against Al Gore, which is mostly true and I admit his very existence troubles me, but I really think he is going to stick with this Social Security attack. It smells like their endgame. They don't know what else to do, so they are going with what has worked before."

Karl cut me off. "How much do you think we ought to run it?"

"Fifty-fifty."

"Good, okay: You got scripts?"

"A million of them."

"Get your best shot to me and I'll run the traps on it. Let's do it."

This was too easy. "But you know in some markets it might be a good idea to go seventy-five percent negative."

Karl laughed and shook his head.

"I had to try," I shrugged.

Laura Crawford and Russ knocked out the spot in an afternoon.

ANNOUNCER: Remember when Al Gore said his mother-in-law's prescription cost more than his dog's? His own aides said the story was made up. Now Al Gore is bending the truth again. The press calls Gore's Social Security attacks "nonsense." Governor Bush sets aside $2.4 trillion to strengthen Social Security and pay all benefits.

GORE: There has never been a time in this campaign when I have said something that I know to be untrue. There's never been a time when I've said something untrue.

ANNOUNCER: Really?

☆   ☆   ☆

Even though the race was, as Dan Rather would say, "tighter than your little sister's shoes," the media was mostly covering the story as though we were ahead and Gore was desperately trying to catch up. We liked this story line and did everything we could to encourage it, spinning our brains out about how we were going to win and win comfortably. Which we had actually started to believe. Even though the race was always within a couple of points, and there were a crazy number of states that were still very tight, it was easy to make a case that in the final weekend of the campaign, undecided swing voters would start to break our way. The model for this was Reagan versus Carter in 1980, a close race in which Reagan sometimes trailed until the final weekend, when the bottom fell out for Carter.

The Gore spin had a whiff of desperation about it: *We are not dead yet. We can still win.* When Gore announced that he was going to campaign nonstop for the last couple of days of the race, everybody made jokes comparing it to Bob Dole's last drive. We even had numbers showing that there was an

outside chance we might win California; the day that Gore announced that he was going to make a trip to California in the
final week of the campaign, we literally cheered. *The final
week and California is in play?* And then when he announced
he was going back to Tennessee it was just too good to be
true. "Can you imagine if George Bush was campaigning in
Texas the last week of the campaign?" Karl asked.

We relished the infighting among the Democrats over
whether or not Bill Clinton should be allowed to appear in
public. Secretly we were hoping that Clinton would embark
on some grandstanding, coast-to-coast final push for Gore.
But in the end the Gore people were smart enough to keep
Clinton on a leash, limiting him to low-key appearances in
Louisiana and Arkansas. Gore, of course, lost both, which only
proves how right the Gore people were to keep the guy out of
sight. If Bill Clinton couldn't carry Arkansas for Al Gore, why
in God's name would anybody think he would help in the rest
of America?

It is not unusual in a campaign to grind out television
spots right up to the final forty-eight hours, fanatically trying to
get one more punch in, one more vote. This didn't happen in
the Bush campaign. It wasn't Karl's style. He hated the frantic
fidgeting that overtakes campaigns in the end, when you fall
into the trap of making spots just to make yourself feel better,
without ever getting to air the spots enough to actually make
an impact. Karl was a planner and we didn't once jerk a spot
off the air and replace it with another simply out of some nervous twitch.

This meant that, a week or so out from the election, those
of us in the Maverick crowd realized we probably weren't going to make any more spots. It was a strange feeling, partly
frustrating, partly a relief. The campaign was entering the stage
in which people like us become irrelevant. The television me-

dia war was done and the day-to-day message of the campaign was less important every news cycle. It was rapidly becoming too late to inject any new messages into the political bloodstream. This was a campaign that was now being fought tarmac to tarmac on the evening news and it was more about execution—phone banks, direct mail, get out the vote efforts—than any of the high and low arts of television ads that I had practiced for years.

It has always made a funny sort of sense to me that the final stage of most campaigns is in the autumn. In my mind there's a bittersweet connection between the season hurrying into winter and the end of the campaign cycle. In New York, late at night, I would leave the editing room and go for a run in Central Park, leaves crunching underfoot, loving the fresh coolness in the air, knowing that in a matter of days this would all be over—the frantic phone calls, the daily trauma of tracking polls, the endless crises that seem so important at the time and so meaningless once the polls have closed.

Austin is not a place noted for beautiful autumns but there is a subtle change in the season, early morning fogs, a dampness, some leaves that fall on Barton Springs to be pushed out of the way when swimming at night. I knew that I would miss Austin and during those last days of the campaign, I tried to devour as much of it as I could. I ate barbeque at the Iron Works, more barbeque at the Green Mesquite, went swimming at night at Barton, even climbing the fence one midnight. I did the Bob Schneider trifecta and heard the Austin rock star play in all his configurations: as a solo artist at the Broken Spoke; with his regular band Lonelyland at Antone's; and finally in a raucous late-night performance by his totally irresistible pickup band, the Scabs. I bought a University of Texas Hook 'Em Horns T-shirt I now wear around New York City. I ate the fabulous grilled quail at Ranch 616, with Daddy-O's huge neon rattler glowing on the outside and Daddy-O himself on the inside, holding court at the bar. "I told you your boy was going to win," he said. "Son of a bitch is going to be president of the United States!" He shook his head. "Poor bastard. Seems like a hell of a nice guy."

Daddy-O's prediction of a Bush victory was looking good. That last week our tracking numbers started to be consistently good—not great, but instead of going up five points one night and down seven points the next, they started leveling out and showing us with a lead in key states like Florida and Michigan. Ohio was in the bag. It looked like we would win Tennessee, Arkansas, New Mexico and Iowa. California had always been a reach too far but Oregon, God bless Ralph Nader, was still very much in play, and Washington State was looking doable. The race seemed to be taking shape, headed toward something more than a narrow victory, maybe four or five percentage points in the popular vote and 310 to 330 in the Electoral College. Not a landslide, but something big enough that you could call it a mandate, particularly when the race has been so tight for so long.

The governor was in a fabulous mood. The crowds on the road were huge, but then they always are at the end. He had taken to calling Karl and Joe and trying to add more events to each day's schedule, trying to jam as much as possible into the last days. This was a race I had never felt very confident about winning but now I did start to feel like it was breaking our way.

"I had accepted losing a month ago," Mike Gerson, the speechwriter, said to me on the Thursday before the election. "But now, I'll just hate it." If we did win, Mike's writing would be one of the major reasons. From the first speech launching the campaign in Iowa to each of the major policy speeches to Bush's acceptance speech at the convention, it was Mike who had created the language that we had used to wage this campaign. Many of his phrases—"Leave no child behind," "The soft bigotry of low expectations," "Let us ask children not how old they are, but what have they learned"—had managed to cut through all the noise and clutter of the campaign and define the Bush candidacy. Gore, for all his focus groups and consultants, had never developed a distinctive voice. This inability to articulate the rationale for his candidacy was one of the things that frustrated the Democrats most. If Gerson had been working for him, he wouldn't have had that problem.

I was rediscovering that when you didn't spend all day making commercials, it opened up a lot of time in the day. There was still the daily message meeting, the daily press spin meeting, the Candy Gram meeting, but that still left some extra time, a deliciously novel feeling. Mark disappeared on the road for the final push. He had always enjoyed traveling inside the campaign bubble more than I did. Maybe I had just done it for too many years, but it tended to remind me of a polite kidnapping, where large men with guns told you where to go and what to do. And it was an impossible place to get any work done.

My good feeling about the campaign lasted for several days. Until Thursday late afternoon, when I picked up my cell phone and saw that I had twenty-six messages. I was leaving the studio where I had just seen an Election Night video that Laura Crawford had made using a lot of the outtakes from our various film shoots. Working on funny videos that had a yearbook feel—this was the kind of end-of-term thing you did when you weren't making spots anymore.

As soon as I saw the twenty-six messages, I got that shot-to-the-stomach kind of nervousness that comes from knowing that something bad must have happened. You never got twenty-six messages in a half hour when the news was good.

Back at the campaign there was an edgy battle-stations feel. By then I had listened to enough of the messages to know the story line: A Maine television station had broken the story that George W. Bush had been arrested for DWI, driving while intoxicated, some twenty-plus years earlier.

Karl was in his office, plugged into his headset. This was an image I knew I'd take away from my days in Austin—Karl sitting behind his antique wooden desk on his headset, dealing with the crises of the moment as they flooded over the transom. He had a naturally buoyant nature that was hard to beat down. Only when he lowered the blinds on the large glass window that looked into his office from the main floor was there reason to believe that he was either in a lousy mood or dealing with a Defcon Five crisis. The blind was still up this night. "He's going out in a minute," Karl said.

"He," of course was the governor, and by "going out" he meant that he would be talking to the press. We looked at each other and shrugged. The cable channels and the nets were moving into a full scandal frenzy, announcing that they were going to take the Bush press conference live. This is what they did for bombshells. It was exactly what you didn't want to happen in the final days of a campaign, when campaign discipline was most crucial. In a campaign, you can recover from almost any mistake if you have enough time. But this was the Thursday before Election Day. There wasn't much time to fix anything.

Karl and I watched Mark on television as he walked past the place where the impromptu press conference would be held. It was to take place in front of a redbrick building; I tried to call Mark on his cell to suggest changing the angle so that the cameras wouldn't be shooting straight against the redbrick, which can give the person speaking a cornered look. But I couldn't get him and then the governor was walking out to take questions and it was too late.

Bush looked tired but not angry or hostile, more resigned to the questions. Several times, when pressed as to why this was coming out now, he made the point that the timing was questionable. He wasn't accusatory, but he didn't shrink from voicing his suspicions.

The obvious question was, How *did* this come out just days before the election? These things don't happen by accident.

Tim Morrison and Bill Clark, the two "oppo dudes" of the campaign, walked into Karl's office. They were smiling. "You know who is from Kennebunk, don't you?" Bill Clark asked. He and Tim were both in their late twenties and looked like very tired, very rumpled college kids. They were in jeans, as always, and Tim was wearing the heavy leather work boots that were his trademark in an office where cowboy boots were the norm.

"Chris Lehane is from Kennebunk," Tim said. These guys had worked together for so long, crammed into their little cubicle, surrounded by stacks of files, newspaper clippings and pizza boxes, that they often finished each other's sentences.

This was interesting. Chris Lehane was Gore's press secretary. The story had been leaked out of Kennebunkport, where the incident had taken place. Was it possible that Chris Lehane, who had been active in Maine politics, whose sister worked for a law firm in Portland, who grew up in Kennebunk, a town of about three thousand, hadn't known anything about this? Sure, it was possible. Was it likely? Not very.

Within hours we knew a lot more and had a lot more questions. The reporter who had leaked the story, a young woman named Erin Fehlau from a Portland television station, maintained that she had stumbled onto the story when she happened to overhear a police officer talking about the incident in the Portland courthouse; the police officer then told her a local lawyer had the information and, when she contacted the lawyer, he provided her with a copy of the court records.

On *Nightline,* Ted Koppel was openly skeptical of the story. "You're pretty confident you weren't set up, here?" Koppel asked the young reporter. By then the local lawyer who gave her the information had been identified—Tom Connolly, a former Democratic candidate for Maine governor and, most interestingly, a Gore delegate to the Democratic National Convention.

The next morning on *The Today Show,* Matt Lauer was even more leery of her account. "When you hear all these facts lined up: the police officer comes to you and says, 'Hey, here's what I heard,' the attorney's name is mentioned, you meet the attorney, the attorney just happens to have the docket, he happens to have been a delegate at the Democratic National Convention. It sounds like the plot of a movie."

"It kind of does," was the reporter's confidence-inspiring denial.

There was no real way to determine how the story was playing. *The Today Show* dedicated the better part of an hour to the story, it led the news on every network and the cable channels were in full Monica mode. Meanwhile, more confusing details surfaced about the leak; apparently Tom Connolly, who constantly wore a duck bill fishing hat that made him look like a marine version of Ignatius Reilly, the hero of *A Confederacy of Dunces,* had shopped the story to at least one other reporter, who had passed on it, believing it to be an old story, not newsworthy. And a local judge, Billy Childs, appeared to have been involved somehow in the acquisition of the court records, only to discreetly disappear from view when reporters were looking to ask him questions. Our best guess was that the energy released by the story tended to pump up the hard core of both sides and would have only a modest negative effect. In any event, there was nothing we could do but wait for it to be flushed out of the political system.

It still amazes me that no reporter has ever tracked down exactly how this story was leaked. Given the closeness of the election, with five states won or lost by less than a total of fifteen thousand votes, there's certainly a case to be made that the story stopped our momentum and cost us, at the very least, enough votes to have won Iowa, New Mexico, Oregon and Maine, as well as enough votes to have thrown Florida out of the recount mode. John McLaughlin, a Republican pollster, has put together some compelling research that strongly indicates that the story had a negative impact on swing voters. If that's the case, the leaking of the story is arguably the most successful last-minute leak in presidential history, the only one that altered the outcome of a race. Yet we still don't know exactly what happened. Who requested the court records? When were they requested? Was the local judge involved and at whose request?

My theory—and it is just that—is that either the Gore campaign or the Democratic party was involved in feeding the information to Tom Connolly. Their hope was for it to leak out as a local story, without fingerprints of any kind. When the first reporter that Connolly shopped the story to didn't bite, he got a little desperate and fed it to the young reporter, even though he realized he would be revealed as the source. On some level, no doubt he *wanted* to be revealed as the source. It's not often that a small-town lawyer in a duck bill hat adorned with fishing lures, a lowly Gore delegate, has a chance to change the outcome of a presidential election.

A small group of us in the campaign—I'm not sure how many—knew of the incident beforehand, and there had been talk about revealing it voluntarily at an earlier time. I never did discuss it with the governor, but it was understood that it was a personal decision and that he had chosen not to do so. Was it the best move politically? Probably not, but he wasn't making his decision based on politics. He had said repeatedly that, as a father, he believed that it was one thing to admit past mistakes, as he had, but that it was wrong to inventory each mistake.

It's interesting that even while this story was crashing all around us, no one in the campaign was second-guessing Bush's decision not to talk about the incident earlier. This is a rare thing in politics, where it is customary for campaign staffers to develop a mind-set that they know best and that if only the candidate would cooperate, the election would be easy. It wasn't that way in Bush world. It was startling how much the staff genuinely liked the man they were working for and seemed to appreciate that he was dealing with difficult choices, balancing his roles as a father, public official and candidate for president. There was something refreshing about this, like falling in love for the first time.

We entered that last weekend thinking we would win but holding our breath.

The Long Good-bye

13

WAITING IN THE RAIN FOR GORE TO CONCEDE, I was as tired as I could ever remember. The rush of winning, standing in Karl's office when the networks called the election for George W. Bush, the cheers, people crying, walking down Congress Street with Karl and Mark—all that was seeping away and now it was late, very very late, it was cold, it was rainy and Al Gore was taking forever to concede. "He is probably focus grouping his concession speech," I said to Chris Henick, who was towering above me—as he towered above almost everybody—wearing a George Bush baseball hat and an old raincoat. Henick had a cell phone pressed to his ear. "You are going to get electrocuted on that thing," I said.

"You seen Karl?" Henick asked.

"He's here somewhere," I said, looking around.

"We've got to find Karl. Something is wrong," Henick said. "The governor ought to come down here and claim this thing and let's get out of here."

The crowd was soaked, but everybody who was still there had stuck it out because they wanted to be part of history and didn't mind being soaked, at least not if we won. Suddenly, on the jumbo screen over the stage, an appalled-looking Jeff Greenfield and Judy Woodruff of CNN were reporting that Al Gore had retracted his concession and that Florida was now within a margin of error that demanded an automatic recount. Nobody cursed or yelled at the screen. Instead, they simply stared at these talking heads with incomprehension, as if they had just heard that the election was in doubt because aliens had landed and seized several ballot boxes in Miami and were refusing to release them until Regis Philbin agreed to return with them to their planet.

"This will kill Gore," I said to Henick. "The only man in history to concede and then retract it." I was starting to get angry.

Henick and I returned to headquarters and found Karl back behind his desk. where he had spent the last twelve hours. He had Randy Enwright, the Florida political operative, on the speakerphone. Randy sounded tired but level-headed. Karl was trying to get the latest vote count.

"I don't really have an answer, Karl," he said. "We are trying to get the number. I can't believe it dropped like it did there at the end." None of us could. We had been fifty thousand votes ahead with 97 percent of the precincts reporting.

We watched Bill Daley give his nonconcession speech. "The campaign continues," he concluded. *The campaign continues—what campaign?* The count might continue but this campaign was over.

"Where is Ginsburg?" Karl asked, meaning Ben Ginsburg. The network coverage had switched back to our rally on Congress Street. One of our Warrior advance women was wiping down the podium with her shirt.

Don Evans came out and read a statement. "We hope and we believe that we have elected the next president of the United States. They're still counting, and I'm confident when it's all said and done, we will prevail."

In the debate negotiations Don Evans and Bill Daley had developed a respect and even a fondness for each other. Now they were both going out for their respective candidates, each unable to claim victory, neither willing to admit defeat.

We were still trying to get accurate numbers from Florida when Don appeared in Karl's office with Ben Ginsburg. A short elfin guy, Ben was the leading Republican expert on campaign laws and recounts. Ben had handled the last famous Florida recount case, when Connie Mack won in 1988 based on absentee ballots. Everyone had marveled at how close the race was—Connie won by thirty thousand votes. Only thirty thousand out of five million. That was amazing. Ben was the only one of us who looked fresh, like a field goal kicker called in to win the game. "We are in a recount," he said. "An automatic recount mandated by the state. Not an option."

"Randy's got the latest count and we are somewhere between fifteen hundred and two thousand votes up," Karl said.

"Man, how did this happen?" Don shook his head. "Unbelievable." He was half-soaked from giving his statement in the rain.

People filtered back into the office; somebody made coffee. The phones were ringing in the office like it was ten o'clock in the morning, not 4 A.M. A few of the kids who worked for the campaign, most of whom had been up for several days straight in the final flurry of the campaign ground war, were back at their desks, asleep. "I'd better get down to Tallahassee," Ben Ginsburg said matter-of-factly.

A plane was organized to fly Ben to Florida. Ari Fleischer of the press shop was back at his office dealing with the networks, who were demanding a Bush representative on the morning shows, which were scheduled to start taping in a couple of hours. Ari suggested that Karl go on.

"I'm cratering," Karl said. "You do it, Ari. No way I want to go on. I've got to get some sleep for a few hours."

"What do you think is going to happen?" Don asked me. "You ever done a recount before?"

"Sure. Look, the law of recounts is that unless there are just a few votes separating the two, what always happens in a recap is whoever is ahead increases their lead. It always happens."

"We'll be okay," Don said, rubbing his eyes. Don was in this situation for one reason—he loved George W. Bush and wanted to do anything he could to help him. He wasn't drawn to politics as a blood sport like a lot of us, and there were times when I felt like I should apologize to him for the craziness of this world, which made even wildcatting for oil in West Texas look logical.

"You two look like hell," Don said to Ari and me.

"I feel like hell. I'm going home," I said.

"I've got to shave and get ready to do these shows," Ari said. We talked a little about what Ari's spin should be for the shows.

"Do the same thing we have been doing for months," I said. "Predict victory. We might as well, it doesn't matter."

"Just don't predict too big a victory," Don drawled.

"Just big enough," Ari said.

"Now you got it," Don agreed. "You're a good man, Ari. We'll be pulling for you. From bed. Let's go," he said to me. "You need a ride?"

"No, I've got my car."

But when I walked out on Congress Street I realized I didn't have my car after all, that my wife had taken it home around 1 A.M., a lifetime ago. I walked down Congress Street in the rain looking for a cab.

☆   ☆   ☆

We thought it would all be over in a matter of days. There would be a machine recount of all the ballots, our lead would expand or stay about the same and Gore would accept defeat and concede graciously. Had anybody suggested that this thing would go on for another thirty-five days, we would have laughed hysterically, then probably thrown the person out of the window. *Thirty-five days for a simple recount?* No way.

"Do you think I ought to stick around for a few days until this thing is settled?" Mark asked me.

He had long planned to disappear after the election for two weeks in Zanzibar, a place he had picked off the map because it seemed far away and he liked the name. I was sympathetic to both instincts. "You ought to go," I said. "I don't know what we are going to do hanging around here anyway." This was actually more true than I realized at the time. From the moment the recount began, another campaign lurched into existence and what Mark and I did, the black arts of television, would have no role. Over the next few weeks, I would become accustomed to a sickening sensation of helplessness. After twenty years of campaigns, I understood their quirks and rhythms, the unpredictability that was almost predictable. Campaigns had made me angry, giddy, exhausted and occasionally deeply gratified. But I had rarely felt helpless. There was always one more spot to make, one more spin, one more missile to launch.

But for the next thirty-five days, I would wake up every morning to the growing realization that whether we won or lost, the race for the presidency was going to have little to do with anything we did in Austin that day. For all our posturing in front of the television cameras, this was now an election that would be decided in the courtroom by lawyers. They were the soldiers now and I was just another well-intentioned civilian.

In those first few days, we were still in campaign mode, instinctively reacting to the recount crisis just as we had every other crisis for the last year and a half. The recount was annoying but the idea that we might lose it and the presidency never crossed my mind. *Gore had already conceded, for crying out loud.* This was just a technicality to go through, one last desperate effort for him to cling to power. (This ignored the reality that the recount was automatic, but who could be rational at a time like this?) I must confess to a stab of glee as I contemplated Al Gore's legacy—as a man pathetically forced to unleash lawyers to snare a prize he'd had every chance imaginable to win cleanly. It would all be so sweet in a few days when the recount was over, our lead confirmed, our victory secure and then Al Gore would go down in history as the only guy who had to concede twice in one presidential election.

"If the will of the people were to prevail," Bill Daley was proclaiming, "Al Gore should be awarded a victory in Florida and be our next president."

We were standing around headquarters watching Bill Daley and Warren Christopher do their best to seem outraged. For all their angry words, they never seemed to have their hearts in the fight.

"What is this 'will of the people' crap?" I muttered. This was outrageous. *What are we going to do, have a national séance instead of an election? Get a big Ouija board out?*

It was clear watching Christopher and Daley that the Gore campaign was improvising a strategy. They had no idea what would work and wouldn't, but each day that dawned without George W. Bush being declared president was a good day. At the moment they seemed most keen on discrediting the butterfly ballot, which they darkly implied was part of some massive injustice that had been wrought by outside forces on the poor voters of Palm Beach County.

"That's the butterfly ballot that was designed by Palm Beach's own election supervisor," Michael Toner, the in-house Bush campaign lawyer said, standing next to me watching the television. "The butterfly ballot that was approved by Democratic County commissioners, published in the paper and never objected to by a single Democrat. Now somehow this is a Republican plot?" He shook his head; Michael already looked tired. In thirty-five days he would move beyond tired into some transcendent state of permanent exhaustion.

In retrospect, it's apparent from that very first press conference that the Democrats made wrong strategic choices from which they never fully recovered. By investing so much of their outrage in the butterfly ballot, they had picked a fight they could never win. If the ballot was confusing, what did they expect to be done about it after the fact? The chance of actually getting a revote was about as likely as a court declaring that the election must be redone because the ballot wasn't written in Esperanto, the true universal language. When the smoke cleared on the butterfly ballot and people began to understand that while it might have been a mess, it was a perfectly legal mess of Palm Beach's own making, it started to confirm the impression that Gore was a victim shopping around for an injustice. Like their mantra to "count every vote," which really meant the votes of their choosing, a fact that was not lost on anybody with an IQ higher than the average daily temperature in Miami. The Gore forces were angry, they were tired, and they were flailing around. All of this was understandable, but it still didn't make up for the lack of an overall strategy.

Of course, no strategy could make up for the Gore team's one inescapable problem—Gore kept losing the election. Had Gore been 1,784 votes ahead instead of behind on election night, he would have been president. Had Gore moved ahead in the machine recounts, so that he was 320 votes ahead of George W. Bush instead of 320 votes behind, he probably would have been president. Had some county uncovered a massive screw-up of underreported Gore votes, he could have won. Gore ultimately lost because he never won. Which may seem a tad obvious, but then this was thirty-five days when Bill Daley from Chicago was the voice of ballot integrity and Warren Christopher whose heart, they used to joke at the State Department, would set off metal detectors, was telling us what mattered was how people *felt* in the ballot booth, not how they voted. Meet the new spokesman for the Friends Psychic Network, Warren "Chuckles" Christopher. Right through the rabbit hole we plunged.

A lot has been made about the networks calling the race for Bush, that massive conspiracy on the part of ABC, CBS, NBC, CNN, Fox News, et cetera. Much has been made of the fact that Fox News employee John Ellis, George W. Bush's cousin, was the first to pull the trigger for Bush, though I don't seem to remember where it was written that NBC, ABC, CNN, CBS, et cetera, *had* to follow Fox News. In fact it's not so unreasonable to think that Dan Rather might enjoy not following Roger Ailes's Fox News. No doubt, if I were a Gore person, I would be furious at the networks, just as we were furious with them on election night when they called Florida without knowing what the hell they were doing. The Gore forces have complained bitterly that the networks declaring Bush the winner created an impression that they were never able to erase and I'm sure they are right. But all it took for Al Gore to undo that impression was to win in Florida. Instead, Gore lost every count, which is why he wanted to keep counting. If you were confident you'd won, why not agree to that? Maybe eventually he would win one. If you could keep playing the Super Bowl until you won, would you blow the whistle?

It was interesting watching the Gore camp's contortions over the popular vote. It was clearly driving them crazy that Gore had won the popular vote and they were still having to troll for votes in Florida before they could move into the Oval Office. I would have felt exactly the same way. But it was deliciously ironic that in the days leading up to the election, they had been preparing for the scenario in which Bush might win the popular vote but lose the electoral vote. Apparently nervous about an attempted coup under this scenario, they had been spinning for days that the Electoral College was sacrosanct and that what happened in the popular vote was just a sideshow. Now that the situation was reversed, they did what any campaign would have done. They backtracked, moaned, groaned, wished to hell they hadn't said those things and tried to stir up a popular uprising against the gross injustice of the Electoral College without looking too terribly hypocritical and opportunistic.

Clearly they wanted to go in front of every camera in America and shout, "We won the goddamn popular vote by hundreds of thousands! This thing should be ours! What is this Electoral College bullshit anyway?" But, alas, they had to make do with a little more subtlety, dropping lines like, "Even though he won the popular vote by hundreds of thousands of votes, Al Gore recognizes . . ." Even Gore couldn't keep from pointing out in his first postelection press conference that he had won the popular vote, just to clear up any misunderstanding, of course. Then he reasserted that he intended to abide by the Electoral College, which was rather touching, I thought, making obeying the Constitution sound like a voluntary option.

☆   ☆   ☆

"You got to see this thing," Gary Edson said, waving a piece of paper in my direction. "I got this from a buddy in the election office," he said. "Cook County, butterfly ballot. The butterfly ballot is such an injustice, they use it in Bill Daley's home county!"

I held Gary's piece of paper in my hand, marveling at it. It was the most beautiful thing I had ever seen. I was in love with this piece of paper.

"Has Karl seen this?" I asked.

Gary shrugged. "I'm not sure."

"He has got to see this," I said, and started to walk off with the piece of paper.

"Give me that thing back," Gary yelled at me.

"Never," I said.

"I am going to make some damn copies of it," Gary said. "It is the only one we have."

Karl was preparing for a press conference with Karen and Don Evans. This was two days after the election, before James Baker had taken center stage in Tallahassee, and would be one of the last times that we tried to stage a campaign-style Austin press conference.

"You've got to see this Cook County ballot that Gary came up with," I said to Karl. He looked better than he had on election night at 4 A.M. It was beginning to sink in that we might be in for a long fight and Karl liked a good fight.

Matthew Dowd came into the office. As usual, he was carrying a computer printout with numbers on it. Matthew loved numbers.

"Do you know that from 1996 to 2000 the total registration of the Independent party, the Reform party and the American Reform party increased a hundred percent?" Karl and I looked at each other. Pat Buchanan was on the Reform party line and the main complaint about the butterfly ballot was that people had mistakenly voted for Buchanan. Maybe it wasn't so unreasonable that Buchanan got more than three thousand votes.

"What's the total?" Karl asked.

"Almost seventeen thousand voters," Matthew said.

"And Buchanan got how many?" Karl asked.

"Three thousand four hundred and seven."

"Sounds like a talking point to me," I said.

The only thing that anyone knows for sure is that Buchanan did get 3,407 votes. No one in the world can tell you exactly why this happened or how many of those votes were intended for Bush or Gore. But at least the butterfly ballot eruption did provide one priceless moment—Pat Buchanan on television vigorously confirming that no one in their right mind could have voted for him. He described people who had mistakenly voted for him as "very anguished and chagrined, and I don't think they're acting." He seemed offended at the very idea that people might have *deliberately* voted for him and wanted to point out as quickly as possible that clearly it was a mistake. He was *Pat Buchanan,* after all. How in God's name could *anyone* vote for him?

☆   ☆   ☆

"We just dropped six hundred and thirty-seven votes in Palm Beach County," Brian Ballard told me.

"That's impossible," I said, as I usually did when something I didn't like happened in Florida.

Brian sort of chuckled. "We're still ahead." This was in the first few days, when the machine recount was underway.

Yeah, still ahead, I thought, but when you got 1,740 votes and you just lost 637, that ain't good. This isn't supposed to be happening. We are supposed to be moving ahead in the recount, *not* behind.

"What the hell happened?" I asked Brian.

"Some kind of computer error," Brian said and sighed. Brian Ballard was, at the ripe old age of thirty-something, one of Florida's most skilled Republican operatives and about as wired in Florida politics as you could get.

"These Gore people are crazy," Brian said. "You are never

going to have a revote done in Palm Beach County. They are arguing for something that is not going to happen. They teach you in law school this is not so smart."

The pictures coming out of Palm Beach County were full of outraged citizens demanding a revote. This struck me as harmless and arguably helpful, especially since the likes of Jesse Jackson and Alan Dershowitz were rapidly becoming the public face of the Gore campaign's assertion that American democracy was imploding. There was a limit to how much sympathy Claus Von Bulow's lawyer could generate. And Jesse, well, he just made it all the more of a farce. Now all we needed was Barbra Streisand to go on *Larry King Live* to guarantee that this had become just another American comic strip.

"There is all kinds of crazy stuff going on in Gadsden County too," Brian said. "You are not going to believe it." The next morning he faxed over an article in which election officials in Gadsden County were quoted as admitting that they were "trying to read the minds of voters" in recounting the ballots. "Mind reading" became a term we latched on to and used to great effect. *How can you pick a president based on mind reading?*

We were still immersed in a thick fog of war that felt like it would never clear. There was confusion as to how many of the absentee ballots had actually been counted in each county. No one seemed to understand exactly what the situation was with the overseas ballots—how many were outstanding or what process each county would use to count the ballots as they arrived. There was a deadline of Friday, November 17, when the ballots were due. But if the ballots came in earlier, each county had different rules about whether they would count the ballots on receipt or wait until the deadline. This was critical since we were trying to figure how many of the overseas ballots were already included in each county's totals. And it became even more important when our lead shrank to 320 votes from the previous landslide of 1,784.

It's a strange sensation to be sitting around campaign headquarters in a presidential race, realizing that basic facts about which you are clueless will determine the outcome of the race. It was sort of like being in the middle of a Super Bowl and not knowing whether field goals were going to count for three points or four points and maybe in the fourth quarter the field goals were going to count for five-and-a-half points, but that would be decided at a halftime meeting of the referees.

"I am going to get Warren on this overseas ballot thing," Chris Henick said. He was talking about Warren Thompkins, not Christopher, the South Carolina political operative who had run our endgame against McCain. The press had fixated on Warren as some dark force, which was probably a good thing since the worst thing for someone in Warren's business is to be considered ineffectual. Far better to be feared than ignored. There's an amusing dichotomy in the way the media tends to treat Republican and Democratic political operatives. Democratic operatives are tough-minded, hard-nosed; Republicans are ruthless. It's like the old complaint that male executives are considered forceful and demanding while women executives with the same style are called pushy and bitchy. Thus, a guy like James Carville is celebrated as colorful, flamboyant and yes, tough, but he is not considered a bad person because the press for the most part supports his goal—to elect Democrats. (Most of them don't realize that Carville's big break was working for the most pro-life Democratic official in America, Governor Bill Casey of Pennsylvania—the same Bill Casey that Bill Clinton refused to allow to speak at the 1992 Democratic National Convention.)

Even Dick Morris got great press for a while when he was

working for Bill Clinton; when he worked for Jesse Helms, he was the evil mastermind. In the movie *The War Room,* you see George Stephanopoulos threatening some poor bastard who wants to spill dirt on Bill Clinton, but George is cute and wears jeans and has that mop of hair and works for the guy who is promising the most ethical administration in history, so the press gives him a pass. Put a Republican working for a conservative in that same scene and the press would shout that the ghosts of Haldeman and Erlichman have returned. The assumption is that Stephanopoulos is a good person being forced to do bad things in support of a greater good. Surely no modern American politician had a tougher crowd around him than Lyndon Johnson, whose Texas operatives practically invented modern vote stealing and dirty tricks, and yet one of Johnson's top Texas aides, Bill Moyers, has established himself as the conscience of American journalism.

Warren knew how to count votes and he knew how to impose order on chaos.

"Warren will get his arms around this thing," Henick said.

In any presidential campaign, at any given moment, everybody in America has advice to offer. Now that we were in overtime, everybody in America still had advice, only now *we had to hear it that very moment and if we didn't listen we were sure to lose the recount.* Most of the advice amounted to the same thing: (1) don't let Gore count only the four Democratic counties—Palm Beach, Broward, Volusia, and Miami–Dade, and (2) you're crazy if you don't ask for a hand recount in the good Republican counties. It was hard to ignore this advice since it seemed so overwhelmingly logical.

We talked about it at headquarters. It was then that we realized the extent to which the world had changed—that ultimately this decision would be made by the governor based on advice by the team that Ginsburg and Baker had put together in Florida. It wasn't a political decision, it was a legal decision. None of the political operatives in Austin wanted to second-guess whatever decision the lawyers made more than we would have wanted a bunch of them calling us to suggest what commercial to put on or what speech to make or what precinct to organize. It was sort of like coming to grips with the idea that once your kids have gone away to college, they can stay up all night and raise hell and there isn't a thing in the world you can do about it. You just have to trust them.

How strange and emotionally wrenching was the Florida recount? Look at just one day, Friday, November 17. It began with Judge Terry Lewis's decision to uphold Katherine Harris's authority to exclude manually recounted ballots. Which meant that Harris would be able to certify the election the following day, without including the incomplete hand recounts. This meant that we would win. Or at least so we thought at the time. We watched Judge Lewis's decision at headquarters and the place erupted in cheers, with everybody high-fiving one another. The networks had set up cameras in an office adjacent to the campaign and they were able to capture the spontaneous celebration. By the next day, we had put up curtains to mask the cameras' views of headquarters.

A week earlier, none of us had the remotest notion that Judge Terry Lewis existed. Now he appeared to have cleared the way for us to end the Florida mess with a victory. It was ten days after the election, an unimaginably long period of time to wait for finality. But now it looked like it was over.

For a couple of hours anyway. Then the Supreme Court of Florida issued a ruling barring Katherine Harris from certifying results until it heard arguments in the case. This meant that there would be no certification for days, at best. We started to get a not very good feeling about the Florida Supreme Court.

Later in the day, the 11th U.S. Circuit Court of Appeals rejected our campaign's request to stop hand recounts. Not good, but then no one really expected to win that case. To cap off the day, the Miami–Dade County canvassing board voted to conduct a full hand recount, reversing a decision they had made two days earlier. This had the potential to be a disaster, as no one was sure what standards they would use for the recount.

"Is this the goddamnedest thing you have ever seen, or what?" Chris Henick said at the end of the day. Everybody was walking around headquarters saying the same thing, more or less. Our lives were beginning to resemble the movie *Groundhog Day,* in which the character must relive the same day over and over until he gets it right. Each day we would win the race, then lose the race. Then we'd wake up the next morning and do it all over again, with no end in sight. Henick and I retreated to the Continental Club on South Congress Street where the music was good and nobody was talking about chads. And so ended a typical day during the recount.

For all the fierceness with which both sides fought the PR war for those thirty-five days, most of it ultimately didn't matter. The judges on the Florida Supreme Court or U.S. Supreme Court or 11th Circuit did not make their decisions based on what they had just seen on MSNBC or the latest spin from either camp.

But occasionally the press wars did yield significant victories and defeats—like the spin battle over the overseas military ballots. For years, overseas military personnel had been granted extra time to return their ballots. The idea was a simple one—a soldier serving in a faraway country should still be able to vote, even if his vote wasn't received by Election Day. No one had ever paid much attention to these votes before in Florida. But now they had become wildly important.

Both sides were extraordinarily anxious about the over-seas ballots since they could potentially alter the outcome of the entire race. Technically they did not have to be military bal-lots; any overseas voters were granted the same grace period and wild rumors surfaced in the press that the Gore–Lieber-man campaign was expecting to receive thousands of ballots from Americans in Israel. No one had any idea if this was re-motely true, but we were concerned enough to have former Florida Secretary of State Jim Smith hold a press conference stressing the legal requirement that each of these votes, mili-tary and nonmilitary, must be cast before Election Day, even if they were mailed later. This was an effort to head off any postelection effort to organize overseas late voting for Gore–Lieberman. We had no evidence that this was occurring but wanted to send a signal that it was something we were watch-ing, as best we could.

The Gore campaign was equally concerned about the military ballots, which everyone assumed would be skewed toward Bush. Behind the scenes they had a lawyer draft a memo detailing a process by which each of the military votes would be challenged. This was sent to Democratic officials in various counties so they would have it available when ballots were counted.

"Man, did they screw up big time," Henick said, as soon as a copy of the Democratic memo surfaced. In the tightly fought spin war, this was a gift from the gods. After days and days of haggling over hanging and pregnant chads, over one arcane legal point after another, this was something that anybody could understand—the Gore campaign was paying lawyers to try to challenge ballots from overseas military personnel.

"Unbelievable!" Mindy Tucker cried. Mindy, aka Xena the Warrior Princess, was on the ground in Florida helping with the spin operation. She grasped immediately what a blunder this was for the Gore campaign. While it might have been hard to get America to rise up in indignation over the question of a dimpled chad versus a hanging chad, this would be easy. "Don't they have any idea how this looks?" Mindy asked. Within hours, the Democratic efforts to challenge military ballots was the hot story out of Florida, and there was no way the Gore campaign could win this battle. We sat and watched in glee as Joe Lieberman retreated from his own campaign's position of challenging the ballots.

"My own point of view," Lieberman said on *Meet the Press,* "if I was there, I would give the benefit of the doubt to ballots coming in from military personnel, generally." Having backed away from the Gore position, he then turned around and began to run in the other direction. "If they have the capacity, I would urge them to go back and take another look, because again, Al Gore and I don't want to ever be part of anything that would put an extra burden on the military personnel abroad."

Thus, Joe Lieberman launched his campaign for the 2004 presidential nomination. That was when it was clear that there was a division in the Democratic ranks, and that at least some people were looking to save their own skins. If in a 2004 presidential debate the subject of overseas military ballots came up, Lieberman could always say, "Well, you know I never supported the challenging of those ballots."

☆　　　　☆　　　　☆

Mark came back from Zanzibar, marveling that nothing seemed to have changed. He spent a day at the campaign and came to the same conclusion I had reached. "This is driving me crazy," he said. "There is nothing for guys like us to do. Can't we make some spots attacking somebody?"

"Actually I have been working on some spots going after

Carol Roberts," I said, laughing. Carol Roberts was the chain-smoking election official in Palm Beach County who had come to epitomize what Republicans hated about the hand re-count process.

"This is the first time in my goddamn life I wish I had gone to law school," Mark said.

This just wasn't how it was supposed to be, we both agreed. A momentous election that determines who will lead the free world should be decided by the peculiar process we had come to accept as normal: endless attack spots, frantic spin, phone banks, direct mail, all of it vulnerable to one bad rain or snowstorm on Election Day. That was how we did it in America, not by rationally arguing cases in front of impartial judges. What kind of fun was that?

"We could always attack the Florida Supreme Court," Mark said.

I loved that idea. "How much do you really know about the Florida Supreme Court?" I sketched out a spot. "Under those dark robes, do you *really* know what is going on?"

"They think they know best," Mark added another line. "What do you think?"

We felt better right away. Nothing like a good attack spot to get you out of a bad mood.

That was when we decided we should volunteer to go to Florida.

"What are you going to do?" Karl asked skeptically.

We hadn't really thought about this.

"We can be election observers," I said.

"Watch them count ballots, like everybody else," Mark said.

Karl started laughing. "Oh that will be great," he said. "That will really elevate the process." We were beginning to feel like aging war veterans being rejected by the Draft Board.

"Guys," Karl said, "we are going to win this thing and the governor is going to go on television. You should stay here and help with that."

It happened at last on Sunday, November 26. This was the date on which Katherine Harris would finally certify the election; once the results were certified, the results would be submitted as the official election results of Florida. We gathered at headquarters to watch the ceremony on television. This bizarre ritual of watching television to find out whether one was alive or dead had come to seem almost normal. As a television spectacle, watching three people sign documents is right up there with live coverage of checkbook balancing, but I couldn't remember ever seeing anything I enjoyed more.

"Well, it is about goddamn time," somebody muttered and that seemed to sum up the mood pretty well. There was some scattered applause but no wild cheers. We were beyond the cheering stage.

The plan was for the governor to make a statement following the certification. We had set up a shot at the State Capitol for his appearance; normally we would have used the governor's mansion, but it was being decorated for Christmas, although appearing with a lighted Christmas tree and Santa Clauses probably would have been the absurd touch the situation deserved. The group of reporters who gathered to watch had the numb glaze of hostages who had been promised release one too many times.

"Is this thing finally over?" Karen Hughes said laughingly, when she arrived with the governor. He seemed preoccupied, very serious, eager to get this over with. Some of the security personnel congratulated him and he smiled. "We'll see. It's not over yet." Seeing him, it suddenly struck me how difficult this whole period must have been for both him and Al Gore. There were no guidelines for how to respond in such strange circumstances. You would want to appear confident, but not presumptuous. And, although it must have been maddeningly frustrating, that was a feeling you could never air in public.

I had long thought that one of George W. Bush's great strengths was that he was truly comfortable with himself; he was ready to be president, but if he lost, he was prepared to go on with his life. But now he had been thrown into this never-never land, a purgatory of defeat and victory.

After the speech, he shook hands with each of us and thanked us for helping. You could see the sparkle, the little wink, the nod, the warmth. But underneath there was a tiredness that offered a glimpse of what he must have been going through. We stood around for a few awkward moments, and then he left with Mrs. Bush and walked out through the State Capitol where a crowd had gathered. From the upstairs window of the Capitol, I watched him work the crowd a little and then drive away. It was November 27, 2000, and America still didn't have a president.

☆   ☆   ☆

I left Austin right after the certification, thinking it was all over. The lease was up on our little limestone cottage and it seemed silly to move into a hotel. The truth was, I had come to hate the recount period, hated the way it made me feel like some kind of hanger-on. Karl was starting to focus on the first hundred days of the new administration, but that wasn't what I did. I was a campaign guy and no matter what Bill Daley said, the campaign had ended on November 7, 2000. The recount had denied me what I loved most about the ritual of campaign life, the definiteness of winning or losing. Either way, you said good-bye to the people who had consumed your life and moved on. It was always abrupt and jarring, but a clean break was for the best. The recount had turned the usual rushed good-bye into the longest of farewells. It was like standing on the platform for weeks, waving and waiting for the train to pull out of the station.

The night it finally ended, Wednesday, December 13, I watched the speeches on television just like everybody else. I was back in my apartment in New York, ready to resume my life, but still held in some kind of suspended animation by this horrible, tedious process. But now, yes, it was over.

Still, there was a moment halfway into Bush's speech when I reached for a piece of paper to make notes for the next message meeting. But of course there wouldn't be any more message meetings, no more Candy Gram Committees, no frantic revising of scripts. The man standing in the well of the Texas legislature would soon become the most powerful individual on the planet. He had made it through a process that was as daunting and humbling as anything the evil gods of politics could conjure, defeating a vastly more experienced opponent riding a wave of peace and prosperity the likes of which hadn't been seen since Eisenhower ran for reelection.

Through it all, these cockeyed optimists from Texas had survived every crisis, always convinced that George W. Bush would be our next president. A long time ago, down in the bunker, Karl had talked about running the ideal campaign. That we certainly hadn't done, but I knew that I would always look back on it with a certain fondness, glad and maybe a little proud that I had joined them and become, if only for a short while, a Texan.

Acknowledgments

A most special thanks goes to Brian Selfon, David Humphries, Matthew Schuerman, Martha Sutro, Doreen Eliott and Rachel Abrams. Rachel Klayman was an extraordinary help and Peter Matson, as always, the best.

About the Author

Born in Jackson, Mississippi, Stuart Stevens is both a writer and a top political strategist. He is the author of four previous books, including *Malaria Dreams* and *Feeding Frenzy,* as well as of some of the earliest episodes of the critically acclaimed television series *I'll Fly Away* and the Emmy Award–winning *Northern Exposure.* His articles and essays have appeared in *The New York Times, Los Angeles Times, Outside, Esquire, The New Republic,* and elsewhere. Over the past eighteen years, he has also helped to elect dozens of governors and senators, as well as international clients, such as Vaclav Havel of Czechoslovakia. He lives in New York City and Stowe, Vermont.